It took 50
a suppo
others
Hitler's "Fi

- Who were these "Soldiers of Evil," and where did the Nazis find them?
- Were they volunteers or were they ordered to the death camps?
- Were all or most of them anti-Semites?
- Did they know what they would be required to do *before* they joined the SS?
- Did any of them protest or try to rebel?
- Was their gruesome work thought of as a duty . . . or a calling?
- How did their families feel? Did their families even know?
- Do those who are still alive feel any remorse?

FOR MORE THAN 40 YEARS, THE CIVILIZED WORLD HAS BEEN ASKING, "HOW COULD THE HOLOCAUST HAVE HAPPENED?" THIS CHILLING BOOK PROVIDES THE ANSWER . . .

Soldiers of Evil

The Commandants of the Nazi Concentration Camps

TOM SEGEV

Translated by Haim Watzman

BERKLEY BOOKS, NEW YORK

This Berkley book contains the complete text
of the original hardcover edition. It has been
completely reset in a typeface designed for easy
reading and was printed from new film.

SOLDIERS OF EVIL: THE COMMANDANTS
OF THE NAZI CONCENTRATION CAMPS

A Berkley Book / published by arrangement with
McGraw-Hill Publishing Company

PRINTING HISTORY
McGraw-Hill edition published 1987
Berkley edition / August 1991

ISBN: 0-425-12171-2

A BERKLEY BOOK ® TM 757,375
Berkley Books are published by The Berkley Publishing Group,
200 Madison Avenue, New York, New York 10016.
The name "BERKLEY" and the "B" logo
are trademarks belonging to Berkley Publishing Corporation.

PRINTED IN THE UNITED STATES OF AMERICA

10 9 8 7 6 5 4 3 2 1

CONTENTS

FOREWORD

THIS book is based on a doctoral thesis written some years ago at the history department of Boston University. Among other things, it was meant to examine the theoretical problems involved in the integration of psychology and history. For this reason a special team of advisors was set up for me, including Professor Bruce Mazlish from MIT, Professor Rudolph Binion from Brandeis University, and scholars from the Psychoanalytic Institute of Boston. My advisor in the history department of Boston University was Professor Dietrich Orlow. My thanks to all of them.

During the course of the research, which lasted several years, I received generous financial aid from Boston University and from the Free University in West Berlin, where I was assisted by the late Professor Friedrich Zipfel.

The material which served as the foundation for this work is kept in the Berlin Document Center, in the German Federal Archive in Koblenz, in the Wiener Library, located first in London and now in Tel Aviv, and in the Yad Vashem Archive in Jerusalem. I received helpful guidance and advice in each of these places. Many people helped me during the research, as well as recently, when I rewrote it as a book at the invitation of the Domino Press, Jerusalem. My thanks to all of them.

INTRODUCTION

MOST of the material on which this book is based is kept in the Berlin Document Center, a small house situated at the end of a shaded passage in the Zehlendorf quarter of West Berlin. This is the SS archive, now the property of the U.S. Army; the card file of Nazi party members is also kept here, totaling millions of names. The house is surrounded by a fence and is protected by an electronic security system. No one may enter without prior arrangement and written permission. The American MP orders visitors to identify themselves. Most are researchers— historians and attorneys. Before allowing them to enter, the MP checks their identities over an internal telephone.

I went there every morning, over the space of several months, beginning in the summer of 1974. The staff was very helpful, and aided me in locating, among the hundreds and thousands of brown cardboard folders, the personnel files of the commandants of the concentration camps. They assigned me my own room, in the basement of the building, and there I went through the files, one by one. Many of the files had been damaged during the bombardment of Berlin. Some contained only a few scorched pages; others were waterstained or faded by the sun and could no longer be read. Some crumbled at the touch of a hand, and there were also files whose entire contents had disappeared. But there were also thick ones overflowing with small details: the SS command wanted to know everything about each member of the organization, starting from his father's and grandfather's professions and ending with the exact locations of the fillings in his teeth. From time to time SS members were required to record their life histories, and what they wrote was kept in their personnel files. The histories joined testimonies concerning the SS members' characters and habits, gathered for the most part without their knowledge from relatives, friends, and neighbors, as well as detailed evaluations by their superiors, medical and psychological reports, and a myriad of other documents. At times I told myself that I knew more about some of these concentration camp commandants than people generally know about their best friends.

I also saw documents in other archives which shed light on the lives of concentration camp commandants—in Germany, the United States, Britain, and Israel. A few of the commandants were tried, and some of the court records are open to scholars. Here and there I was shown classified legal documents. Afterwards I set out on a long journey through all of West Germany, looking for the three concentration camp commandants who were then still alive, and for the deputies, assistants, widows, children, and acquaintances of those who had passed away. It was not easy; it sometimes resembled detective work. West Germany has no central population register, but each of its citizens must, by law, notify the local registry of his address. Whenever a person moves, his name is erased from the local register and he is listed at his new location. I had no reason to believe that the people for whom I was searching were still living at the addresses I found in the personnel files, but it was at least a start. I wrote to the registry offices. They are very well organized: they had sometimes succeeded in preserving records from the ravages of war. Through our correspondence they directed me from one address to the next—from city to city and from village to village—each time informing me that the person had moved from here to there, from there to elsewhere. At the same time I spent weeks poring through telephone books. I found people with names identical to those for whom I was searching, and some were able to help me. I also made use of organizations of veterans, including that of the Waffen SS. In Berlin there is an office with the names of all the German soldiers wounded at any time during World War I. Among other things, they locate relatives. They also helped.

At times I went to the addresses I found in the personnel files of the concentration camp commandants in order to ask the neighbors if they, perhaps, knew something. I would go into the local *Kneipe* and engage the bartender in conversation, or visit the minister's house. People remembered something— "Yes, you mean the one who became something important in the SS. Hard times, hard times and everything happened so many years ago. Maybe ask the widow of the manager of the train station, she knows things like that." This is how I found, among others, Fritz Hensel, brother-in-law of Rudolf Höss, commandant of Auschwitz; Jörg Hoppe, son of the commandant of the Stutthof concentration camp; and Hans Hüttig, commandant of the Natzweiler concentration camp. (I also located two other concentration camp commandants who were still living and spoke with them.) Hensel and Hoppe helped me formulate questions; Hüttig suggested an answer.

Rudolf Höss's widow refused to speak to me. She was not well, she informed me, and lacked the strength to relive, again and again, the horrors of the past. She asked her brother, Fritz Hensel, to speak with me instead. Hensel had known Höss in his youth. They had been members of the same agricultural-romantic-nationalist youth movement and lived on the same commune in northern Germany. We met in a *Lokal* in Hannover. The blaring music made conversation difficult, so we left to wander through the streets of the city, for three hours, in pouring rain. Hensel was a painter. During World War II he was conscripted into an artists' unit, which was sent from front to front to memorialize in their drawings the heroism of the army. Whenever he was given leave, he traveled to Auschwitz and stayed with his sister and brother-in-law, commandant of the camp.

"A nice family," he told me. He was not the only guest who came to the camp. From time to time there were visits by Nazi government officials, Red Cross representatives, and others. It seems, however, that there was no one who stayed as a guest at Auschwitz for as extended a period as Hensel—four straight weeks. He would walk freely through the camp, alone or in the company of his brother-in-law. He saw much and drew much.

Once he drew a pile of bodies. Sometimes he would ask Höss how he was able to function in the hideous reality of the camp. Höss answered that Hensel could not understand, since he belonged to a different world. Once the commandant of Auschwitz used the expression "another planet" to explain what he meant. Many years later that became a very common expression in the historiography of the Holocaust, in particular after the testimony of the writer Yehiel ("K. Zetnik") Dinoor, a survivor of Auschwitz, seconds before he collapsed and fainted at the Eichmann trial.[1] Hensel also told me much of himself and of those days. I asked him how he survived as a guest in Auschwitz. He looked at me in surprise. "I never asked myself that question," he said. "You know what? It's a good question."[2]

The Stutthof concentration camp was situated not far from the city of Danzig. About 120,000 prisoners were held at the camp, and some 80,000 died there.[3] A few hundred were killed in the gas chamber erected in the camp for that purpose. At the beginning of 1975 I believed that the commandant of the camp, SS Colonel Paul Werner Hoppe, was still living, and I wrote to him requesting an interview. I was wrong: Hoppe had died just a few months before my letter arrived. I received a reply from his eldest son, Jörg, then 34 years old. He suggested we meet. We sat over a bottle of wine, in a little restaurant in West Berlin. He spoke as if in spiritual torment, almost without a break, deep into the night. "Maybe I shouldn't say this," he said, "and actually I've never said it before, even to my wife, but all in all it was a great relief when Father finally died."

At the end of World War II Jörg Hoppe was 4 years old; his brother was 2. Their mother told them that Father, like three million other Germans, had not come home from the front. Some time after the war a man who presented himself as their Uncle Werner began paying visits. He generally came at night. "I would hear him come in after we were already in bed," Hoppe told me. "I knew he was there, but when we woke up in the morning—he was already gone." From time to time soldiers from the British army of occupation came to the apartment and asked about Uncle Werner.

"I remember how they came once to look for him when he was with us for supper. Suddenly, they knocked on the door.

Mother jumped up and before we could understand what was happening, she pushed Uncle Werner into the closet. Everything happened very quickly. Mother opened the door. Outside stood three British soldiers. Mother invited them in. They asked about Uncle Werner. Mother swore that she had no idea where he was. She hadn't seen him since the war, she said. She suggested that the three soldiers search the apartment for him: 'Look everywhere!' she shouted hysterically. 'Look under the bed, look in the closet, maybe you can find him for me!' But the soldiers only mumbled something and left. All that time Uncle Werner was hiding in the closet. A quarter of an hour later he left, and years passed before we saw him again."

Much time would pass before Mrs. Hoppe revealed to her sons what they may already have sensed: the mysterious Uncle Werner was, of course, their father. He tried to hide his identity from the military police of the British army of occupation, but could not do so for long. Within a few weeks of being pushed into his wife's closet, Hoppe was discovered and arrested. The British intended to bring him before a court-martial as a war criminal. At some stage the Polish authorities requested his extradition and then, in circumstances which have never been clarified, Hoppe managed to escape. He settled in Switzerland, took a false name, and made a living as a landscape designer.

"We missed Father a lot," his son told me, "and we felt that Mother also missed him a lot." At the beginning of the 1950s Paul Werner Hoppe returned home, joined his wife and children, and went back to using his real name, as if nothing had ever happened. He apparently believed that in the new Germany no one would bother to confront him with what he had done during the war. His son Jörg was instructed to tell his friends in the neighborhood and at school that his father had been released suddenly from a Soviet prison camp, in which he had been held since the war. The neighbors believed the story. The authorities did not. A short time after he came home Hoppe was arrested, given a lengthy trial, and sentenced to nine years in prison. His son related: "It was a terrible blow. First were the years without him, then they returned him, and now they took him away from us again. No one told me why they put him in jail. My classmates said he was a murderer. Mother told me not to pay attention to what they said."

From time to time Frau Hoppe was allowed to bring her sons for brief visits with their father at the prison. He never spoke of the reasons he had been brought there. Only by chance, in one of his history lessons, did Jörg Hoppe learn that his father was a war criminal. He was then 16 or 17 years old. The teacher said something about the concentration camps and looked at him out of the corner of her eye; the other pupils whispered among themselves. That is how he learned of his father's role in the war. From that point onward he began searching out and reading books on the history of the Nazi regime, World War II, and the murder of the Jews. In one of the books he came across the name of Hermann Baranowski, commandant of the Sachsenhausen concentration camp. He identified the name immediately: Baranowski was his grandfather. It was not difficult for him to figure out the connection. His father, a young officer in the SS, married the daughter of another SS officer, older than he and perhaps his superior. Grandma Baranowski was then alive, but he did not dare to ask her about Sachsenhausen. The subject was taboo in the house. Grandfather, he had been taught to believe, had fallen on the Eastern front. Only once did he gather the courage to ask his mother about it. She advised him to forget about it.

In 1962, Paul Werner Hoppe was released from prison and found a low-level position with an insurance company in the city of Bochum in the Ruhr district. His son Jörg was already 21, a student at the Technical Institute in West Berlin.

"Immediately upon his release from prison I asked my father to talk with me about what he had done in World War II. I thought I had the right to hear an explanation from him. I did not demand a report and did not intend to sit in judgment on what he had done. I only hoped that he would help me understand the matter. Only understand. I felt that only a frank talk, even if a painful one, could free me of the agony which had accompanied me all those years."

Hoppe spoke much about the war, and at times even met with his comrades to exchange memories from the past. Of his position as concentration camp commandant he refused to speak. His son would not understand him anyway, he argued; all of West Germany does not understand, since it is still early to speak of it. But the day would come, Hoppe promised his son, when he would retire and have the time to write a book, like Rudolf Höss, the commandant of Auschwitz. Then the world would know that he, Hoppe, had only done his duty.

His son was not convinced. The subject continued to torment him, unceasingly. During one of his trimester breaks he traveled to Poland and visited the site of the Stutthof concentration camp, which had by that time become an official memorial. The visit shocked him, despite all he already knew about the horrors of the Nazis. Among the photographs on display in the museum he identified a picture of his father, in uniform. It was the first time he had seen how his father had looked when he was his age: he noted the great similarity between them. As he stood there, a class of Polish schoolchildren, 10 or 11 years old, came in. Hoppe hurried out, before the children arrived at the picture of his father. "Now that seems stupid, of course," he told me, "but at that moment I really was afraid of those children."

When he returned home he tried once more to get his father to talk. He traveled to see him at Bochum, told him of his visit to Poland, and also showed him illustrated guide books he had taken from the museum at the camp. "So you went there," his father murmured. "You went there." It was clear that he was hurt. He glanced quickly at the Polish guide books and stated: "All this never happened. It's all lies. Communist brainwashing." He claimed that the Poles had brought to Stutthof instruments of torture and murder which had existed only at Auschwitz. "At Stutthof there was nothing like that," he argued, but again refused to go into the details. Everything would be made clear in the book he would write, he said. The son felt that his father was lying to him and from that day onward they had nothing to say to each other.

Jörg Hoppe settled in West Berlin, worked in a firm of economic consultants, and for all intents and purposes cut off all contact with his father. One summer day in 1974 his mother called and told him that his father was very sick and asked him to come to Bochum to be with him at the hospital. The father, 64, was unconscious and only occasionally woke up and babbled fragments of sentences, as if in a dream. From his words it became apparent that he thought the doctors and nurses around him were secret Communist agents who were conspiring to extradite him to Poland, in order to try him again. In his delirium he thought his son Jörg was an agent of the Israeli secret service. In a final attack of terror he sat up in his bed and screamed that his son was plotting to take him to Jerusalem, in order to have him hanged as they had hanged Eichmann. Minutes later he died.

His son made one more attempt to understand his father's actions, after his death. "It was immediately after he passed away," he told me. "I was still under the influence of his last outburst in the hospital. On the way home I remembered that book my father promised to write about himself and about his deeds during the war. I returned to my parents' apartment, searching through the things he had left behind, in drawers, in suitcases, and in the attic. Maybe he nevertheless tried to leave some sort of explanation, I thought. I hoped very much that he had done so. I so needed a word of explanation from him, my father, the war criminal, but I could not find anything and I could, of course, have predicted that in advance: the book was a lie, too."

That same day Hoppe decided he would never again think about the past, as his mother had advised him when he was still a child. But sometimes he would tell himself that his son would soon be going to school and within a few years would learn about the Nazi era. Maybe he also would come across the names of his grandfather and great-grandfather and discover their part in the crimes of the war. "If he asks me about that—I really won't know what to answer him," Jörg Hoppe said.[4]

Afterwards we went through his father's personnel file together; for a certain moment we almost became friends.

In April 1975, after great effort, I found Hans Hüttig, then 81 years old, formerly one of the commandants of the Natzweiler concentration camp in the Alsace region, some 20 miles southwest of Strasbourg. About 25,000 people died at the camp.[5] Hüttig first agreed to talk with me, then changed his mind and sent me a telegram telling me not to come. I ignored the telegram and traveled to see him. We sat in the sun, by the well in his village, Wachenheim, on the Weinstrasse running parallel to the Rhine, with a view of vineyards of breathtaking beauty. Hüttig wanted, as I expected, to persuade me that I had come to him by mistake, and that he was not the man I was looking for. Afterwards he admitted his identity, but said he had only done his duty, in accordance with the orders he had received, a small cog in a large machine which he did not control and did not understand correctly. The French who sentenced him to death, Hüttig said, had done him a great injustice. He had sat in jail for eleven years before being released. His years of imprisonment were, he said, the hardest thing he had endured in his life. At this point he broke into tears. People from the village who passed by pretended they did not see the elderly Hüttig sobbing into his foreign guest's tape recorder; I imagine they knew what was going on. After he calmed down I asked him what had motivated him to enlist in the SS. Hüttig answered that I could not understand it unless I could see things as he saw them fifty years previously. "Today it seems so cruel, inhuman, and immoral. It did not seem immoral to me then: I knew very well what I was going to do in the SS. We all knew. It was something in the soul, not in the mind."[6] Something of this sentiment was also apparent in his personnel file.

The personnel files do not contain a clear-cut answer to the great historiographic question: "How could it have happened?" Many of them, however, tell how certain people, Nazis, members of the SS, consented to making terror their profession, and how they were able to implement the murder of millions of people as part of their daily routine. There were some twenty main concentration camps scattered through Europe, and six major facilities for the extermination of the Jews, all on Polish territory. All together there were about 50 commandants; towards the end of the war a staff totaling approximately 40,000 was serving at the camps. This book tells their stories—who they were, what brought them to join the Nazi movement, what induced them to enlist in the SS, what brought them to serve in concentration camps and what gave them the relentlessness required of them in their duties. The terror and the Holocaust would not have been possible without them.

1
JOSEPH KRAMER
FROM DACHAU TO
BERGEN-BELSEN

ON March 21, 1933, Joseph Kramer read in *Völkischer Beobachter,* the Nazi party's morning newspaper, that on the following day, Wednesday, a concentration camp would open some 9 miles north of Munich.[1] The local police chief told a press conference that the camp, the first of its type, would have space for 5000 inmates. The buildings in the camp had been a gunpowder factory during World War I. Not far away, at the foot of an old castle, lay a picturesque town called Dachau. The newspapers published the item concerning the opening of the camp inconspicuously. Outside of Germany it evoked only limited interest: *The New York Times* gave the announcement a few lines on the front page, but the name of the man who had made the statement was not yet known to American readers in those days at the dawn of the Nazi regime. It was Heinrich Himmler.[2]

Joseph Kramer was an unemployed electrician of 27, and lived in the city of Augsburg.[3] He was a member of the Nazi party and had already served for half a year as a volunteer in the SS. The *Völkischer Beobachter* reported that the concentration camp at Dachau had been established as part of the redoubled efforts to wipe out Communist subversion. Kramer was pleased. He hated the Communists. Within two years of reading about the opening of the camp at Dachau, he had joined its staff. He was to serve in concentration camps over a period of more than a decade. During this time, camps were set up all over Europe. They expanded and became more brutal from year to year. Kramer was party to this development from the start and accustomed himself to it gradually, step by step, from Dachau to Auschwitz to Bergen-Belsen. When soldiers of the British army entered Bergen-Belsen in 1945, they found 60,000 prisoners, wasting away from hunger and disease, many of them on the edge of insanity. Tens of thousands of bodies were strewn between the barracks; there were signs that some of them had been eaten. "It was not always like this," Joseph Kramer told his captors, and he was right.[4] When he looked back, a short time before he was executed, a few months after the camp was captured, he noted in a letter to his wife, "Yes, we came a long way."[5]

The night before the opening of the camp at Dachau several supporters of the Communist party were led to imprisonment at another abandoned munitions plant, near Oranienburg, nine miles north of Berlin. The Nazi propaganda authorities would in the future allow, from time to time, outside visitors, journalists, and representatives of foreign embassies to tour the site. Werner Schäfer of the "storm troopers" (*Sturmabteilung,* or SA) was there to receive them. He was always careful to emphasize to them that the Oranienburg camp was, in fact, the first concentration camp in Germany. His pride for what, in his words, he had created from scratch and through his own efforts and "pioneering devotion" was so great that he wrote an entire book about his camp; Dachau was not even mentioned.[6]

In those days there was still confusion about internment. No one knew for sure who was responsible for what. Within weeks of Hitler's ascension to power the regular jails were filled to bursting. As the arrests continued, from Berlin to Munich, there was a need for new prison facilities. Before the establishment of the official concentration camps, improvised prisons sprouted up all over Germany, set up by the SA and the *Schutzstaffel* (SS) on their own initiative in abandoned factories, sports fields, and farms, in order to confine—and sometimes obliterate—their enemies. Even before the Nazis took over, brown-shirted hooligans would often kidnap anyone who had crossed them personally—debtors, business competitors, bothersome neighbors, even relatives. These activities were part of the atmosphere of general anarchy which pervaded Germany in the last days of the Weimar Republic. Law and order collapsed, and their place was taken by violence, crime, and political terror. In the course of the purge of the ranks of the SA in 1934, the SS took control of the Oranienburg camp and, within a year, closed it.

The Dachau camp served the official law-enforcement agencies from the start, and as such it truly was the first of its kind. With the exception of a short period in which it was closed for construction and renovation, it served continuously as a concentration camp, throughout the Third Reich's twelve years of existence, until it was captured by the U.S. Army some three weeks before Germany surrendered.

When Dachau opened, a few weeks after Nazi rule was established, only a few dozen prisoners were held there. On the eve of its capture by the U.S. Army their number was 50,000. A total of more than 200,000 prisoners from thirty-eight countries passed through the camp, most of them during the war. At least 30,000 of them died there.[7] In the six years before the war, concentration camps were also established at Sachsenhausen and Buchenwald in northern Germany, Mauthausen in Austria, Flossenbürg in northern Bavaria, and Ravensbrück (this was a women's camp) in northeast Germany. At the outbreak of the war these camps held about 20,000 prisoners; towards its conclusion their number was more than 385,000.[8] Some 975,000 prisoners passed through the six large camps in operation before the war; some 360,000 of them died. The International Red Cross located, after the war, close to 2000 prison facilities and forced-labor camps. The great majority were set up during the war, in all the areas of the Nazi occupation. Only about twenty were considered major concentration camps; the others all functioned as secondary camps, branches, and labor details.

The first concentration camp established outside Germany opened in May 1940 in Galicia, about 90 miles southeast of Warsaw, not far from a small village known as Oświecim—in German, Auschwitz. The site was originally intended as a transfer camp for Polish citizens on their way to concentration camps within the borders of the Reich. With time it became the largest of all the camps. Its original facilities, which once served the Polish artillery forces, were known later as

Auschwitz I. They were expanded in October 1941 in the direction of the village Brzenzinka or, in German, Birkenau. This part of the camp later became known as Auschwitz II. There, in a farmhouse, the gas chambers for the annihilation of the Jews were installed. In 1942 a special camp was set aside for the chemical concern I.G. Farben, which manufactured synthetic rubber there. This part of the camp, near Monowice, was called Auschwitz III.

In June 1940, concurrent with the establishment of the camp at Auschwitz, a concentration camp opened in Neuengamme, one of the suburbs of Hamburg. Neuengamme was among those concentration camps which originally functioned as branches of other camps, before they were granted independent status with their own command. Neuengamme first served as a branch of the Sachsenhausen camp, as did a camp set up in 1941 in Lower Silesia, not far from the town of Rogoznica—known in German as Gross Rosen. The prisoners at Neuengamme were employed in the manufacture of bricks for construction. The prisoners at Gross Rosen worked first in granite quarries; at a later stage chemical and electronic works owned by the Krupp and Siemens companies were transferred to the vicinity of the camp.

The first camp set up west of Germany also opened in the summer of 1941, near the village of Natzweiler, which lies about 20 miles southwest of the city of Strasbourg in the province of Alsace. Its location was also chosen for its proximity to quarries of valuable red granite. A single camp of its kind was opened at the foot of a medieval castle in Westphalia known as Wewelsburg; Heinrich Himmler housed the cultural-ideological center of the SS there. Between the years 1933 and 1941 prisoners from Sachsenhausen labored on the renovation of the castle. Other prisoners from Sachsenhausen, Buchenwald, and Dachau were brought to a special camp for construction workers established in the Niederhagen forest, on the other side of the road leading to the castle. In September 1941 the Niederhagen-Wewelsburg camp became independent.

Stutthof was first opened as a prisoner-of-war camp, some 20 miles east of Danzig; in January 1942 it was classified as a major concentration camp. A year later, in January 1943, a concentration camp was set up in Holland, not far from Hertogenbusch, about 45 miles southwest of Amsterdam. Three months later, in late March, the small concentration camp at Kaiserwald opened. Not far from Riga in Latvia, it contained only six barracks, three for men and three for women. Some weeks later the prison facility the Germans had set up in Lublin, 80 miles southeast of Warsaw, was declared a major concentration camp. The last remnants of the Jews who remained in the city were brought there. The camp was later used for the extermination of Jews as well. It is located in one of the city's neighborhoods, Mejdan Tatarski; the inhabitants called it, for short, Majdanek. At the same time that Majdanek became a concentration camp, in April 1943, a camp was established some 50 miles north of Hannover in northern Germany, originally intended for Jews with dual citizenship. The intention had been to exchange them for Germans who had been taken prisoner by the British. The camp is located on the main road connecting two villages, Bergen and Belsen. During the last stages of the war prisoners evacuated from camps in the east were transferred there, just before those camps fell into the hands of the Russians. In June 1943 Himmler ordered that the Warsaw Prison also be given the status of a concentration camp. The ghetto was no longer in existence at that point, since it had been destroyed almost completely during the course of the famous uprising that had rocked it that spring. A few hundred inmates in Warsaw Prison had been meant to turn the area of the ghetto into a huge park, but a short time later the project was shelved and Warsaw Prison was added to the command of the Majdanek camp.

September 1, 1943, marked four years since the eruption of the world war. On that same day a main concentration camp opened in Vaivara in Estonia, 100 miles west of Leningrad. The Russians at that time had already broken through the great siege of Leningrad, and masses of Jews, most of them from Vilna in Latvia, were brought to the Vaivara camp in order to work on the erection of the east wall of Narwa Bay, which was meant to stop the advance of the Red army. A few of the camp's prisoners were also employed in a project for the manufacture of synthetic fuel on the shores of Peipos Lake. On the day the Vaivara camp opened the SS overran the Kowno ghetto, 55 miles northeast of Vilna, and from that day onward the ghetto became a concentration camp. Another Estonian camp was set up in Klooga, also in September 1943. Starting in January 1944, the work camp which had operated for a year in the Jewish cemetery in Plascow in Cracow became a concentration camp. About half a year before Germany's surrender one of Buchenwald's subsidiary camps was also added to the list of major concentration camps. That was in November 1944. The place was 40 miles northwest of Buchenwald and was known by the code name of "Dora," the place the V-2 rocket was manufactured. This was the last prison facility to be officially designated a concentration camp.[9]

It is impossible to be certain how many people were held as prisoners in Nazi concentration camps. The registration records of many camps were destroyed or lost. The numbers of some inmates were given to others after their deaths. But there were also prisoners who were listed more than once, as they were transferred from camp to camp. There were some who were never registered. In any case, on January 15, 1945, there were some fourteen camps still functioning, holding close to 700,000 prisoners, among them 200,000 women.[10] During the trial of Oswald Pohl, who headed the camp administration during the war, it was estimated that not less than 10 million people ended up at the camps.[11] According to the same estimate, more than 1 million prisoners died in the concentration camps; in addition, close to 6 million Jewish prisoners were murdered in the six extermination camps.[12] The great majority of the victims died during the war. As defeat approached, the camps in the east were evacuated and the prisoners were forced to endure long marches to other camps in the west. Thousands died or were killed along the way. At the same time the camps in the west were in total chaos—the overcrowding, the lack of sanitary facilities, the epidemics, the hunger and cold raised the death rate to a level much higher than it had ever been before. When Joseph Kramer wrote before his death that he had gone "a long way" from Dachau to Bergen-Belsen, he spoke from personal experience.

It began not unreasonably, from his point of view. When Heinrich Himmler explained that the Dachau concentration camp was meant to protect the nation from communism, he had in front of him the results of the German general election three weeks previously. Adolf Hitler was already chancellor, but almost 5 million Germans still voted for the Communist party, and more than 7 million for the Social Democrats—together some 30 percent of the vote.[13] "Needless to say, they had not all been enemies of the state," Hermann Göring would later testify in all generosity. "In fact, the overwhelming majority were honest Germans who had been seduced to support an insane ideology. . . . We had to rescue these people, to bring them back to the German national community. We had to re-educate them." It was for this purpose, Göring argued, that the concentration camps were set up.[14]

Many of the opponents of the Nazi regime were brought to the concentration camps to be destroyed, but many others were brought in the sincere hope that they would accept the principles of Nazism and become loyal to the government. A correspondent for *The New York Times* allowed to visit Dachau some time after it was opened received the impression that Theodor Eicke, commandant of the camp, and his men were very serious about the educational goals they set for themselves. "They honestly and sincerely believed that their task was pedagogic rather than punitive," the correspondent wrote. "They felt sincerely sorry for the misguided non-Nazis who had not yet found the true faith."[15]

Documents captured after the war confirm the impressions of the correspondent, at least in part. An internal memorandum written at Gestapo headquarters in 1934 stated that the victory of the Nazi movement would not be complete until all its opponents learned to support it—not from fear or for practical reasons, but through complete identification with it. The author of the memorandum emphasized the educational value of ideological indoctrination, and suggested imbuing the concentration camp prisoners with the knowledge that, upon their release, they would be able to find their place among those loyal to the regime and become, like them, outstanding citizens and members of society. This document was not written as propaganda.[16] Another document warned state authorities not to harass prisoners after their release, in order not to make their reintegration into society more difficult.[17]

SS commandants would sometimes use the term "education camps" when referring to the concentration camps in memoranda and letters they sent to one another; they did not do so to try to hide anything. The use of this term reflected what they saw as one of the purposes of the camps. In the summer of 1942 Himmler was still emphasizing the "educational value" of internment in the concentration camps in a letter he sent to Oswald Pohl, and even a year later language of this type was included in secret briefings given to camp guards.[18] Each of them, the instructions read, must try to make his behavior a personal example for the prisoners, in order to imbue in them respect for the regime and to teach them to behave properly.[19] The education of the prisoners was to reflect the traditional values of the German bourgeoisie: hard work, strict discipline, frugality, law and order in the family and at work, and respect for the regime and the Nazi movement and its Führer. Here and there something of this sort was actually done, with programmatic lectures on the foundations of Nazism delivered to prisoners.

It is difficult, of course, to believe that the brutal conditions turned any opponents of the Nazi movement into its disciples. At the most they learned to keep quiet during their time as prisoners. In any case, the fact is that tens of thousands of them were, over the years, released, after it was established that they were no longer dangerous to society or to the regime. Many times the authorities determined that the prisoners had learned to honor the Nazi movement and accept its direction. A document from October 1944 deals with some, if not many, Communist prisoners who abandoned their previous convictions and became loyal Nazis.[20]

The first inmates were, for the most part, opponents of the regime, Communists, Social Democrats, or their supporters. Later, the concentration camps were used to imprison criminals, prostitutes, homosexuals, vagrants, gypsies, clergymen, Jehovah's Witnesses, and pacifists. All were considered by the new regime to be negative elements harmful to society and dangerous to its stability. Not all were considered appropriate for re-education—many were described as hopeless cases, unable to change their ways or opinions. There were some Jews among these prisoners, but arrests of Jews simply because they were Jews did not begin, for the most part, until after the pogroms which raged all over Germany on the night of November 10,

1938, known as *Kristallnacht*. Most of the prisoners in Nazi concentration camps were not Jews, although Jews were by far the largest number killed in them.

There were those who were sent to the camps by court order, for fixed terms; there were those imprisoned without trial, on the basis of a law which allowed the police to hold a person in "preventative detention" or "protective custody"; there were those interned in the camps at the conclusion of their sentences in regular prisons, in accordance with the measure of justice meted out to them by the courts: on the day of their release they were transferred to concentration camps. Some were there without any legal authorization. The great majority of the prisoners did not know for sure how long they were to be held in the camps, and many did not know why they had been arrested.

Vast numbers of prisoners were brought to the camps as forced labor for various factories. In 1938 the SS founded a company for stone quarrying and cutting, Deutsche Erd- und Steinwerke (DEST). The company based its activities on the work of the prisoners at Sachsenhausen and Buchenwald. The wave of mass arrests in Germany during the second half of the thirties was meant, in part, to provide laborers for the SS factories. The camps near the village of Flossenbürg, not far from the Czechoslovakian border, were set up near granite quarries, as part of a program to expand the economic activity of the SS. In time the concentration camps became the foundation of a huge economic empire and a central component of the political influence of the SS.[21] The camps also provided forced labor for military industry.

With time, the camps also served to camouflage various activities that required secrecy. At Sachsenhausen the prisoners were employed in forging passports, stamps, and foreign banknotes for Nazi intelligence. Underground factories in the Dora camp manufactured rockets, and in some camps the prisoners were used for "medical experiments" and "scientific research" in race theory. During the war some POWs were brought to the camps for execution. At one point, close to 2000 prisoners were even conscripted into a special combat unit and sent to the front, under the command of one Oscar Dirlewanger, an unbalanced embezzler and adventurer and one of

Heinrich Himmler's protégés.[22] Extermination facilities were set up at two concentration camps, Auschwitz and Majdanek, which were used from 1942 onward in the liquidation of Jews in the framework of the "Final Solution." (Four other extermination facilities were not officially designated concentration camps.)

After the war, many argued that they knew nothing: "All I know about the atrocities of Gross Rosen I learned during the trials against me," said the camp's commandant, Johannes Hassebroeck.[23] That was, of course, a lie. The Nazi regime never knew what would best serve its interests—hiding the truth about the camps or publicizing it. In reality they did both. The power of totalitarian authority is not only the strength of the support it receives from its subjects, but also the power of arbitrariness and fear. For this reason the authorities made sure that all citizens, even if they supported the regime and observed its laws, knew that they could find themselves at any time, and without any reason, on the other side of the electrified fence of one of the concentration camps, and not necessarily after due process.

German newspapers frequently reported the internment of citizens in concentration camps; they did not hide the fact that people were sent to the camps for unlimited terms, sometimes after they had served their full court-mandated sentences in regular jails.[24] Information about what was going on in the camps made its way into Germany through radio broadcasts from across the border. Tens of thousands of prisoners were released, in time, from the camps. Before they were allowed to return home they were forced to promise to keep secret what had happened to them, but there is no reason to believe that they all did. There were judges, lawyers, members of the clergy, social workers, and repairmen who were allowed in to perform various tasks, and suppliers who came to unload merchandise. Many camps employed local civilians on a regular basis, and nearby factories and even farmers sometimes hired prisoners as day laborers. There were also the tens of thousands of staff members who served in the camps.

Details about what was being done in the camps also leaked through by chance. Heinrich Deubel, Dachau's commandant, threatened to drag a policeman who had insulted an SS man at a train station to the camp, "where he would be whipped as he deserved." Himmler complained that the story spread and even found its way into the foreign press. The commandant of another concentration camp gave a local printer the job of printing the disciplinary regulations of his camp, and Hans Helwig, one of the commandants of Sachsenhausen, told of the cruelties customary in his camp as he sat drunk in a bar in the company of foreigners.[25] When some of the prisoners at the Hertogenbusch camp in Holland were killed, the news spread all over the area within a few hours. A local worker employed at the camp's telephone exchange told a friend in a neighboring village what had happened.[26] It was not possible to hide the brutal treatment of prisoners while they were being led from camp to camp in civilian passenger trains. One document, written during the war, tells how Soviet prisoners of war died while being led to the camps. When their bodies were shipped from train stations to the camps, the local population began asking questions.[27]

Various documents indicate that rumors of what was being done in the camps were disseminated among the population after relatives discovered bloodstains on the clothing returned to them from the camps along with the death certificates.[28] The bodies themselves were seldom returned. Hundreds of letters from worried citizens, preserved among the documents of the Buchenwald command, show that the public knew the truth about the conditions in the camps.[29] The ashes of those who had died in the camps were often buried in demonstrative ceremonies of protest.[30] Individual members of the clergy occasionally dared to include bits of criticism in their sermons, and here and there open protests arose against repression and the execution of the retarded and the mentally and terminally ill in the framework of the euthanasia program—"mercy killings" which preceded the liquidation of the Jews. A letter sent in 1941 to the justice ministry in Berlin indicates that the children of the city of Hadamar, near Frankfurt, were acquainted with the house in which such "mercy killings" were carried out and knew that those brought there would be killed.[31] The children of the city of Dachau could likewise have known something of the camp at the edge of their city; their parents could read in the Nazi party newspaper an item on the agitation aroused in one city when gypsy peddlers greeted their customers with the words: "May you be healthy and may you not end up in Dachau."[32] This was a typical news item—the German papers were full of similiar ones; it was also a warning and a reminder to the readers: the Dachau concentration camp was not far away.

The Nazi propaganda authorities also made great efforts to give the public a positive impression of the concentration camps, to the extent that it was possible. Adolf Hitler took the trouble once to tell his citizens that it was really the British who had invented the concentration camp, in their colonies. "We only copied the invention," the Führer said.[33] The British had, in fact, set up concentration camps during the Boer War. In addition, Hitler protested the "waves of incitement and slander" against Germany. German newspapers also complained frequently of what they termed anti-German slanders spread, they said, by the world media, on subjects including the establishment of the concentration camps. The newspapers denied the reports of atrocities in the camps. Photographs appeared in the papers from time to time, picturing prisoners in the camps as deformed and retarded creatures: here, this is what we have taken off the city streets, the photographs explained. Alongside them were photographs which showed prisoners at work and at rest, engaging in sports, playing chess, eating their fill in a pleasant dining room.[34] In his book on the Oranienburg camp, Werner Schäfer claimed that many citizens asked permission to send their children to be educated in his concentration camp, and that there were prisoners who refused to return home when they were released. "Among them were those who performed physical labor, for the first time after many years of unemployment," he boasted.[35] He listed the types of food given to the prisoners and computed how much weight they gained during their stay at the camp. German citizens thus had reason to see the concentration camps in a positive light. They could support the regime's efforts to reinstate law and order and they could support them as national patriots, citizens loyal to the regime. The staff of the camps knew the truth, but they also had a basis for seeing themselves as part of the security and legal apparatus. Preserved in one of the files is a unique document signed by Himmler, which contains several comments on the principles of imprisonment in the concentration camps, and which, unlike Schäfer's book, was not meant for publication and propaganda. The document, classified "secret," carries the date 27 May 1942. It was intended for distribution among the senior officers of the Gestapo, and it contains the following language:

> Recently, various officials in the party and the government have begun threatening to lodge complaints with the police against citizens, or to have them imprisoned in concentration camps, in order to give greater force to various orders and decrees. In this manner, for instance, one office threatened a citizen that he would be sent to a camp for "police interrogation" if he did not produce within five days a certain form, as he had been told to do by one of the officials. I request in all seriousness that the parties involved be instructed to cease this practice immediately, and if this is not done I will take upon my self to declare publicly that citizens are not liable in such instances to either police investigation or imprisonment in a concentration camp. The most severe punishments lose their deterrent ability when they are threatened at every opportunity, or when the impression is given that every official, in every office, is authorized to make use of it.
>
> Imprisonment in a concentration camp, involving as it does separation from one's family, isolation from the outside world, and the hard labor assigned to the prisoner, is the most severe of punishments. Its use is reserved exclusively for the secret police, in accordance with precise regulations which specify the form of imprisonment and its term. In this matter I have retained for myself a large measure of authority and exclusive discretion. All in all the German people are uniquely fair-minded. Most Germans obey the instructions of the authorities of their own free will and desire. Instructions accompanied by threats will, however, be received with disrespect and will be obeyed only unwillingly, not to mention that the multiplication of threats of this type will give a completely false impression, both here and abroad.[36]

The watchtowers on the wall which surrounded the concentration camp at Dachau allowed a striking view of the Bavarian Alps. The mountain peaks could be seen at times from within the camp as well. Along the inside face of the walls ran barbed wire fences, including an electrified one. Powerful projector lamps were set on the walls and on the inside fences, lighting the camp and its surroundings from sunset to dawn. The guards in the towers and those who sat above the single gate which led into the camp were armed with machine guns. The positions were guarded twenty-four hours a day. Armed patrols in black uniforms circled the camp on the outside, accompanied by terrifying guard dogs.

Some thirty identical wooden barracks were built within the camp over the years, and served as living quarters for the prisoners. They stood one after the other, in two parallel rows separated by an avenue of poplars. Each barrack was meant to house about 200 prisoners in eight rooms, four for sleeping and four for daytime activity. Towards the end of the war more than 1500 prisoners were packed into each one. Other barracks in the camp served as sick rooms, a canteen, and work rooms. One was used for so-called medical experiments on prisoners, another as a morgue. During the course of the war a crematory was built by the camp and was used to burn the bodies of the dead. A gas chamber was also constructed, but at Dachau it was never used.

The tree-lined avenues dividing the barracks led straight to the camp's parade grounds. Behind this were stone buildings, containing the headquarters, the administration, the warehouse, the kitchen, and the laundry, as well as rooms for interrogation, torture, and isolation. Paths, marked in white paint and lined with flower beds, connected the houses. The staff quarters and its service facilities were built next to the camp, to the northwest. The Dachau camp was a model. As long as it was possible, exemplary order was preserved. The structure of the camp, its internal organization, and the conditions there were imitated by other concentration camps established thereafter. At least ten concentration camp commandants received their first training at Dachau.

Within the whole of the hierarchy of the SS, the camp commandants were towards the middle, generally lower rather than higher. Their rank was usually parallel to that of lieutenant colonel (*Obersturmbannführer*) or major (*Sturmbannführer*) in the army. Heinrich Himmler interviewed each one personally before his appointment was confirmed, and sometimes even gave them direct orders. In general, however, the commandants were subordinate to the many-branched bureaucracy of the concentration camp administration, which worked out of the SS headquarters in Oranienburg near Berlin, first headed by Theodor Eicke, and later in the framework of the head office for administration and management headed by Oswald Pohl. The commandant was not party to the considerations that brought about the arrest of a person, and his influence in the decision to free a prisoner was limited. During one period he was expected to fill out a form on the behavior of each prisoner and his report was taken into account before a decision to free a prisoner was made, but later this order was rescinded. It became clear that the commandants were careless in filling out the forms, perhaps as a result of their workload, and perhaps because they were not interested.

A large proportion of the instructions sent out to concentration camp commandants were sent on purple mimeographed paper, directed to all of them at once. These instructions went into technical details and practices. But some of the commandants acted in their camps as supreme rulers with practically no limits to their power over life and death: "The camp was a kingdom to its commandant, and within it he was its king," the widow of Amon Göth, commandant of the camp at Plascow, recalled.[37]

The camp command was divided into several departments, which dealt with matters of administration, personnel, transport, communications, mail, equipment, kitchen, supplies, health and sanitation, and so on. The commandant was assisted by a deputy, an adjutant, a master sergeant, a medical officer, an education officer, a legal officer, a fire officer, and others. With the exception of the final months of the war, the concentration camps were never in real danger of attack from outside. The major task of the commandant was, then, to see to the internal security of the camp, to prevent the prisoners from rebelling and escaping.

Only rarely did prisoners try to rebel; many tired to escape and at times succeeded by, among other methods, using SS uniforms and vehicles. Close to 700 prisoners succeeded in escaping from Auschwitz, including its branches and extensions, during the five years of its existence. Beginning in 1941 the concentration camp commandants were required to send a report to Himmler himself whenever a prisoner succeeded in fleeing. Himmler demanded to know what had been done to try to capture the escapee and if the escapee had, in fact, been captured. "The increase in the number of prisoners escaping from the concentration camp worries the commander in chief of the SS in the extreme," was written in his name to the concentration camp commandants. Himmler wanted to give notice that in the future he would be more severe in punishing those responsible for the escape of prisoners, and instructed that from now on specially trained dogs should be used in the search for the escapees.[38]

The concentration camp commandants would frequently pay visits to the secondary camps and work extensions set up over the years. For this reason they were often absent from their headquarters. Their subordinates nevertheless did not free them from dealing with a long list of administrative matters which demanded their personal attention. Each commandant spent a large part of his time sitting at the desk in his office, signing memoranda, letters, reports, and uncountable forms. The files of the headquarters at Buchenwald, for example, include tens of thousands of documents, all of them signed by the commandants of the camp, including equipment inventories: "11 winter coats (gray), 76 pairs of socks, 59 handkerchiefs."[39] The commandant spent no small part of his time drafting his daily orders. These reflect not only the daily routine of the staff, but also something of his routine as its commanding officer: "While on duty within the camp, staff members may leave the upper button of their shirt open; upon leaving the camp they must fasten it," wrote one commandant, and Hermann Pister, commandant of Buchenwald, left behind a lengthy correspondence, the purpose of which was to find out whether members of the camp staff were allowed to travel on trains free of charge when they left on furlough, or only when they returned.[40]

The commandant's responsibilities as the direct superior of the camp staff took up a great part of his time: his measure of success in this area at times determined his chances for promotion. Hermann Baranowski, the commandant of Sachsenhausen, was once demoted to a minor position, because, among other things, he had not succeeded in establishing proper relations with his staff.[41] Otto Förschner, commandant of the Dora camp, was always described as "too soft" in his relations with his men; his friendly approach to his subordinates delayed his promotion.[42] The concentration camp commandants asked more than once that their authority be broadened to include the SS units stationed by their camps; for years this was the subject of unending power struggles. At a certain stage it was established that the concentration camp commandant would also be the commander of the district brigade of the SS.

The commandants were also responsible for the re-education of those prisoners not considered "lost cases," that is, those who were not homosexuals, Jews, and so on; commandants were also required to exhibit a measure of political sensitivity. The Sachsenhausen camp was opened at times to outside visitors as a result of its proximity to Berlin. For this reason it required a well-mannered, trustworthy, and responsible person who could accompany the guests and answer their questions properly. In 1937 Theodor Eicke recommended that Arthur Rödel be deposed from his position as commandant of Sachsenhausen "since the manner of his contacts with foreign visitors may cause us diplomatic problems."[43] The political instincts of the commandants often left something to be desired. One forced a Polish prisoner to sign a form declaring that he revoked the vow of celibacy he had taken upon himself as a Catholic monk. The incident was mentioned in a letter sent by the head of concentration camp administration to all the commandants, with a warning that they should abstain from such political initiatives, lest they leak out and serve the purposes of anti-German propaganda outside the country.[44] The administration apparently did not trust the political instincts of the commandants, and made a point of warning them, in writing, that while touring the camps with outside visitors, SS men, government officials, industrialists, and sometimes with foreign visitors, they should not include the extermination facilities, the furnaces for burning bodies, and the brothels.[45]

The concentration camp commandants were also responsible

for the proper financial operation of the camps. At times they became tangled in financial improprieties and some were tried for various acts of corruption. Hans Aumeier kept unrecorded sums in a safe at Auschwitz. Hans Loritz was asked to explain how funds had disappeared from the canteen in his camp, Esterwegen. "It is not fair," thundered the elderly commandant. "Such things can happen. No one has ever taught us how to keep proper accounts."[46] Two concentration camp commandants, Karl Koch and Hermann Florstedt, were sentenced to death in an SS court-martial for acts of corruption at the Buchenwald camp. Many of the commandants did not know how to manage properly the industrial factories the SS set up within their camps. In 1943, Oswald Pohl complained that some of the factories were not managed as they should be. He threatened that, if the situation were not corrected, he would suspend the special bonuses the commandants received for running the factories in their camps.[47]

The concentration camp commandants thus had full responsibility for everything that happened in the camps, except for part of what was done in the political departments. Starting in 1942 they were also relieved of responsibility for the work of the doctor and the medical staff. The political department operated in the camp as an extension of the Gestapo and it was headed by a plainclothes member of the secret police. This department dealt with the reception and registration of inmates, and was also in charge of their release. When the department functioned as it was meant to, it had a file card for each prisoner which included, along with personal details, the prisoner's picture and fingerprints. The department also acted as a sort of census bureau. For instance, it filed death notices of prisoners and was responsible for passing this information on to government authorities that requested information on prisoners. The department also corresponded with the prisoner's relatives in cases when there was a need for a permit of one sort or another for arranging personal matters—guardianship, insurance claims, and so on. The political department could decree, at its own discretion, special conditions of internment. It was responsible for interrogation, and for the torture and brutality which accompanied it. The department also dealt with prisoner informers, censorship, field security, prevention of rebellion, escape, and communication with outsiders. On occasion, the political department oversaw the entire concentration camp—prisoners, staff, and the commandant himself. Within the camp the department enjoyed a unique status, powerful and fearsome; at times its relations with the camp command were strained.

Not all members of the command had direct, daily contact with the prisoners. The prisoners were kept in a special compound, a sort of camp within the camp, with its own commanding officer, or even two or three of them, aided by their own staff. Some staff members were responsible for head counts, others for work arrangements, others for accompanying prisoners when they went out to work, and others for each of the living quarters, each *Block*, as it was called in German. The man in command of each Block was called *Blockführer*, an SS man with the rank of corporal or sergeant. Oversight of the prisoner division was given to an officer with a senior position in the concentration camp's hierarchy; in the absence of the commandant, he filled in for him. He often served also as deputy commandant of the camp.

Soon after Theodor Eicke was appointed commandant of the concentration camp at Dachau, he drafted a series of orders which were supposed to provide for the punishment of prisoners according to fixed criteria. Up until that point, the prisoners had been subject to the whims of the guards: each guard had brutalized them at his own discretion. The criteria for punishment at Dachau were updated from time to time in order to bring them into line with other camps and with changing circumstances. Eicke's orders established iron discipline. "Lenience is a sign of weakness," he stated in the introduction to his rule book. He promised to punish ruthlessly those prisoners involved in political incitement and intellectual subversion. They should be grabbed by the throat to teach them to be silent, he decreed. Well-behaved prisoners were not meant, he said, to be hurt. In the rule book, Eicke set out the following punishments:

Incarceration within the camp for eight days, with 25 lashes at its beginning and 25 at the end, for prisoners who insulted an SS man or gave any reason to believe that they were not willing to obey the rules of order and discipline of the camp; a similar punishment was meted out to those prisoners who took advantage of the command authority they were given and discriminated between prisoners for political reasons.

Fourteen days of incarceration within the camp for a prisoner who went to sleep in another room without receiving permission to do so; for anyone who tried to smuggle something out of the camp in parcels of laundry; for anyone who entered or exited a building other than through its main door; and for anyone who smoked where it was forbidden. If a prisoner smoked and, as a result, a fire broke out, the prisoner was to be charged with attempted sabotage.

Fourteen days of incarceration within the camp, with 25 lashes at the beginning and 25 at its conclusion, for anyone who left the prisoner's wing without an escort and for anyone who entered it without permission, for anyone who joined without permission a group of prisoners leaving for work outside the camp; for anyone who included in letters comments harmful to the Nazi movement, the government, or the state; for anyone who included in their letters praise of Marxist rulers or leaders of liberal parties or the Weimar republic; for anyone who gave foreigners details of what was being done in the camps; and for anyone in whose belongings were hidden small weapons, such as sticks and stones.

Forty-two days of incarceration within the camp or unlimited isolation for anyone who funded a forbidden activity in the camp; for anyone who received or passed on money from the outlawed Communist "Red Aid" fund; for anyone who gave one of the members of clergy information outside that permitted in the relations between prisoners and clergy; for anyone who tried to pass, by way of the member of clergy, letters or messages; and for anyone who desecrated the symbol of the Nazi movement or the state.

Whoever was caught in actions which constituted political subversion, including making speeches, painting slogans, spreading rumors, smuggling news out of the camp, organizing escape, and similar offenses, was sentenced to death by hanging. Capital punishment was also imposed on anyone who tried to attack the guards and who was not shot on the spot, and on anyone who was caught while sabotaging one of the camp facilities.

Conditions of incarceration within the camp were laid out in the disciplinary regulations—a cell without a mattress and food consisting only of bread and water, with a hot meal once every four days. Disciplinary labor was extremely difficult or particularly disgusting. The term in the camp of a prisoner sentenced to internal incarceration was automatically lengthened by at least eight weeks; the prisoner would not be released in the forseeable future. The disciplinary regulations detail additional punishments, each one accompanied by at least a four-week extension of the prisoner's term: warning; rebuke; disciplinary exercises; confiscation of mattress, cigarettes, and food; and prohibition of the reception of mail.[48]

One of the most common methods of punishment, also mentioned in the regulations of Dachau, was hanging the prisoner by his wrists on a tree or column, with his arms tied behind his back. Willy Apel, one of the prisoners at Buchenwald, later described this in the following words:

May 1938. A labor detail was delayed on the parade grounds. After I stood there for an hour I went to the barracks to rest, because I was sick. SS Master-Sergeant Brauning submitted a complaint against me. I was sentenced to hanging for half an hour. Brauning refused to hear my explanation. The punishment remained in force and I was led up to the tree. The hanging is carried out as follows: the arms are tied with rope behind the back, and afterwards the prisoner is raised up to the column and the rope is tied onto a large nail fixed at a height of two meters, so that the prisoner's feet are off the ground. All the body's weight is concentrated on the wrists. The result of this was often fractures in the shoulder bones, involving horrible pain. I was hung there, together with three or four of my fellows, for half an hour. Others were hung for three or even four or five hours, until they lost consciousness and in some cases even died. The screams of pain filled the forest. SS Sergeant Sommer would even beat the legs, faces, and genitals of the hanging prisoners. The torture brought the hanging prisoners to the point of insanity. Many pleaded with the SS men to shoot them in order to put them out of their misery.[49]

There were also lashings. Their number was fixed—25, 40, or 50, on the prisoner's buttocks. The prisoner was tied for this purpose to a special tree stump. The lashings were carried out every day, in public, on the parade grounds, with a stick, whip, or other instrument. This also was performed in accordance with precise guidelines. In a letter which the head of the camps authority sent to the camp commandants on April 4, 1942, he made it clear to them, in the name of Heinrich Himmler, that whenever a prisoner was sentenced to lashes "in serious circumstances," the intention was always that his pants should be removed beforehand.[50]

The SS leadership did not satisfy itself with having the standing orders on record. The organization warned the concentration camp commandants that they must follow the instructions strictly and not deviate from them. The commandants were also required to prevent cruelty beyond what was permitted. "What is completely prohibited a camp guard?" asked a training manual for guards. "Answer: under all circumstances he is forbidden to strike prisoners at his own initiative, outside the framework of the disciplinary regulations." Reinhard Heydrich wrote his men in 1935 that "it is not becoming an interrogator to insult a prisoner, demean him, or behave with rudeness and brutalize or torture him when there is no need to do so." He warned his men if they beat a prisoner in violation of the regulations, they would be court-martialed.[51] "The guards should be instructed to abstain from mistreating prisoners," Eicke wrote in 1937. "Even if a guard has done no more than slap a prisoner's face, the slap will be considered an act of brutality and the guard will be punished."[52]

Whenever a prisoner was sentenced to a lashing, the commandant had to apply to the concentration camp authority in Berlin in order to receive prior permission to carry out the punishment. In the winter of 1942, the commandants received the following memorandum:

The Commander in Chief of the SS and the head of the German Police [Heinrich Himmler] has instructed that, in the future, lashing will be the punishment of last resort. Prior approval to carry out such punishment will be given in the future only in the following cases:

A. When the inmate has been given all other possible punishments in accordance with the camp regulations, such as internal imprisonment, denial of food, or disciplinary labor, and on condition that none of these has been effective. Denial of food will, or course, be imposed only on those inmates who can physically endure this punishment, in accordance with a doctor's certification.

B. As a deterrent in special cases, such as in connection with attempts to escape or attack guards. Care should be taken that the punishment be carried out in a way that makes it a deterrent.

The commandant of the SS has decided that lashings should not be imposed for the convenience of commandants and guards who are too lazy to take upon themselves the effort involved in the education of the prisoners, in order to reform them. If, for example, one inmate is caught stealing food from another—he should be punished by withholding his food, on condition that this is possible from a medical point of view and on condition that this was his first offense of this kind. When, for medical reasons, this is not possible, he should be punished with internal imprisonment for three to five days, and fed only bread and water. Only in cases of repeated offenses should a request for lashing be submitted for prior approval. Lashing is the most severe of punishments. From the requests which have arrived here, it would seem that its purpose was not understood properly. The concentration camp commandants are requested to observe the disciplinary regulations strictly in the future, and restrict lashings to cases in which they are really justified.[53]

Preserved among the SS documents are a number of judgments condemning camp guards for brutalizing prisoners in excess of what was permitted. In 1937 Theodor Eicke publicized the case of SS Sergeant Paul Seidler. Seidler, Eicke wrote to his men, beat one of the prisoners at Sachsenhausen "with sadistic cruelty" and was as a result put on trial, demoted to the rank of private, and expelled permanently from the SS. "I am making this incident public so that it can serve as a warning. The camp guards should once more be told the serious results of brutality to inmates . . . the commandant may impose extremely heavy and serious punishments on troublesome inmates; there is no need to add private initiatives to these. Whenever a guard is illegally brutal to an inmate, he will be expelled from the SS. We will do our best to preserve the good name of the organization."[54]

The archive of the Buchenwald camp command contains a document from 1944, a report on the Kapo Stanislaw Zarenc. This man made a habit of whipping and mistreating prisoners in violation of orders, and was for this reason dismissed from his position.[55] Hans Loritz was relieved of his command of the Esterwegen camp because of his cruel treatment of prisoners. The story current among his friends was that the dismissal order came from Adolf Hitler himself.[56]

Two concentration camp commandants, Adam Grünewald and Karl Chmielewski, were tried and found guilty of the deaths of prisoners as a result of brutality in their camps. A total of several hundred staff members of camps were tried for mistreatment of inmates. "As a result of my personal attention to the matter, and the repeated irregularities recently noted, I have learned that many of the guards at the camps are aware only in the faintest way of the obligations imposed upon them," Oswald Pohl complained in one of the mimeographed letters he sent from time to time to the concentration camp commandants.[57]

The standing orders for dealing with prisoners helped the concentration camps exclude themselves from the authority of the civil judicial powers. These were in the end forced to recognize the judicial independence of the camps. Himmler corresponded frequently with the Minister of Justice.[58]

The judgments of courts in various countries which tried Nazi crimes after the war contain uncountable testimonies of the bloodcurdling atrocities which were an inseparable part of the daily routine in the concentration camps. They involved acts of brutality against individual prisoners or groups of prisoners. They were performed in public, in broad daylight, with the full knowledge of the camp commandants, and often at their initiative and with their active participation, deliberately ignoring the disciplinary regulations. Random brutality, forbidden by the regulations, became the norm in the camps. In this a unique dichotomy was created. Regulations that precisely defined the permitted and the forbidden coexisted with arbitrary cruelty practiced in opposition to the regulations. Such lawlessness and unbridled impulses often reflected sadistic perversions. To the extent that the camp guards restrained themselves and treated the prisoners "according to the book," carefully observing what was permitted and what was forbidden by the camp regulations, the suffering of the prisoner was reduced. To the extent that the guards deviated from the regulations, the prisoner suffered more. Survivors of the camps testified after the war that at times they were made to suffer twice. When lashes were imposed on them, they were generally administered without waiting for permission from Oranienburg. Concurrent with this the commandant requested permission, and when it arrived two or three weeks later, the prisoners were whipped again, "according to the book." Those of the camp staff who wished to explain their deeds to themselves or to guests could find institutionalized legal and moral justification for what they did in the standing orders. These were an inseparable part of their job. If they wanted, they could pretend to themselves and to others that they were only doing their jobs, following orders which they justified but did not initiate, following set and written rules in accordance with the law. Anyone who wanted to find in the camps an outlet for violence or sadistic perversions could also find it as part of the collective routine: "everybody does it," they could tell themselves. They supported each other, members of the same gang, comrades in cruelty.

In the spring of 1937, Theodor Eicke appointed a chief education officer to his staff. Along with the company education officers, the chief education officer was charged with strengthening the ideological and political commitment of the staff of the camps. The goal was to present the daily life in the camp as part of a recognized and legitimate military routine; along with this was emphasized the danger the prisoners presented to German society as a whole and to the guards in particular. This was done, as was the custom in the SS, in the form of questions and answers.

Question: What is the relation between the guard and the prisoner?

Answer: The guard is the commander of the prisoner.

Question: What does that mean?

Answer: It means that the prisoner must treat the guard with respect.

Question: How is that expressed?

Answer: The prisoner must greet the guard, while removing his hat, and must present himself at attention when he has an announcement connected with his assignment.

Question: From what distance does the prisoner deliver his announcement?

Answer: From a distance of at least six meters.

Question: Other than this, what is forbidden while on duty?

Answer: Any conversation between the prisoner and the guard which is not part of one's duty.

Question: Is it permissible to allow a prisoner to present himself before you in a careless pose, or with his head covered?

Answer: No. I must demand that he present himself at attention.

Question: What must be prevented at all costs in relations between the prisoner and the SS man?

Answer: Any sign of friendship or familiarity. . . .

Question: Experience shows that prisoners try to make the guards like them through all sorts of favors and services they propose to them. How should this behavior be treated?

Answer: In all cases such favors must be rejected.

Question: What is the intention of a prisoner who proposes favors to a guard?

Answer: He wants to bribe the guard. He expects repayment.

Question: What interests the prisoners more than anything else?

Answer: They want to induce the guard to smuggle mail out of the camp for them, without going through examination or censorship.

Question: Through whom do they often try to achieve this?

Answer: Through civilians, women, and children who come into contact with them in their work.

Question: This being the case, what must the guard take special care to prevent?

Answer: Contact between prisoners and civilians.

Question: What else can be achieved through careful observance of this rule?

Answer: Preventing prisoners from receiving things from outside, such as food, cigarettes, news, and mail.

Question: What does a guard, who, despite all this, maintains overly close connections with one of the prisoners, prove?

Answer: He proves that he is not fit to serve in the SS, that he himself is one of the enemies of the state, and that his place is among the prisoners in the concentration camp. . . .

Question: What kinds of people are kept as prisoners in concentration camps?

Answer: Criminals, antisocial elements, perverts, enemies of society, people who are disloyal politically, and many others.

Question: What do you think of such people?

Answer: In my opinion they are people who are dangerous to the community, the nation, and the fatherland.

Question: What would happen if they were set free?

Answer: They would renew their dangerous activities and extend them.

Question: Under what circumstances is this danger especially severe?

Answer: Today, in a period of war.

Question: Why?

Answer: Because people of this type destroy the unity of the nation, destroy Germany's ability for military action, and call victory into question. . . .

Question: A guard is forbidden to take his hand off his weapon even for an instant. Why?

Answer: Because if he does so, the prisoners may grab the weapon from him, aim at him, and force him to open the gate for them.

Question: Why is it forbidden for a guard to light a cigarette?

Answer: Because at that very moment prisoners may attack him, beat him to death, and escape. . . .

Question: The most serious of offenses is sleeping during guard duty. Before what court will the man caught sleeping on guard duty be brought?

Answer: Before a military court.

Question: What is the maximum punishment he may expect?

Answer: Death.[59]

All these were clear ideological and practical reasons for treating the prisoners in the camps severely, in accordance with the standing orders. "The prisoner must know," said the SS catechism, "that the guard represents a philosophy superior to his, an unblemished political approach and a higher moral level, and the prisoner must take these as a personal example as part of his efforts to correct himself so that he may once again be a loyal citizen in his community."[60] This was part of the ideological and practical foundation of the work of the staff.

Theodor Eicke also instructed his education officers to strengthen the anti-Semitic consciousness of the camp guards: in accordance with his instructions, issues of the pornographic anti-Semitic *Der Stürmer* were posted on company bulletin boards. He wished to imbue anti-Semitic hatred in the non-Jewish prisoners as well, and for this reason distributed copies of *Der Stürmer* among them, too.

The prisoners in the camps were not equal. There were those kept in worse conditions than others; there were those who received extra privileges and even power to issue orders, all in accordance with the regulations and the circumstances as they changed from time to time and from camp to camp. Those who were returned to a camp for a second term of imprisonment were sent to perform more difficult work than others, and for longer hours. Limits were put on their right to smoke, receive letters, and so on. Certain jobs, such as in the kitchen or in the camp central office, carried with them extra perquisites and rights, which sometimes determined the prisoner's chances of surviving. Jewish prisoners were allowed to see the warrants issued against them, but unlike other prisoners they were not always allowed to keep these in their possession. Different groups of prisoners could be identified at the camps through the use of colored cloth triangles attached to their clothes—red for political prisoners, green for common criminals, and so on. Documents from the Buchenwald headquarters note no less than twenty-seven different combinations of identity tags, such as green and yellow for Jewish criminals and black and pink for clergymen with homosexual tendencies, each group with its cloth triangles, each with its special conditions of imprisonment.[61]

In April 1939 Adolf Hitler celebrated his fiftieth birthday. In honor of the occasion there were plans to pardon several hundred prisoners from the camps and send them home. The instructions that determined who was to be freed and who would remain in prison also reveal something about the different kinds of prisoners in the camp. The intention was to free prisoners who were brought to the camps in 1933, in other words, six years previously, "with the exception of special cases such as [Ernst] Thälmann [the well-known Communist leader]." It was decided to consider the release of repeat offenders who were first arrested in the years 1933 to 1934 for short periods and who had currently served at least a year; political and white-collar offenders who were sent to the camps for minor offenses and who had served at least half a year; criminals who had not been convicted in court or who had been acquitted and who had been imprisoned for at least a year; prisoners of 60 or more years of age, including Jehovah's Witnesses who refused to sign loyalty oaths, forbidden by their faith; so long as they had not been accused of moral offenses; homosexuals who were currently imprisoned for the first time, had not been imprisoned in a civil court, and who had not been accused of sexual relations with minors and who had been held in the camp for at least a year; and prisoners who had been in the past members of the Nazi party, in particular if they were among the senior fighters for the movement and had not been convicted in a civil court.[62]

In 1941 the camps were classified into four groups, in accordance with the severity of the discipline and conditions of imprisonment imposed upon them. To the extent that they felt that a prisoner could be re-educated and released, they tended to ease the conditions of his imprisonment. But this differentiation of the camps was not observed in practice. From time to time the camps were reclassified and at all times each camp held prisoners of different types. There was occasionally a certain improvement in conditions, whether as the result of the appointment of a new commandant, more efficient or less cruel than his predecessor, or in order to preserve the prisoners' ability to work and lower the death rate among them.

Towards New Year's Day 1944, Heinrich Himmler ordered that certain prisoners should have their conditions of imprisonment eased. These prisoners were allowed to wear civilian clothes and would be identifiable only by an insignia on their sleeve. Himmler instructed that these prisoners were to be given a special barracks within the camp.[63] From the very start there were "privileged prisoners" among the rest, including some who had made names for themselves in politics, culture, and the media. Among these some were accorded better treatment than others; in contrast, there were those who were tortured and humiliated because of their notoriety. Christian clergy were also often subject to more difficult conditions than were other prisoners.[64] Some prisoners received authority over their comrades, and as such became part of the camp hierarchy, headed by the commandant. At the head of the prisoners stood the "dean of the camp," who served as liaison between the prisoners as a group and the camp command. Alongside him sometimes functioned officials whose area of responsibility was limited to certain facilities, such as the hospital. The dean was responsible for, among other things, the office work in the prisoners' compound, almost all of which was done by the prisoners, as well as for the work of those prisoners who were employed as clerks in the camp headquarters, in the political department, or in the clinic. A prisoner-overseer was in charge of each of the barracks, subordinate to the dean, and under him were prisoner-overseers of each of the rooms in the barracks.

A prisoner was appointed *kapo* (which in Italian means "head") over each labor detail. Subordinate to the kapo were assistant overseers and work directors who were also prisoners. Prisoners with such positions in the camp were supplied with special sleeve insignias: black for the dean and the dean's staff; red for the barracks overseers; yellow for the kapo. The entire system was based on two hierarchies which were actually one, said the prosecutor at the Neuengamme trial—from the last of the prisoners to the commandant of the camp.[65]

There were among the prisoners those with authority who greatly mistreated their fellows, sometimes no less than the SS men themselves. There were those who were careful to observe the rules and those who violated them, sometimes with sadistic cruelty. Certain prisoners were chosen to carry out death sentences on other prisoners, though never on Germans. An instruction sheet for the implementation of death sentences, written in January 1943, noted that execution by hanging was to be assigned to prisoner-executioners. As payment for this work the executioner received three cigarettes.[66] In 1942, the violence of prisoners was described as a real problem: "Camp prisoners brutalize each other; in one incident prisoners tortured one of their fellows to death. Such prisoners are brought before civilian courts. The increasing number of such cases is in danger of damaging the image of the concentration camps in the eyes of the judicial system."[67]

The daily life of the camp staff was a mixture of military routine and blood-curdling atrocity. Both of these aspects are represented in the documents captured during the war.

For immediate implementation: work hours at headquarters (1938) will be, on weekdays, from 0730–1200 and 1230–1700 (nine hours). On Saturdays work will be from 0730–1200 (four and one half hours), afternoon free. Sundays are free.[68]

. . . work hours for prisoners and guards (1942) on weekdays and Saturdays are from 0645–1200 and from 1230–1830 (11 and one quarter hours); on Sundays, from 0645–1200 (five and one quarter hours), afternoon free. These are actual work hours, not including morning, noon, and evening inspections.[69]

It has come to my attention that the prisoners often do not work at all and the guards stand by, apathetic and bored. When asked, they say they can not do anything, because they have been forbidden to raise their hands against prisoners. This is ridiculous. The guards are responsible for making sure that the prisoners work, even though it is needless to note that it is forbidden to beat them.[70]

Question: When must you open fire on a prisoner?
Answer: When I suspect that he intends to escape.[71]

. . . SS Corporal Kallweit would not have been killed [by an inmate] had he kept all safety precautions. . . . I intend to ask the Führer's permission to have [Kallweit's murderer] strangled in public, in the presence of the camp's three thousand prisoners and the entire staff.[72]

Commandants have recently often been recommending lashes for prisoners caught in acts of sabotage in arms factories. I request that in future cases of this sort you submit requests for death by hanging. The execution will be carried out in public, in the presence of all the inmates of the camp.[73]

. . . SS Commander in Chief Himmler's visit to the camp . . . extremely satisfied . . . extraordinary team work . . . every officer and man did his best . . . deepest gratitude . . . extra day off for the entire staff.[74]

Guards have invited their wives and children to keep them company while on duty . . . [75]

Many irregularities have been discovered in the completion of identity forms for inmates when they are transferred from camp to camp. Interrogation of inmates is frequently careless, leaving out basic information such as birth date and location of birth. It is most important that each inmate be registered immediately upon his arrival at the camp, and care should be taken to register him accurately.[76]

Inmate Registration Form: . . . height, build, face, eyes, nose, mouth, ears, teeth, hair . . . character.[77]

. . . do your work quickly, accurately, and without unnecessary paper work.[78]

. . . in small camps the gold teeth pulled out of the mouths of prisoners should be made into an annual shipment. The teeth should not be transferred in small, monthly parcels.[79]

Staff members may not leave the camp without permission . . . I have recently had to discipline irresponsible guards who were late in returning to the camp, in violation of orders.[80]

The village of Natzweiler is off limits, effective immediately, due to an epidemic.[81]

. . . outside visitors and, in particular, visitors from abroad, will not be allowed to tour the camp except when accompanied by the commandant himself, or at least by a senior officer with political training. . . . The information given to the visitors is to be as brief as possible. It is to be delivered politely and in a matter-of-fact way. The misimpressions visitors are likely to suffer can cause problems not only in specific camps, but will also damage the good name of Germany.[82]

. . . staff members shall not waste electricity. Possession of private electrical appliances is forbidden . . . an order has been issued to conduct searches of the rooms of men in order to discover electrical appliances being held illegally.[83]

Wood lying around the camp is essential to ensure the supply of hot water in the coming winter. If the wood is wasted now there will not be hot water in the winter.[84]

. . . shortage of toilet paper . . . only five grams per person per day can be allocated.[85]

It has become apparent again and again that SS men are borrowing money from each other . . . this is totally forbidden. It is unworthy for an SS man to spend more than he has . . . those who violate this order will be court-martialed.[86]

. . . any SS man caught stealing food from a package sent to one of the prisoners—will be executed.[87]

. . . our victory in this war is certain beyond a shadow of a doubt. It is nevertheless the duty of every SS man to contribute to the defense fund in order to ease the financial burden the state is carrying.[88]

. . . it is strictly forbidden to put the SS skull symbol on automobile windshields or bicycle handlebars.[89]

. . . most camps, especially those in the east, are situated far from large cities and main roads . . . the staff works long hours and under a heavy physical and mental load and they have only minimal free time. They are thus dependent on the possibilities for entertainment in the camp itself. In this light, I request that you send us urgently books, games, radios, and so on.[90]

. . . receipt: four accordions, 125 SS song books. One hundred copies of the book *Germany Forever*. . . . Book catalog: *Faust* (part one) . . . Hitler: *Mein Kampf* . . . Saint Exupéry: *The Little Prince;* von Klauswitz.[91]

. . . and 16 phonograph records were discovered among the effects of the above mentioned prisoner, on which were English lessons meant for Russian students. I suggest transferring the records to the intelligence division of the Waffen SS and in their place I request that the camp be supplied with records of light music, since we have a record player but no records.[92]

The prisoners' hair is to be sent to Alex Zink, Fur Manufacturers, Ltd., Nuremberg. The company will pay 0.50 marks for every kilogram of hair.[93]

. . . staff members who received orders to participate in the performances of the chorus will also participate regularly in its rehearsals.[94]

. . . anyone who had been present at the movie last night

would have been likely to think that he was not among disciplined soldiers but rather had somehow found himself among a wild and neglected horde. Many officers and soldiers were late for the film, sat in the back rows, made noise, laughed, and shattered beer bottles, all without consideration of their comrades. If this sort of behavior repeats itself, all future movies at the camp will be canceled.[95]

. . . staff members who visit the camp prostitutes are to pay two marks for each visit. One mark is for the prostitute and the second will be deposited in a special bank account. The head office of the SS has ordered that steps be taken to see that all the prostitutes' rooms are clean, orderly, and of pleasant appearance.[96]

. . . the sanitary conditions are nauseating . . .[97]

. . . Dachau: typhus epidemic . . .[98]

The life of the camps was run according to a grotesque and unique internal logic. "Time there is not like it is here, on earth," said the writer Yehiel ("K. Zetnik") Dinoor. "Every fraction of a second goes on one wheel. And the inhabitants of that planet did not have names. They did not have parents and they did not have children. They did not dress like they do here. They were not born and they did not give birth. They breathed according to other laws of nature. They did not live according to the laws of this world and did not die. Their name was a number."[99]

The barracks were segregated by sex, but in certain cases prisoners were allowed to marry, with the registration carried out by one of the SS officers; immediately after the registration the couple was separated again.[100] In the framework of the policy meant to encourage production in the camps, it was decided in 1943 that a prisoner who excelled in his work would be allowed to submit a request to visit, as a special reward, one of the camp prostitutes. The request, it was decided, would be submitted to the prisoner's immediate superior, who would pass it on to the commandant of the prisoner division, who would in turn pass it on to the commandant of the camp, who would consider it "without delay," as stated in the order.[101]

At the end of a long line of legal examinations it was decided that the heirs of a prisoner who died while being held at a concentration camp would be eligible to collect his life insurance, but only on condition that the prisoner paid the monthly premiums regularly during his term of imprisonment. For this reason, a special fund was set up in 1942 which paid the insurance premiums of prisoners until the day they died.[102] Preserved in one of the files is a draft of a letter to concentration camp commandants on the subject of foreign currency regulations. The document carries the date 12 October 1944 and reads as follows:

> With the transfer of the prisoners from the concentration camps in the conquered territories, large amounts of money in foreign currency have accumulated in some of the camps. Inasmuch as this money belongs to prisoners there is a possibility of exchanging it for German currency, in accordance with the regulations of the Reichsbank [the German central bank]. From an economic point of view the purchasing power of the public should not rise. For this reason the camp commandants are requested to see that the above mentioned money is deposited in savings accounts . . . the Reichsbank recently decided to allow camps to open collective savings accounts, in the names of the camps, in which the prisoners' money will be deposited. The list of names will remain with the camp command. . . .
>
> The bank has set new regulations for the exchange of foreign currency belonging to prisoners, as follows: until now, in order to carry out the transaction, a list of names of prisoners wishing to exchange their money has been required. Since the camps notified the bank that they are unable to produce such lists, the bank has decided to suffice with notification of the number of prisoners whose money is to be exchanged, by nationality. The camp will accept responsibility with regard to the bank that none of the prisoners are violating the currency regulations. As such, the bank will forgo the submission of the identity documents, such as passports and the like, of the prisoners who own the

deposits, so long as the camp command obligates itself to record the foreign currency exchange transactions on the prisoner's passport, when he is released from the camp. The camp command is to promise the bank that all the information it gives is correct, complete, and in accordance with the foreign currency regulations.[103]

In 1936 the authorities had to deal with the question of who would take care of children when both their parents were prisoners in concentration camps. At the conclusion of a wearying discussion it was decided that the father and mother would be released on an alternating monthly basis. Each one would spend a month incarcerated and the next month would take care of the children, until one of them was released for good.[104]

Dozens of the standing orders sent to the concentration camp commandants were meant to establish procedures for the execution of prisoners, the cremation of their bodies, and the notification of their relatives. In 1943 Himmler signed a six-page work paper on this subject. When a prisoner was executed within the area of the camp, Himmler ordered, as if this were a unique event, the commandant must be present, along with his deputy and a doctor.[105] A new order was issued a few days afterwards, forbidding the execution of German women within the area of the camp. The camp command was required to transfer them for this purpose to the local police in their place of residence.[106] In 1938, the camp commandants were told to send telegrams to the relatives of prisoners who had died, without noting the circumstances of their death. The relatives could notify the camp within twenty-four hours of their desire to see the body before it was cremated. They were required to arrive at the camp within three days.[107] This arrangement was later canceled. In 1942 the camp commandants received instructions not to notify relatives directly of the deaths of prisoners, since these notices, it was said, had caused disquiet among the population. Instead, the commandants were to notify the authority in the prisoner's place of residence that brought about the prisoner's arrest. The local authorities would deliver the death announcement to prisoners' families.[108] At a certain point the camps were freed of the obligation to make notification of the death of Jewish prisoners. Afterwards, this order was also amended: as before, notification was to be made of the death of a Jewish prisoner—if the prisoner's relatives were not Jews. There was no obligation to make notification of the death of a Jewish prisoner to Jewish relatives.[109] In 1942 one of the heads of the SS complained that death notices were sent to the relatives of prisoners on postcards. "This is not proper," he rebuked the camp commandants. "It is only fitting that you show some manners and send the death notices in sealed envelopes."[110]

The first extermination facilities were set up on an experimental basis in the Chelmno camp, in December 1941. After the Wannsee conference, during which the details of the execution of the Final Solution were clarified, facilities for extermination in gas chambers were activated also in the Belzek camp (March 1942), Sobibor (May 1942), and Treblinka (June 1942), all within a radius of 300 kilometers of Warsaw. These camps were in operation for close to a year and a half. They were extermination facilities, not concentration camps: they were not used to imprison people, but to murder them. Extermination facilities also operated in Auschwitz and Majdanek. Camps for the liquidation of Jews on a more modest scale operated also near Vilna, Riga, Minsk, Kowno, and Lvov.

"The freight trains," stated the verdict against Adolf Eichmann, "which carried the Jews earmarked for destruction, arrived at a special platform at the camp, near the extermination facilities. Advance notification was sent by Eichmann's office, which dispatched the trains, and they were marked with special numbers and letters, in order to prevent their confusion with shipments of other prisoners. There was an average of 2000 Jews on each train. After removing the Jews from the trains and counting them—lists of names did not exist—they all passed by two SS doctors who divided those fit for work from those unfit. On the average, 25 percent were found fit. The belongings of the Jews remained on the platform and would be brought afterwards to storage rooms for sorting. Among the unfit for work, the men were separated from the women and children, and they were brought to the closest vacant extermination complex. There they had to strip, in rooms which gave the impression of being delousing facilities.

The hesitant were told to hurry so that those after them would not
have to wait long, and to pay attention to where they laid their
clothes in order to be able to find them after the shower. From
there they were brought to the gas chamber, which was disguised
as a shower room by the installation of showerheads, pipes, and
drains. After they had all entered the door was locked and the
Zyklon B gas was dropped from the top, through a special
opening. It immediately vaporized and did its work. Death came
in from three to fifteen minutes. Thirty minutes afterwards the gas
chamber was opened and the bodies were transferred to the
crematories, after the women's hair had been cut off and gold
teeth removed. There were five crematories in which 10,000
bodies could be burnt every day. The ashes were crumbled into
dust and thrown into the Vistula River."[111]

The following also could only be written in that particular
system of values which established good and bad, permitted
and forbidden, life and death, on that other planet.

"On that same pile of trash," it says, "not far from the camp,
were used articles of clothing and blankets. It was a terrifying
sight. What horrible waste. A large portion of the uniforms
thrown there were still usable. It is hard to believe that
something like this could happen here."[112] The man who was
so disturbed by the waste at his camp was a senior officer at
Auschwitz. That was in January 1945. The number of people
destroyed in the camp had at that time already exceeded one
million.

All in all, the life of the staff of the camps was more
comfortable and secure than service on the front. The appointment of an SS officer as commandant of a concentration camp
often involved an improvement in living standards. "I have in
my hands an order, signed by the Commander-in-Chief of the
SS, according to which I am to move with my family to
Dachau," said one of the officers to his superiors at the camp's
authority. "At Dachau one may obtain only four-room apart-
ments. Today I live in a two-room apartment. Unfortunately, I
do not have the means necessary to pay cash for the additional
furniture I will need in the new apartment. If I pay for the new
furniture in installments I will have to add between 25 and 30
percent of the price. I therefore apply to you with a request that
you approve me a loan of 1000 marks with the arrangement of

monthly payments to return the debt, at a rate of between 25-30 marks."[113] The base pay of SS Colonel Wilhelm Goecke, the commandant of the concentration camps in Warsaw and Kowno, was 740 marks in 1942. Supplementary payments, including child allowances, raised the sum to 955.40 marks. After various deductions, including a pension fund, he had 666.13 marks.[114] A nice sum, but not excessive.

SS department heads in Berlin received higher salaries, but the commandant's residence as well as, it seems, his uniform, his board, and that of his family were supplied by the camp. The standard of living of many of the concentration camp commandants was higher than anything they could have expected to achieve at the beginning of their careers, whether in civilian life or in the SS. There were those who lived in spacious houses, with cooks, servants, gardeners, and drivers, some of them from among the camp inmates. The Villa Koch at Buchenwald and the Villa Höss at Auschwitz were the talk of the entire SS. Thirty years later Rosina Kramer would still remember with longing the commandant's house, with its servants, in Bergen-Belsen.[115]

Joseph Kramer was born on November 10, 1906, in Munich, and he grew up in Augsburg.[116] His was a middle-class family. As a public official, an accountant, his father's future was secure; he could look forward to a monthly pension upon retirement. Kramer was an only child and received, as was the custom, a strict Catholic education. He remained close to his parents until his death. They lived for thirty years after his execution.

Kramer began elementary school in 1912. World War I raged during half of his school years and left an indelible impression on him, even though his father, whose profession was in demand, was not sent to the front. In 1920, when he was 14 years old, Kramer decided to be trained as an electrician. He registered as a student in a local school for commerce and studied there for more than a year, and was afterwards employed for three years as a trainee in a department store. In 1925 he received his first steady job, but his employers needed him only a few months and then fired him. During the next nine years, until he began receiving a regular salary from the SS at the beginning of 1934, he was for all intents and purposes unemployed, with the exception of the temporary jobs he performed here and there as a door-to-door salesman. During this entire period he lived, single, with his parents. "That situation caused him no small amount of difficulty," his widow related in an interview. "He felt that he was not going anywhere; at one stage he lost all hope. From his point of view, those were years of failure."[117] In December 1931 Kramer joined the Nazi party.

"Over the years he had not shown any interest in politics, did not believe in it, and did not understand it," his widow said. "For that reason, it would not be correct to say that suddenly, close to Christmas 1931, he discovered politics. It was actually the other way around: his personal problems became those of millions of other people. What bothered him now bothered the entire country. I don't think that he ever wanted the party to represent his political views, because I don't believe that he had any solid political views. What happened was much simpler. At a particular point he found himself surrounded by a huge public, all bitter and close to despair like he was, and they joined the Nazi party. So he joined, too. They identified not only with the party, but also with each other. My husband identified with them, and like them believed in the party. He probably asked himself how he had not discovered the party earlier; after all, the party promised solutions to all his problems. From the day he understood this, he gave himself over to Nazism with all his heart. I think he remained ever grateful to his movement. Without the party and the SS he would have remained a failure for the rest of his life."[118] The party did not immediately improve his financial situation; the SS, in which he enlisted in June 1932, did not pay him a salary at the beginning, either. He served in the organization as a volunteer.

"My husband would always tell me how much the movement changed his attitude towards the future and to life in general," his widow related. "The movement gave him great hope. He would say that, for him, Nazism was a deep emotional experience. The movement caught him. It allowed him to believe in himself once again. He would tell me that what drew him to the SS more than anything else was the desire to be in the company of other young men, of his age, in the same situation. He found close friends in the organization and their friendship was very dear to him. They would always enjoy themselves together. After all, all his friends then found themselves, like he did, with a chance to escape the despair they had fallen into years ago, and to start all over again. That happened thanks to the party and the SS. This joint effort, the new faith, brought them closer to each other. They had something to give each other. When I thought about that years later I said to myself that my Kramer felt more comfortable among men than among women."[119]

Some time after the party gained power, it became apparent that it could help Kramer find permanent employment as an official of the municipality of Augsburg, but in the spring of 1934 he preferred enlisting in the regular service of the SS. The organization offered him a full-time job. It would seem that during the two years he belonged to the organization as a volunteer, his commandants came to the conclusion that he should be brought among them as an officer. His widow remembered that he was very pleased with the change in his status. At the age of 28, he could for the first time allow himself to leave his parents' house.

"He told me once that until he enlisted into regular service in the SS, he could not free himself of the feeling that he was still a boy. Only after he left his parents' house did he begin to feel like a man."[120] It was a good job, on the bottom rung of a promising ladder of advancement. He had never been so close to his father's status, a public official. He was stationed at Dachau.

When he was first sent to Dachau, Kramer did not come into direct contact with the prisoners at the camp; he was employed as a clerk in the payments department of the SS. He knew, of course, of what was being done at the camp, but only rarely visited there himself. The first camp he served in was at Esterwegen; here, too, he had an administrative position in the headquarters. He had no connection with the prisoners themselves. With the closure of that camp, in 1936, he was returned to Dachau, once more as a clerk. In 1937, he was transferred to the Sachsenhausen camp, where he was put in charge of the mail. There, too, he knew what was going on, but his personal involvement in the atrocities were still marginal and indirect.

Four years would go by from the day he first entered the gates of a concentration camp before he arrived, in August 1938, at the Mauthausen camp. He was appointed deputy to the commandant, Franz Ziereis. This was the first time he took on part of the overall responsibility for one of the camps, the first time he personally dealt with prisoners.

So long as he could, he did his duty efficiently. His superiors praised him. Over the years, his widow remembered, Kramer became more serious, introspective, and unbending.[121] In the meantime, he also rose through the ranks. In 1940, he served for several months at Auschwitz, as deputy to Rudolf Höss, the commandant. He was trained in a special course at Dachau to serve as commanding officer of the prisoner section of the camp. He served in this role for more than a year at the Natzweiler camp, until being appointed commandant of the camp in July of 1942. He was then a 36-year-old captain. At that time the mass murder program was already underway in several places. There is good reason to believe that Kramer knew of this. In any case, in August 1943, Kramer supervised the gassing of eighty prisoners at Natzweiler; in accordance with orders, he sent the bodies to the University of Strasbourg, for scientific research. When he was asked, years later, how he felt while carrying this out, Kramer answered: "I didn't feel anything. I received an order to kill the prisoners, and that is what I did."[122] Eleven years after he enlisted in the SS, nine years after first passing through the gates of a concentration camp, after his experience at Natzweiler, he seems to have been able to do anything. His superiors probably knew this, and for that reason recalled him eastwards in May 1944, and made him commandant of Auschwitz II, in Birkenau, one of the extermination camps.

"At the sight of those people being pushed into the gas chambers," he said during his trial, "I asked myself if it was a correct action, and I wondered if whoever ordered it would know how to justify it in the future."[123] It is doubtful whether Kramer really ever asked himself such a question. His responsibility was limited, he did not initiate the orders he received; his job was to carry them out. He was not expected to consider whether the orders he received were legal—he never doubted that they were. He took no initiatives—that was not his job. Even during the last days of the war he did not ask the army to help him overcome the catastrophic situation at Bergen-Belsen, even though he could have done so: his orders told him to function solely through the civil system. The first British soldiers who entered Bergen-Belsen had the impression that Kramer did not see the prisoners as human beings like him, and in fact those of the prisoners who had held on did not look like living human beings: it was a large crowd of walking skeletons. The bodies of the dead were scattered in piles all over the camp.[124]

Kramer never exceeded what was permitted and forbidden him when he joined the SS. He served the organization with a deep sense of duty, both ideological and emotional. He developed as the system itself developed, and became part of the brutality escalating from year to year, from Dachau to Bergen-Belsen.

Rosina Kramer said that her husband "did not like Birkenau," and for that reason asked to be transferred to Bergen-Belsen. According to her, he supposed that the atmosphere there would be "nicer" and hoped to establish a model camp, "clean and orderly, with lots of flowers."[125]

———————

IT was not easy to find Rosina Kramer. After her husband was executed, she remarried, changed her name, and moved to a small town where she became a teacher. When she retired, she returned to the house of her son, Karl Heinz, only a few kilometers from the site of the camp, between Bergen and Belsen. She answered my letter immediately, as if she had been expecting it. Afterwards she told me that some time before his death her husband told her that one day, perhaps in twenty-five years, perhaps in thirty, someone would come and ask her to tell the truth about what he did at Bergen-Belsen. He asked her to cooperate with that person, for the sake of history. She received my letter two months before the thirtieth anniversary of her husband's death. That day she had been sitting at the hairdresser's, and while waiting she leafed through a magazine. She found an interview with her husband's executioner: "Kramer was a frightening man," the executioner told the reporter. "But he was not frightening," his widow told me when we met. She always called him "Papa." Her son, who was identical to his father, was present during our conversation. They invited me to dinner. When it became late, they asked me if I would like to spend the night at their house. Among their books was one on the Holocaust. "Horrible," said Karl Heinz Kramer. "It's horrible what they did, but my father was not part of all that," he argued.

Rosina Kramer kept in her possession several letters her husband had written. She read them into a tape recorder for me. Some of them were from the period before Kramer was involved in the camps. In a letter to his parents he described, in Bavarian dialect, the birth of his son. How the contractions came early, how he took his wife to the hospital in an old car, how the car broke down on the way. "Still not born and already making trouble," Kramer wrote of his son. "I'll have to talk to the guy as soon as possible and make it clear that I absolutely dislike this kind of independence." Some of the letters were sent from jail. "What do they want from me?" Kramer wrote. "Maybe they are putting me on trial just because I was in the SS." In an emotional letter to his wife's parents he wrote, "I'm a good man, otherwise our Rosie would not have married me." The letters give the impression that he did not quite understand the nature of his crimes. Perhaps he fooled his widow and his son, and perhaps he fooled himself, also. The impression is that he did only what he thought was right. "Papa believed that everything happened as it was supposed to happen," his widow said, and once he even told her that they should be thankful that they were not born Jews, since that would mean that they would have to die.

———————

2
THE UNDEFEATED ARMY

DURING the first half of November 1925, Adolf Hitler's driver hired eight muscle men to serve as the Führer's bodyguards. They had just been released from the same prison in which Hitler had been incarcerated after his abortive attempt to overthrow the Bavarian government in the "Beer Hall Putsch," fifteen months previously.[1] Additional thugs were hired during the four weeks that followed. These were the founders of the *Schutzstaffel* (SS), the "Defense Corps" of the Nazi party; within a short period of time it had become a fearsome terror organization as well as a source of tremendous political, military, and economic power. By the time Henrich Himmler became its commander in 1929 it had 280 men, and at the end of that same year there were 1000. In December 1930 the SS had 2700 members, in December 1931 there were close to 15,000 and on January 30, 1933, the day Adolf Hitler became chancellor of Germany, they had reached 52,000. A year after Hitler's assumption of power there were close to 200,000 men in the SS; during World War II their number came close to 1 million.[2] Hundreds of thousands of them were not German, but rather volunteers and draftees from a number of other European countries.

After the war many senior SS men claimed that they had joined the organization because they had not found any other employment. "My father died in 1928," Max Pauly, commandant of the Neuengamme camp, testified at his trial when asked why he had joined the SS. "I was 18 years old, and suddenly we faced great economic difficulties; I had the responsibility for providing for the entire family. I saw no other way."[3]

Actually, the SS did not improve Pauly's economic situation. Like most members of the organization, he served as a volunteer, during the afternoon and evening and on weekends. Until the Nazis came into power at the beginning of 1933, the SS had practically no way to offer salaries to its men. Only a few individuals received modest economic support from time to time. Even after the Nazi regime was founded only a handful of SS men received compensation; in 1938 the organization paid a monthly salary to only 3500 of its 14,000 officers, that is, only about 25 percent of them.[4] The number of volunteers rose steadily, even though the German unemployment rate went down. Most members of the organization did not, therefore, serve for economic reasons: they joined the SS because they identified with it. Those who later became commandants of concentration camps stood out from the start in their fanaticism and emotional allegiance to its struggle. They came to the Nazi movement in the same way that millions of other Germans came to support it. Like others, they were also reacting to the political, social, economic, intellectual, and psychological chaos of post-World War I Germany. The revolutionary image of the movement, the hope it nourished and the hatred and anti-Semitism it spread were attractive, and the charismatic nature of Adolf Hitler intoxicated them.

The camp commandants were part of the nucleus of the movement. Most of them joined it early on. One out of three joined before 1930; two-thirds joined before the Nazis gained power in 1933, at a time when the SS could not reward them for their service and when there was no certainty that it ever would. Indeed, supporting the party at such an early stage often involved personal and economic risk, and sometimes legal problems.

During the first years of its existence, while its major responsibilities were still protecting Adolf Hitler, keeping order at party rallies, and disrupting the gatherings of other parties, the SS functioned in the framework of the party's "storm troopers," the SA, and was under its command. The men of the SA, or the "brownshirts," as they were called, were among the first Nazis, from the year 1921. Among other things, they carried out political terror in order to help the Nazis seize power and, beginning in 1933, to fortify their hold on it. The members of the SS, the "blackshirts," saw themselves from the start as a select group. The SA was more plebian, and the SS considered its members rabble and asked to be freed of their control. The turning point came on the night of June 30, 1934, the "Night of the Long Knives." That night, and during the days that followed, Hitler used the SS to carry out a bloody purge of the SA ranks. From this point onward the SS gained strength steadily. Within a few weeks it was no longer under the SA command and operated as an independent organization. Its source of authority was Adolf Hitler himself.

The SS functioned in every respect as a military organization, and its men saw themselves from the very beginning as soldiers in the service of the party and the state. It aimed at gaining members from all areas of the country, and the more members it gained the more it was able to establish itself in new places. It did all this while preserving a centralized structure and vertical command. Its members wore uniforms and held ranks parallel to those of the army. As years passed, and especially after the Nazis gained power, the SS spent more time engaging in military exercises. The SS built itself communications, transport, and supply systems—including weapons and ammunition—as well as an officer training program. By the time the SS set out for the Second World War it had a well-founded legal and disciplinary system similar to the army's disciplinary code but independent of it.

The army watched the development of the SS with mixed feelings. During the days of the Weimar Republic, while it was still limited by the Versailles Treaty to 100,000 men, the army tended to look with favor on military or paramilitary associations, whether legal or not. This attitude changed when the Nazis gained power and the SS came to see itself more and more as a military organization independent of the Wehrmacht (the German Army) and in competition with it. From this point onward the army made every effort to keep the SS as small as possible. Hitler at first tended to support his generals in this matter: the SS was assigned police functions for the most part. The missions it took upon itself were described as "special activities to preserve state security," and everyone understood that this meant internal security, or in other words, political activity meant to shore up the Nazi regime.[5] The division of authority between the SS and the army was therefore clear, or so it seemed; in fact, the SS aimed to be a standing army.

Heinrich Himmler was 29 years old when he received command of the SS; his story is similar to that of many of the concentration camp commandants. A combination of his world view and the circumstances of his life brought him to the SS. He was born in 1900, the son of a private teacher in Munich, and grew up in an established, conservative, and royalist house; he studied at a gymnasium and received a diploma. In those days he dreamed of serving the army. When World War I broke out he was only 14 years old. When he reached the age of 17 he asked to be sent to the front. His father, a patriot, helped him. He had connections in the imperial court, but by the time Himmler was enlisted and put through basic training, the war ended. He did not get to the front, but he considered himself a soldier for the rest of his life. He once tried to enlist in the navy but was rejected because he wore glasses. He tried several times to enlist in the Republican Army, but for various reasons did not succeed. The defeat of Germany and the establishment of a republic led people like Himmler—bourgeois, conservative, royalist—to the extreme nationalist right; they aspired to revenge and dreamed of re-establishing the monarchy. Hundreds of organizations representing these sentiments sprang up all over Germany, among them paramilitary organizations and even real private armies. Himmler joined one of them. When Adolf Hitler attempted to over-throw the government of Bavaria, Himmler and his comrades went to help him. Himmler was then 23 years old. The Beer Hall Putsch failed and Hitler was imprisoned, but Himmler remained loyal to him and his platform, waiting patiently for his release. In the meantime he drove his motorcycle from town to town, from beer hall to beer hall, spreading Hitler's ideas. He was at the same time studying agriculture at Munich University. Now he dreamed of buying his own farm in the country. This also, like his dream of serving in the army, was an expression of his conservative ideology. Agricultural romanticism was fundamentally antimodern, antiurban, anti-industrial, anticapitalist, and anti-Jewish. Life in the country was meant to express the true spirit of the German nation and was also a response to the shock of the shameful defeat in the war. In time Himmler would foster and encourage an entire mythology of the links of blood between man and the soil, the basis of the SS philosophy. All this also brought him to the agricultural movement where he met, among others, Rudolf Höss. Years later he would send Höss to set up Auschwitz and oversee the extermination of the Jews.

Hitler was released from prison at the end of 1924. Himmler helped him reorganize the party, which paid Himmler a modest salary. At that time he had no other work. He married, but unhappily, living alone most of the time and devoting himself to the SS.

In 1936 Hitler appointed Himmler to be "commander in chief of the SS and chief of the German Police." This was a new title. It gave the SS official status as a political army, part of the security forces. By this time the SS had already been divided into three parts: the General SS (*Allgemeine* SS), the Militarized Formations (*Verfügungstruppen,* or VT), and the Death's Head Formations (*Totenkopfverbände,*or TV). Hitler signed a secret document defining more clearly the status of the different parts of the SS. This document was of tremendous importance. It established the status of the SS as the party's army. It emphasized the "close link" between the SS and the police. Hitler ruled that if, for instance, it would be necessary to put down internal riots in Germany, the SS would do so and not the Wehrmacht. The army had good reason to be satisfied with this distinction: the generals saw themselves as above politics.

The SS's military ability was not up to that of the Wehrmacht. Frustrated by the army's low opinion of it, the SS forged a self-image according to which it was an elite force competitive with the Wehrmacht. The competition between the two armies was expressed daily in verbal exchanges and even fistfights between SS men and soldiers in beer halls and other meeting places; it was also expressed in the highest levels of the government. In February 1938 General Freiherr von Fritsch, army chief of staff, wrote that the Militarized Formations of the SS were demonstrating a negative and sometimes inimical attitude to the army. "There is a distinct impression that this enmity is purposely fostered in its ranks," the general wrote.[6]

Von Fritsch knew what he was talking about. In February 1938 he was the victim of one of the best known intrigues in the history of the Nazi regime. There is good reason to believe that, in addition to reflecting the decay and corruption in the army, this action was also rooted in the competition between the army and the SS. A few days before von Fritsch made his statement about the SS, Adolf Hitler was told that the general, a Prussian bachelor of 58, had been for three years a victim of extortion and had paid to prevent exposure of his homosexuality. Hermann Göring showed Hitler documents he had received in this connection from Himmler, presumptive evidence of the truth of the story.

Von Fritsch was summoned to the Führer's office the next day. Göring and Himmler were also there. Hitler recounted the story to the thunderstruck general. Von Fritsch denied it, and swore on his honor as an officer that there was no truth to the accusations. Himmler suggested bringing the general face-to-face with the source of the story, and on the spot, in the presence of the Führer, he brought in a known criminal named Hans Schmidt. Schmidt told those present that he had been spying on homosexuals for some time in order to extort money from them. He claimed to have seen the general during a meeting with a man, in a dark alley, not far from the Potsdam train station in Berlin. He claimed that each time he had been released from prison General von Fritsch had paid him hush money up until his next arrest. Von Fritsch was silent. His shock and outrage were so great that he did not know what to say. The spectacle of the head of the German state, the successor of Hindenburg and the Hohenzollerns, introducing such a shady character in such a place for such a purpose, wrote William Shirer, was too much for him.[7] Hitler demanded his resignation. Von Fritsch demanded a court-martial to allow him to clear his name. An investigation by the army and the Ministry of the Interior found that von Fritsch had fallen victim to a plot cooked up in Himmler's headquarters. The findings of the inquiry did not, however, help the general, and he was removed from his command (in the end he was acquitted). A few weeks later the Wehrmacht invaded Austria and annexed it to the Reich. Several SS regiments participated in the operation. Despite the guidelines Hitler issued the previous August in order to placate the army, it was impossible to mistake the trend: in both the secret and open struggle between the Wehrmacht and the SS, the party organization had been immeasurably strengthened; its aspiration to be an army in every respect was now closer to realization than it had ever been.

Close to two weeks before the Nazi invasion of Poland the Militarized Formations were put under the army high command, and when war broke out they took part in the occupation. From here on out they began to be called the *Waffen SS* (the Combat SS).

The commandants of the concentration camps also saw themselves first and foremost as soldiers: two-thirds of them had served in the army before joining the Nazi party and the SS. Most of them had volunteered for the army before, during, and after the First World War.

A young man at the beginning of the century who chose to serve several years in the German army often found that he had made the right decision. If he had been born into the middle or lower-middle class, as had most of the camp commandants, he did not have many options. After completing their elementary education, most of the commandants had been meant to enter an apprenticeship in carpentry, baking, or some other craft, or sometimes in a small store, as a way of training themselves to be self-employed artisans or storekeepers. As soldiers in the standing army they were public employees with a higher social status than that of artisans or even storeowners. Public employees received monthly salaries and a small pension upon retirement. At base, the difference between public employees and those in other sectors was not measured by income; the income of a mailman was not necessary higher than that of a cobbler, but the mailman was an official of the state and as such could lay claim to part of its authority. A young man who decided at the beginning of the century to serve several years in the army was likely to base his decision on the income and social status it granted, even if the salary of a young soldier did not raise him much above the social class into which he had been born, and even if there was only the faintest of chances that he could advance to the highest, or even middle, ranks. With the exception of only two or three of them, the camp commandants had not completed their high school studies and did not have the high school diploma that was a condition of receiving an officer's insignia. The officer corps was open, almost exclusively, to the sons of the aristocracy. The future concentration camp commandants must have known this, but they enlisted anyway. In civilian life they could not go far without a diploma either, and military service could eventually become a jumping-off point. After twelve or sometimes twenty years of service, the army man had gained experience, contacts, and a position he could not have attained had he worked in a bakery all those years. And in wartime there was nevertheless hope of becoming an officer, or so they chose to believe.

There were also other reasons for joining the army. As soldiers, they shared in the state's status and strength. The vast majority of them grew up in families which instilled their sons with patriotism, often of an extreme nationalist type. The middle and lower middle classes did not teach their sons to doubt or rebel. They taught them to obey and to toe the line, an expression of the social and political conservatism that was a sort of imitation of bourgeois society, a sort of self-deprecation, and a desire to become part of a higher class. The state, the family, the church, the Kaiser (or king or duke), the father, and the Pope (or the Protestant minister) represented absolute values, as did the army and the general.

The army was, therefore, more than just a way to make a living. It represented a system of values that the volunteers had learned in their childhood. Their self-image as soldiers flattered them, as did the uniform they wore. A uniform meant a lot in the Germany of the beginning of the century. When a man enlisted in the army, he knew his place in a clear and well-defined framework. The future, at least for the next few years, was certain, and that certainty, like the framework itself, provided no little security and self-confidence. The soldier did not stand alone, like his father the carpenter or plasterer who got by only with difficulty; the army shielded him. He did not have to take initiative himself or do any original thinking, nor was he responsible for his actions. He was expected only to obey. Military service was dangerous, adventurous, and challenging, and was an outlet for violence as an expression of toughness and manhood. The arms, like the uniform, flattered the soldier and were symbols of his virility and patriotism. Many soldiers received a measure of personal power as sergeants. Personal data, and in many cases medical reports in the personnel files of the concentration camp commandants, indicate that they were in exceptional physical condition. For this reason they naturally tended to find their place in a framework which needed solid young men like them; furthermore, most of them did not excel at anything else. A young man enlisting in the army left his parents' house and immediately turned from boy to man, at least in his own eyes and those of his friends and commanders. The law defined him as a juvenile until he reached the age of 21. Many of them saw it as the only way of getting out of their parents' house, other than becoming a journeyman in some craft. Moreover, the army put off the day-to-day drudgery of family life for them, and this also attracted many.

The national, political, social, economic, personal, and psychological factors which led young Germans to enlist in the army before World War I were just as important afterwards. It was not long after the armistice that the defeat was being presented as the fault of the politicians. Had the political leadership not knifed the army in the back—or so the Germans believed—Germany would not have been defeated. Even after the army continued to be part of the social elite and, as before the war, represented the values of patriotism, heroism, and manhood. War stories stirred people's imaginations despite the defeat. A young man who decided to be a soldier after the war could perhaps hope that he could make up for what he had missed then, and perhaps believed that he and his friends would not repeat the mistakes that the previous generation of soldiers had made.

Many camp commandants joined the SS at a time of personal or family crisis. They found hope and encouragement in the organization, and this in an age of despair. It was a new social order—a substitute for what they had lost—in which there was a place for each of them. It was more than the Nazi party offered. The party only united people of common views and sentiments into a political force. Membership in the SS brought with it a unique way of life, a mentality, an ethic. The SS was a male aristocracy, a religious order, a mob, and a large family, all in one. More than anything else it was an army: brutal and sentimental, pragmatic and dogmatic, insensitive and romantic— all at the same time. It fostered its own worldview and system of values, a mixture of overbearing pride and self-pity, violent nationalism and supernatural, pan-European racism, an almost ascetic self-denial, and an erotic cult of youth and manliness. Its attraction was very strong. After the Nazis came to power, the SS offered its men a share in the prestige and power of the movement. "We were the best and the toughest," Johannes Hassebroeck, one of the commandants of the Gross Rosen camp, said thirty years later, still very proud.[8]

Hilmar Wäckerle, the first commandant of the Dachau camp, was 14 years old when his father, a notary public from Munich, sent him to the officers school of the Bavarian Army.[9] The school painstakingly defended the monarchist values of the state and set itself the goal of protecting the country from corruption. Its headmaster gloried in its tradition, beginning 150 years before Wäckerle was accepted as a cadet. In the fifty years before World War I the school trained about half of the generals in the Bavarian Army. Of the kingdom's seven Ministers of War, five had been graduates of the school, as were seven of the thirteen army chiefs of staff. An entire set of officers who were to lead the Wehrmacht during World War II also came from this school, including Hitler's chief of staff, Alfred Jodl. In choosing the 200 new cadets accepted every year, the school's administration tended to prefer the sons of officers in the standing army, continuing the military tradition, but several places were also reserved for the sons of senior officials in the government and local administration, as well as for the sons of lawyers, doctors, and the like.[10] Hilmar Wäckerle was one of these. When he was accepted to the school he swelled with pride, as did his father and his relatives. They saw it as a great honor. One of the commandants later wrote of the conservative atmosphere that prevailed at the school: "During the years of plenty at the beginning of the century, which brought with them various manifestations of permissive decay, the school redoubled its efforts to maintain the true spirit of the officer staff as it had always been, fostering the consciousness of national duty, sacrifice, toughness, chivalry, and brotherhood-at-arms."[11] Like the Wehrmacht, the SS would attribute such characteristics to itself and try to foster them in its ranks. The young men in the school divided their time between lessons in the classroom and military training and physical education, including fencing without face protectors. The curriculum was identical to that used in the academic gymnasia, with particular emphasis on the study of physics and mathematics. Military discipline was imposed on the cadets and they had to observe it precisely. Exceeding the permitted could bring, among other things, a beating. From the day they arrived at the school they were expected to behave like men, soldiers, and patriots, in the spirit of the officer ethic, both within the school and outside it. They lived and grew up in dormitories, always in uniform, always part of a group. The atmosphere was competitive. Each cadet could at any moment suffer the worst humiliation he knew: expulsion from the school. If he remained at the school he was considered a cadet for three years, at the end of which he enlisted for a period of six years in the army, as an officer.

World War I broke out ten months after Hilmar Wäckerle became a cadet. Three years later, in August 1917, he was assigned to the Bavarian Infantry Battalion, and in March 1918 found himself at the French front. "The soldiers lay packed together, one next to the other in the trenches," his battalion's battle log records. "The shriek of the bullets and thunder of the shells did not cease even for a moment. . . . The bodies of their comrades piled up before their eyes, piles and piles, no one took time to care for the wounded, they died in horrible agony."[12] Sergeant Hilmar Wäckerle was wounded in September and sent to an army hospital; within a few weeks he was told that Germany had been defeated and had surrendered. Defeat meant that there was no chance that Wäckerle would ever be an officer in the standing army. He had not had time to complete the matriculation examinations before going to the war, and after the war the German army was disbanded. A dream he had cherished since the age of 14 was snatched away from him. Naturally, he was disappointed. With the end of the war he found himself, like millions of others, in the midst of political, social, and psychological chaos. Economically, he was better off than others. Upon being released from the hospital, two months after the surrender, he completed his examinations, studied English and French, and became a student in the faculty of agriculture at the Technical University in Munich. One of his fellow students was Heinrich Himmler. Wäckerle continued to see himself as an army man. His war continued, but the enemy changed. His enemy was now Marxism. Wäckerle went to anti-Communist rallies, took part in demonstrations and street fights, and joined one of the numerous veterans' organizations established in Germany after the army was disbanded in the wake of the defeat. Each of these saw itself as a *Freikorps*, or "free militia." The Freikorps Oberland was founded in Ingolstadt, Bavaria, a short time after the establishment of the Bavarian Republic in April 1919. The organization was made up of 1500 officers; among other things, it aided Adolf Hitler's putsch attempt.[13]

Wäckerle, by 1922 already a member of the Nazi party, was there. He took part in additional activities of the force, including an attack on the life of Heinz Orbis, prime minister of the republic established under the protection of the French in the Palatinate. The plot to murder Orbis involved a reckless trip to Speyer, using forged identity papers. Orbis was shot as he dined at a local hotel on January 19, 1924; Wäckerle was there. He would later list these among the battles he had taken part in.

Among the members of the Freikorps were those who tended to describe themselves as the first political soldiers of the Third Reich, a sort of early incarnation of the SA and SS. It would seem that the shock of the degrading defeat, the political and social disconnection and the inability to find their place in Germany after the war all influenced them more than it did others. Unlike the members of the SS, they never really knew what they had fought for. Ernst von Salomon, their leader, described their mood in the following words:

> We could not answer the question presented to us so often from the other side of the divide: "What do you really want?" We could not answer the question because we did not understand it and those who asked it could not under-stand the answer. . . . There, on the other side of the

divide, they wanted property and security in life. . . . We rejected all those things: we did not want order or routine or plans of activity. We did not act in accordance with any plan; we did not aim at any defined goal. In fact, we did not act at all. Something acted within us and operated us. The question of what we wanted seemed to us incomparably foolish and unnecessary. . . .

They ask us what we believe in. We do not believe at all, in anything, except in action itself. Action for the sake of action. Nothing, only the ability to act. We were a group of warriors, drunk from the desires of the world. Full of impulsiveness and the joy of action. We did not know what we wanted and what we knew we did not want. War and adventure, stormy emotions and destruction. Our job was to attack, to rule.[14]

By the age of 25, with military education, combat experience, injury, disappointment, and paramilitary political involvement behind him, Wäckerle had a profession and was never to be unemployed. He was appointed manager of a cattle ranch. He had no reason to fear that his professional expectations as a civilian would not be realized. From this standpoint he was not a typical Freikorps man; his early membership in the Nazi party expressed a political awareness that most members of the Freikorps lacked. He was nevertheless partner to the mood von Salomon described, as were many other concentration camp commandants. They, like the rest of the members of the Freikorps, identified with the force that operated within them and pushed them into battle.

The SS later became expert at directing this battle lust to its purposes, giving its soldiers good reasons to fight. Wäckerle maintained his connection with the Nazi party, and rejoined when it reorganized in 1925 after Hitler's release from jail. He now appeared at rallies the party held in beer halls and on farms, and was one of the drafters of the agricultural plank in the party platform. He was, in fact, involved in everything that the Nazis later identified with the image of the "old fighter" they so admired, son of a family with the military in its blood. He continued to see himself as a soldier, as befitted an old fighter, and when he was able, he set up the SS volunteer regiment in Kempten. In February 1933 Himmler chose him to be the first commandant of the Dachau concentration camp. He served in the Militarized Formations which later became part of the Waffen SS and there, finally, became what he had dreamed of since his youth, a combat officer. During World War II he served at the Dutch and Russian fronts, was again wounded and received a multitude of citations and medals. He fell in July 1941 not far from the city of Lvov, wearing the rank of a colonel;[15] he had become a happy man. The Dachau camp was only an episode in his life.

The stories of many of the other concentration camp commandants of Wäckerle's generation are similar to his. The greater part of them volunteered for the army a few years before World War I. Hans Helwig, commandant of Sachsenhausen, served in the army for eighteen years; Jakob Weiseborn, commandant of Flossenbürg, served in the navy for eighteen years; Hermann Baranowski, also of Sachsenhausen, served for twenty-one and a half years; others had similar records.[16]

As military men by their own choice, they were more affected by the defeat of the German Imperial Army; many of them, though not all, went on fighting as Wäckerle did, in various paramilitary organizations and the Freikorps set up after the war by demobilized soldiers like them; with only one or two exceptions, they were among the earliest men to enlist in the SS.

World War I interrupted the lives of several future camp commandants at a point that had a decisive influence on their future. It cut short the studies of Wilhelm Goecke. Had he not enlisted in the army at the age of 16, he might have finished high school and earned a diploma.[17] The war interrupted the vocational training of Wilhelm Gideon: had the war not broken out while he was still a trainee, he might have realized his dream and become a mechanical engineer.

"I was an optimistic boy," Gideon later said. "Machines fascinated me. The professional possibilities I saw before me were excellent. Then the war broke out. For some reason it caught me up. It's hard to say why. Until then I had not thought of being a soldier, and they didn't send me a draft notice. But everyone volunteered, there was a sort of patriotic enthusiasm in the air, and militarism took hold of all of us. Everyone volunteered, and I did, too." He was 16 years old. "The inexperienced, somewhat naive boy who volunteered for the army came back from the front a man, tough and full of bitterness," Gideon said many years later.[18]

Friedrich Hartjenstein had not yet celebrated his ninth birthday when World War I began.[19] He was born in July 1905 in the city of Peine in Lower Saxony, the son of a cobbler. After completing ten years of schooling, two of them in high school, he decided, like Hilmar Wäckerle, to specialize in agriculture, with the goal of becoming the manager of a farm. He worked as a farm hand for four years and then, in December 1926, enlisted in the shrunken army the Allies had allowed Weimar Germany. Hartjenstein had just turned 21. When he had dreamed of agricultural management, he had still been very young; without a high school diploma he could not study agriculture at the university, as Wäckerle did. For this reason there was also no chance that he could ever become a degree-holding farmer with a good salary and possibilities for advancement. He probably was not aware of this when he decided, at the age of 16, to work on a farm. In 1926, after four years as a farm hand, he almost certainly thought that the army offered him the best possibilities. His decision to become a soldier marked a turning point in his life. He was assigned to an infantry unit. Twelve years later, in December 1938, he was promoted to first master-sergeant and found fit to serve as a reserve officer—not a glorious career. Not long before Hartjenstein left the army, while he was still trying to decide what to do in civilian life, he was offered a place in the Death's Head Formations of the SS. The Nazis had already established their power and World War II was at the door. He was offered the rank of second lieutenant in the Brandenburg Death's Head Formation, then stationed not far from the Sachsenhausen concentration camp. Hartjenstein, now 34, accepted the offer; within two months he found himself at the front. In 1942 he was sent, apparently as a punishment for his failure as an officer, to manage the extermination site at Auschwitz-Birkenau.

Karl Künstler, among the commandants of the Flossenbürg concentration camp, was also a professional soldier, and he also saw the SS as a military organization.[20] He was born in Zella in Thuringia, in January 1901. His father was a barber. After completing elementary school he left his parents' house and against their will began working as a clerk in one of the post offices in Kassel. That was in November 1915. It seems that he did not have any trouble finding employment, since many workers were at the front; he was not old enough to go into battle, but in 1919, "I put myself at the service of my country," he later wrote. He joined the army and was apparently happy, because he extended his service to twelve years, until 1931.

Künstler went through several courses in the army and was sent to the military management school. In 1929, at the age of 28, he married. By the time he decided to leave the army in 1931, he had acquired the rank of master sergeant and had two children. Aside from what he had learned in the army he had no professional experience. Immediately upon his release he joined the SS on a full-time basis. Apparently, he saw his job as commandant of a concentration camp as one of his military assignments. Künstler was a chronic drinker. As punishment for this he was transferred to the Prinz Eugen Waffen SS division, made up mostly of Romanians of German descent. This was humiliation. Künstler was killed in April 1945, during the battle of Nuremberg.

Otto Förschner's military career lasted for twenty years, including nine years of service in the SS.[21] He first spent a few years on his parents' farm in the Bavarian village of Dürrenzimmern, about 50 miles southeast of Nuremberg. In 1922, when he was 20 years old, Förschner joined the army. He served for 12 years. By the time he completed his service in 1934, the Nazis were in power. On the day of his release Förschner enlisted in the Militarized Formations of the SS. He was 32 years old, the father of two children, without a profession. He remained in the same unit until World War II broke out, and was then transferred to the Death's Head Formations. Two years later he was stationed in the Buchenwald Camp. He was to become commandant of the Dora camp. Towards the end of the war he had attained the rank of major, as had Adam Grünewald, commandant of the Hertogenbusch concentration camp in Holland.

Grünewald was a carpenter's son from the village of Frickenhausen, not far from Würzburg, Bavaria. His father died when he was 8, and the war broke out when he was 12. By the end of the war he was 16 years old. Grünewald worked then as an apprentice in a bakery. Just as he was about to begin his career as a baker, Germany was flooded with millions of demobilized soldiers, and all of them found themselves, like Grünewald, at a crossroads. Like him, they faced a new beginning and uncertainty. Grünewald did not find it difficult to identify with them. With their return from the front an immediate and tremendous labor surplus was created. The young baker, still without much experience, found it hard to find work. He joined one of the Freikorps and soon thereafter enlisted in the army. He signed up in advance for a period of twelve years. By the time of his release, in April 1931, Germany was deep in an economic crisis. Grünewald was now 28 years old, married, and the father of a two-year-old boy. He had no professional experience. For this reason he was thankful that luck worked in his favor and he was accepted, as a salaried worker, in the SA. Within two years he had been promoted to the rank of lieutenant colonel. The rank flattered him, despite the fact that the army did not recognize the ranks granted by the SA. Grünewald had finished his army service as a staff sergeant. A few months after the slaughter of the Night of the Long Knives, he transferred his allegiance from the SA to the SS.

The factors which drew many of the concentration camp commandants to enlist in the army in their youth also led them to the SS afterwards. The SS was a new, undefeated army. It offered its men senior officer rank without regard to their social origin or level of education. Although the army never recognized these ranks in full, they were enough to allow SS men to "play soldier," as Hans Hüttig later described it.[22]

SS men were often transferred from unit to unit—from the Death's Head Formations to the Militarized Formations, from concentration camps to the battle front and from the front to the camps. Members of the General SS were often dispersed among units of the Waffen SS. Many SS men went to serve in the army and army men came to serve in the SS, both the general and the militarized units, as well as in the Death's Head

Formations. In 1944, Heinrich Himmler warned the chief administrator of the camps, Oswald Pohl, not to be too harsh on Wehrmacht soldiers requesting to serve in the camps. Up to that point about 30 percent of those who offered themselves for service in the camps had been rejected, and Himmler thought that more should be taken.[23] Among the camp commandants were many who had been transferred from the front to the Waffen SS and from the Waffen SS to the camps. Fritz Suhren, later commandant of the women's camp at Ravensbrück, joined the Nazi party in 1928, at the same time that he enlisted in the SA. In October 1931 he transferred to the SS on a part-time basis, as a volunteer. From 1934 onwards he belonged to the General SS as a permanent, salaried worker. In the framework of his service he underwent a series of training programs at a Wehrmacht base, but was never used as a combat soldier. In 1941 he was stationed in the Sachsenhausen concentration camp.[24] Paul Werner Hoppe came to the camps, like other commandants, after having been wounded at the front and being found no longer fit for combat. He had, however, previously served in the Death's Head Formations and had been adjutant to the supervisor of the concentration camps, Theodor Eicke.[25] When Eicke went to the front in 1939, in the framework of the Waffen SS, he took several hundred officers from the concentration camps with him. Johannes Hassebroeck served in the Death's Head Formations beginning in 1936. His unit was stationed not far from the Esterwegen camp, and afterwards next to the Sachsenhausen camp. In the wake of a series of military exercises in the Wehrmacht, Hassebroeck was stationed in Eicke's combat Death's Head Division. In 1942 Hassebroeck was wounded also, and returned to one of the camps.[26]

Richard Baer enlisted in the SS in 1931, served in the Dachau camp, in the Gestapo prison on Columbia Street in Berlin, and in one of the Death's Head Formations, the Thüringen, which was stationed near the Buchenwald camp. In that unit he was a training instructor and did not come into direct contact with the prisoners. From there he was transferred to the Neuengamme camp, from which he was sent in 1940 to the front. Upon finding himself in the Waffen SS, he already had rich experience behind him as an officer in a concentration camp. Within a year he was wounded. In 1942 he went to work for the central camp administration in Berlin, and in 1944 became commandant of Auschwitz.[27] The fact that a man like Baer wore the uniform of the Wehrmacht did not testify, as one can see, to his not having taken part in the war crimes committed by the SS; the fact that he served in the Waffen SS did not automatically clear him of the crimes the SS committed in the concentration camps. The Waffen SS committed war crimes at the front as well. They were political soldiers and war criminals.

A PHOTOGRAPH discovered in one of the SS archives after the war shows an admissions committee at work screening candidates for the SS. Two officers with glasses and short haircuts, about 30 years old, stand in a large hall next to a desk covered with paper, a window behind them. Their faces express authority and a hint of disdain. The light falls on one of the candidates, a boy of 17 or 18, his hands stiffly at his sides, at attention before the officers of the committee. Behind him additional candidates await their turn, arranged in pairs. All the candidates are stark naked. They look tense, somewhat defenseless. They are not comfortable. Each one holds a form of some sort, perhaps a questionnaire, perhaps a card with personal details, in his hand, instinctively using it to cover his genitals; the presence of the photographer must have added to their discomfort.[28]

The scrutiny to which these boys were subjected was based on SS philosophy. The leaders of the SS believed that the residents of Germany, like most other Europeans, could be divided into six races; they credited the Nordic (northern) race with attributes of leadership and believed there was no more perfect breed of people. The Nordic man was described as tall, of flexible body and limbs, with strong bones and muscles. His skin was delicate and fair and not hairy. The hair on his head was straight and blond, his eyes blue.[29] This was the model the acceptance committee wished to find among the naked boys who presented themselves to them, one after the other. It was a humiliating situation, but the self-image and, to a large extent, the social status awaiting whoever was found fit to serve in the SS was an attractive one. Each one of them could say of himself that his quality as a man was better than that of other Germans, since according to the philosophy of the organization—later the official ideology of the state—he belonged to the best stock of the master race, the new elite. The superiority they attributed to themselves derived from their being young, strong, and blond; they were not demanded to display other attributes and they often had none— neither social status, nor money, nor education. Heinrich Himmler, on a tour of SS units, once took notice of a solid, handsome SS man. The man was a private. Himmler was enchanted by his looks. "He looks just like my SS officers should look," he cried happily and ordered that the man be promoted to first lieutenant on the spot.[30]

Most SS members were placed in educational seminars meant to acquaint them with the organization's ideology, which reflected elitist closed-mindedness: "We do not deign to debate the fundamentals of our faith with any man," said one SS publication.[31] Members' personnel files preserve compositions written at the conclusion of these courses. SS member Joseph Altrogge wrote as follows:

> Along with the responsibilities assigned the SS in preserving internal security, the organization also serves as the ideological vanguard of the movement. Among other things, it is invested with the responsibility for ensuring the racial renewal of the nation. Our political achievements have no value, after all, if purity of blood is not victorious. Our entire struggle will be for naught, the German revolution will be nothing but an episode in the last duel between the Nordic soul and foreign blood. Purity of blood and the idea of the extended family are at the foundation of the existence of the SS; our task is to ensure that the Nordic blood flowing in our veins is preserved and reproduced. Only thus can we guarantee the achievements of the revolution and the future of Germany. History is rich with examples of nations which, at the height of their power and cultural development, intermixed with races lower than they, until they declined and were defeated by healthier peoples. Rome against the Germans, for example. Race is the key to the history of the world, said a British statesman of Jewish extraction, Benjamin Disraeli, and he was right. The SS is based on the idea

of the extended family. This is not a new idea. It is a renewed idea. For generations it was suppressed by the power of a strange spirit and rotten thinking. Our German forefathers saw the idea of the extended family as a cornerstone of their world view. The source of livelihood of the extended family is the common yard. This was the property of all, a gift of the sun, source of all life. This was a true nobility: more than anything else they were careful that only women of equal or greater quality were accepted into the family—a nobility of blood that has absolutely nothing in common with the nobility of capital and title which exists today. The theory of blood was the nucleus of the idea of German existence, and is the nucleus of the ideology of National-Socialism.[32]

As the ideological vanguard of the movement the SS saw the idea of the extended family as a central mission. "We are not an order of men," Altrogge wrote, "some kind of brotherhood of German knights, but a community of extended families. Each of us is only a link in the chain of generations beginning with our forefathers and continued through us—by our children. If it is not cut short—we will live in our children and grandchildren and great-grandchildren and our descendants for countless generations, and this will be eternal life. For this reason we must marry and sire pureblooded children. We are the first. We must succeed. We will succeed and Germany will live forever."[33]

Somewhere in there, in the books, lies a system of ideas that can be described as the Nazi ideology. But the compositions preserved in the SS personnel files indicate that their authors were captivated by the organization's slogans, and did not delve into the organization's creed, and probably did not understand it entirely. This does not seem to have bothered them. They were not men of thought. The slogans were sufficient. "I was full of gratitude to the SS for the intellectual guidance it gave me," Johannes Hassebroeck later commented. "We were all thankful. Many of us had been so bewildered before joining the organization. We did not understand what was happening around us, everything was so mixed up. The SS

offered us a series of simple ideas that we could understand,
and we believed in them."[34]

For the most part it was the words themselves which caught
hold of them, some of them bold, imagination-firing words;
their emotional weight was greater than their actual meaning.
They broadcast a sense-numbing link of sorts to primitive
German tradition and an intimacy between men with a sexual-
historical mission to maintain the purity of blood and race. The
expression "blood and soil," widespread then, expressed birth,
life, belonging, rootedness, heroism, sacrifice, death, and
decay. It was a secular religion, extremely stimulating, which,
like all religions, involved practical rules of the permitted and
forbidden in everyday life. The SS man was commanded, for
instance, to put racial and national considerations above his
emotions in choosing a wife. "We much choose her for her
physical, racial, and genetic characteristics and not consider at
all her name, status, or money," SS man Joseph Altrogge
wrote obediently. The natural role of the woman, he continued,
was to give birth to children and see to their earliest education.
"We want strong women, ready to take upon themselves the
mission the German nation assigns them. German women
recognize their responsibility. Those who avoid it are not
worthy of being called German women."[35]

The historical responsibility of the SS for the continuation
and fortification of the race was expressed in endless books and
articles, and received artistic expression in drawings and
sculptures reflecting great, almost ritual, admiration of the
virility, youth, and sexual prowess of members of the organization. The women chosen to live at the side of these muscular
bronze gods, whose statues were on display throughout Germany, were supposed to be obedient, faithful, and responsive
to the sexual urges of their husbands and the needs of the
nation.

The marriage order Himmler issued on December 31, 1931,
established that the future of the German nation depended on
its preservation of its genetic purity. Every SS officer who
wished to marry had to receive advance permission. He and his
chosen woman had to go to a doctor, who examined them to
see whether they carried any sort of hereditary disease and if
she could bear children. They were also required to submit

documents containing exact details of their family history. Officers and their wives were required to prove that there had been no Jewish blood in their families from 1750 onwards. Privates and sergeants were required to supply proofs that their blood had been pure from the year 1800.[36] The request for a marriage permit had to include, among the wealth of papers, testimonies, and other certifications, two clear photographs showing the couple dressed in bathing suits. Each and every request was examined minutely, with the help of a large office staff established especially for this purpose. It was not merely a formal process. Months and sometimes years passed before the couple managed to gather all the necessary documents. When there was doubt as to the reliability of the information provided, the secret police were sometimes put to use.

The medical questionnaires preserved in the personnel file of, for example, Max Kögel, required him to report information about himself, his siblings, his siblings' children, his father, his mother, his uncles and aunts on his father's and mother's sides including their children, his grandfather and grandmother on his father's side and his grandfather and grandmother on his mother's side, their illnesses, and the causes of their deaths. He also had to report whether they drank and smoked, who their doctors were, when they had last undergone a general physical examination, and what the results were. Menstruation, births, abortions: "Please give precise details," this section requests. A large part of the questionnaire was devoted to defining their racial features. The applicant was asked to underline the correct answer and cross out the inappropriate:

Color of skin in areas unexposed to the sun: pinkish-white, ivory, brown-olive; color of skin in areas exposed to the sun: pinkish-white, etc., golden, light brown, brown; eye color: blue, gray, greenish, light brown, dark brown; hair color: light blonde, blonde, dark blonde, brown, brown-black, red; type of hair: straight, wavy, curly, kinky; build: weak, tall, rounded, muscular (athletic); posture: careless, comfortable, soldierly; walk: tired, good, energetic; chest: fallen, medium, good, muscular, barrel-like; stomach: flabby, sagging, fat, tight; skin: oily, firm, spongy, dry; age; weight; height—standing and sitting; teeth; genitals: sound, damaged.[37]

Everything was examined.

In addition to the information on the racial descent of the woman, her health, and the health of her relatives, the SS man wishing to marry her was required to supply his superiors with two signed testimonies, on a special form in duplicate, including, among others, the following questions: "Can she be depended on? Does she love children or not? Is she friendly or not? Frugal or wasteful? A homebody or does she like to enjoy herself? Do you know of mental illness in her family? Do you know of any suicides in her family? Has she or someone else in her family worked for the victory of the movement? Do you think she is worthy of marrying an SS man?"[38]

Emmy Hirschberg, a clerk from a small town in the Sudetenland, asked to marry an officer from the Death's Head Formations, Günther Tamaschke, who served at the women's concentration camp at Lichtenburg. The SS sent someone to investigate her family history. "Her grandfather on her father's side committed suicide at the age of 58 for unknown reasons," the investigator wrote upon returning. He also discovered that "one of her uncles and one of her cousins on her father's side were arrested for political reasons and were imprisoned for a time in a concentration camp." With a green pencil, as was his custom, Heinrich Himmler demanded explanations. "Grandfather Franz Hirschberg committed suicide in 1919 after his third wife made his life miserable because he was unemployed," Hirschberg wrote in explanation. "Uncle Leo Hirschberg, a baker by trade, was arrested because he was a member of the Social Democratic Party, but thousands of members of the party received the opportunity to improve their ways and there are even among Nazi party officials people who in the past were Social Democrats and were forgiven. Uncle Hirschberg was sent to Dachau for no good reason. I hope that they will now expunge the past and not oppose the realization of my love." Permission was granted in the end.[39]

"I hereby inform you that your request for a marriage permit has been rejected," Death's Head Formations officer Heinrich Schwartz was notified, with the following explanation: "The woman you wish to marry has passed her forty-second year. There is no chance that she will bear you a baby and you are only 28 years old. We may assume that you will produce descendants. You must decide, therefore, whether to waive your request or resign from the SS." Schwartz, later among the commandants of Auschwitz, did not relent: "I cannot resign from the SS," he wrote to Heinrich Himmler, "but as an SS man neither can I break my promise to marry her." Himmler allowed the marriage.[40] The personnel file of each member of the organization included detailed information about his sex life and, at times, this information affected his chances for promotion. Before being promoted, Franz Ziereis, later commandant of the Mauthausen camp in Austria, was commanded to explain to his superiors why his wife was no longer bearing children. "Our three children were born by Caesarean section," the officer explained. "My wife cannot undergo another operation and for this reason we have had no more children."[41]

The SS observed a bourgeois, almost puritan ethic in family matters. The wives of SS men were also accepted into what was called "the family of the SS," and were expected to adjust themselves to its ethical rules and behave in accordance with them even if their husbands died. For this reason the SS made a great effort to rid the commandant of Auschwitz, Arthur Liebehenschel, of the woman he loved, Aneliese Huttmann, because in their opinion she was not fit to be the wife of a senior officer in the organization. Huttmann was younger than Liebehenschel by fifteen years. She had previously been sentenced to a short prison term in a concentration camp for an affair she had with a Jewish man, in violation of the Nuremberg laws. Her acquaintance with Liebehenschel led him to divorce his wife after almost sixteen years of marriage, during which his wife bore him three sons. The supervisor of concentration camps, Oswald Pohl, sent his deputy, Richard Baer, to Auschwitz, in order to deal with the incident. Baer reported:

> I sat with L in a side room at the officers club. After we spoke of a few matters connected with work, I gave him the letter [that Pohl sent] and told him that I had instructions to do my best to help him in his troubles [the letter contained information on Huttmann's past]. After reading the letter two or three times, L broke into tears. When he recovered somewhat, he tried to cast doubt on the information I had

brought. I told him that Frau Huttmann had signed a confession confirming the content of the letter. I added that, in light of the circumstances, I had been sent to arrange matters. L spoke much of his loyalty to the SS and the Führer and afterwards said that he understood the matter and would act as befit an SS officer. In his emotion he ordered champagne and drank large quantities. Under the circumstances I do not blame him. Afterwards I spoke with Frau Huttmann. I promised her and her mother assistance in finding an apartment and work. There is no reason she should not marry whomever she wishes, even the director-general of a government ministry, I said, just not a member of the SS. She claimed that her signature was taken from her under false pretenses. I said that, based on my long experience in concentration camps, no one signs an untrue confession. Liebehenschel claimed that the Gestapo has methods of squeezing confessions like these from people. I told him that this was a serious charge and required proof.[42]

Some while later it was discovered, to her good fortune, that Frau Huttmann was pregnant. This fact finally brought Heinrich Himmler to approve the marriage, if unwillingly: a scandal involving one member of the organization threatened to stain all his comrades as well. For this reason, when Günther Tamaschke ceased paying alimony to his divorced wife, his superiors intervened. They also put Otto Förschner on trial for paying a fixed sum of money to one of the officers in his unit so that he would acknowledge paternity of a baby born to a woman that both officers visited. Förschner was married, and the officer who acknowledged paternity was not. SS leaders acted similarly in the case of Elfriede Wäckerle, widow of the first commandant of the Dachau camp. His comrades apparently expected the widow to bear the memory of her husband in noble sorrow to the end of her days, but she preferred moving into the apartment of another man, Johann Herzog, without having married him first. The incident caused a storm in the SS and in the end Himmler himself decided to send Herzog to a concentration camp. Elfriede Wäckerle sent him heart-rending love letters, but they never reached their destination. Instead, they were all filed in her dead husband's personnel file.[43]

Alongside this bourgeois conservatism, SS men were expected to do their part to increase the numbers and quality of the master race and sire as many descendants as they could, as racially "pure" as they were—even outside their marriages. The SS allowed its men—and in some cases encouraged them—to put their sexual prowess at the service of the nation by having relations with women who, in Himmler's words, "felt lonely" and longed for a baby of their own, so long as they could prove the purity of their ancestry. Some of them were prostitutes, and some were seduced into pregnancy against their will. This was done in special homes established around Germany just for this purpose. A special organization, the *Lebensborn*, the "spring of life," was set up in order to support women impregnated by SS men and to provide for their children.[44] It seems that the SS did not see any contradiction between the bourgeois conservatism that typified its attitude to family life and the baby factory it established. The attempt to create people of "pure" race in a methodical way for the good of the nation was never operated on more than a relatively small scale; it is worth mentioning mostly because it expresses a unique ideology, fundamentally different from the humanism common to the Christian world from the time of the Renaissance. The Nordic man, son of the master race, not man as man, stood at the center of the SS's world. This, in condensed form, is the essence of the Nazi revolution. The ideology which claimed that members of the master race could be created in a methodical way could just as easily advocate the methodical extermination of lesser races.

Lowest of all was the Jewish "subhuman." A pamphlet put out by the SS command described the Jew in these words:

From a biological point of view he seems completely normal. He has hands and feet and a sort of brain. He has eyes and a mouth. But, in fact, he is a completely different creature, a horror. He only looks human, with a human face, but his spirit is lower than that of an animal. A terrible chaos runs rampant in this creature, an awful urge for destruction, primitive desires, unparalleled evil, a monster, subhuman.

The pamphlet's fifty pages are full of photographs taken, it seems, in a concentration camp. The pictures depict abused and tortured people, accompanied by an explanation that these horrors were committed by Jews. One photograph showing a Jew in fairly normal-looking traditional dress carries the caption: "the monster disguised as a man."[45]

The SS made a great effort to provide its members with substitutes for the religious customs, holidays, and rituals the members knew from home. This included reviving primitive nature rituals practiced among the ancient German tribes. It competed successfully with the churches, but just as it preserved something of the conservative, bourgeois family ethic, it conceded in advance any attempt to compete with God himself.

In a book of questions and answers it published, the SS taught its men as follows:

Question: What is the wording of the SS oath?
Answer: I swear before you, Adolf Hitler, as the leader and Chancellor of the German Reich, that I will be faithful and courageous at all times. I will carry out your orders and those of the commanders you appoint until the day of my death, so help me God.

Question: In other words, we believe in God?
Answer: Yes. We believe in God; his spirit is with us at all times.

Question: What does the SS think of those who do not believe in God?
Answer: The SS thinks that whoever does not believe in God suffers from a superiority complex. They are arrogant and foolish and the SS has no interest in them.

Question: Why do we believe in Germany and the Führer?
Answer: Since we believe in God we believe also in the Germany he created in his world and in Adolf Hitler whom he sent us in the greatness of his benevolence.[46]

In this spirit, the SS also created a new concept to define the religious affiliation of its members: there was no longer a Catholic or a Protestant faith but only faith in God. SS men were not required to leave the church formally, but those who did so were considered more loyal and their chances for promotion were better. There were those who detached themselves from the church without hesitation: "From the day I finished school," wrote SS officer Alfred Bauer, "I went to church only on rare occasions, for special events like weddings and such. Even then I did so only to satisfy my relatives. In essence I decided long ago to leave the church, but only now did I do it formally."[47]

These words are included in a composition Bauer wrote at the end of one of the ideological courses he participated in. The personnel files of many other SS officers also contain compositions on their attitude towards their churches. Those who thought that the religious tradition in which they had been educated was important often endured difficult pangs of conscience before deciding to leave the church. SS Colonel Lothar von Bonin did not hide, even in 1941, his loyalty to the church, and according to a secret report of the Gestapo, he did not intend to abandon it. It seems that his superiors had already pressured him, but he stood his ground and in the end they decided to expel him from the organization.[48] The personnel file of Hans Helwig contains a note criticizing him because he allowed the benefactors of the village in which he lived to engrave his name on the church bell, in accordance with local custom.[49] The family connections of some SS men and the desire not to hurt their parents often made it difficult for them to cut their ties to their church in an official way, even when they did not see those ties as important. A letter discovered in one of the SS archives, sent from a God-fearing father to his son's commander, reads as follows:

In leaving the [Catholic] Church my son betrayed the good and omnipotent God, his parents, and his family. He made himself an enemy of God and, as such, an enemy of his parents, family, and the heritage of his fathers. I do not let enemies into my house. For this reason I have decided to banish my son from the family. All my relatives will receive an announcement telling them that my son has betrayed God and so all of us. As a traitor he will no longer find shelter among us. He was my only son. In leaving the church he destroyed my family . . . and if he is wounded in battle and remains a heretic, even if his life is in danger—we will not help him. Not I nor any member of my family.[50]

Theodor Eicke said that he received many letters of this type.[51]

The more the rift grew between the SS man and his past and the values his family held, the greater became his isolation and his dependence on the organization. This in turn could be expected to increase his internal identification with the way he had chosen and his willingness "to overcome himself," as Johannes Hassebroeck said, and fight his weaknesses, such as excessive drinking, wastefulness, and homosexual tendencies (homosexual activity was punished by death).[52] Their motto was "my honor is my loyalty." It was not easy: each of them needed physical strength and great willpower to meet the demands of the organization. The more he fulfilled them, the more he became part of the organization and the organization part of him.

The SS invested much effort in hardening its men. Toughness towards others was supposed to derive from toughness towards oneself. It was a process beginning with the harsh discipline they accepted, voluntarily, during their basic and officer training. The two SS officer schools operated not far from the spas of Bad-Tölz in Bavaria and from a medieval palace in the city of Braunschweig. The courses lasted for ten months, with about 250 trainees in each session. The schools followed the training program for army infantry officers. After finishing the course the graduates were meant to serve in the organization on a career basis, for a salary.

Basic instruction in the SS included ideological indoctrination along with physical education and military training. Here the molding of the officer's personality and of his tenacity began.

Since they were volunteers who had enlisted in the organization of their own free will, the intention was not to break SS men into submissiveness. It was to put their endurance to the test and increase it. Those members who did not meet the demands—

several thousand each year—were expelled. "The great majority of those who enlisted in the SS," Johannes Hassebroeck later recalled, "were children; the SS made them into men."[53] One SS man related:

There was a special method of humiliating a man. If anyone, while loading cartridges into a magazine, let a cartridge fall to the ground, he had to pick it up with his teeth. I made up my mind that I would not do that. They can do what they like with me, I said, but I will not pick up a cartridge with my teeth; I shall use my hand. Naturally I took care not to let the situation arise and determined to do everything I could not to let a cartridge fall to the ground. One day of course it happened. On these occasions no one gives an order; the NCO simply turns down his thumb and the man concerned knows what he has to do. In my case of course he turned down his thumb—and I bent down and picked the cartridge up with my hand. He rushed at me like a wild animal, stuck his face close up to mine so that there was hardly an inch between his nose and mine and bellowed whatever came into his head. Of course I could not understand a word because he was bellowing so loud that he was choking. Eventually I gathered that he was yelling: "Have you forgotten what to do?" When he had finished bellowing he handed me over to the deputy section commander who made me do a ten-minute "showpiece." That's a long time when you're double all the time. And it's embroidered with all the usual well-known "extras." After such a chasing your shirt is wringing wet. Then the deputy commander handed me back to the commander himself. His first order was: "Chuck that cartridge away." I was not ready for that. I was practically all in. I threw the cartridge away; it fell some six feet away from me—and he turned his thumb down once more. I hesitated for a second. Seeing this he came up to me. I was almost at the stage of picking it up with my teeth. But then—I just wasn't thinking and I don't know why—again I picked up the cartridge with my hand. That was it! He went scarlet, bellowed out something unintelligible, handed the section over to his deputy and took me on himself. He began with fifty knee-bends with rifle held out at arm's length. I had to count out loud. I was fairly fit and I had got used to anything here, but to be asked to do fifty knee-bends with your rifle held out in front of you, following ten-minute "showpiece" which has left you little better than a jelly—that's a tall order. I'm not saying that it's physically impossible. The only question is whether one is ready for it mentally. And this was what happened. After twenty knee-bends I stopped counting. I just couldn't go on. I did one more knee-bend and then I lowered my rifle and stood up. I can't say that I thought this out; I just knew that I was all in. I heard him bellowing all over again but that left me cold because suddenly I could control myself no longer. I felt I had to weep although I knew that it was neither manly nor soldierly. I couldn't answer his questions because I was so shaken with sobbing that I couldn't speak. I was not in a rage and I was not in pain. I had just had enough. When he saw that he bellowed: "Look at this!" and then: "Mollycoddle! Mother's little darling! Crybaby! Who's ever heard of an SS man blubbering! All our dead will turn in their graves! Is this what we're trying to take to war—etc. etc." Then "assembly" was blown and the training period ended. He ordered me to clean out all the first floor latrines for a week and then report to him so that he could inspect them. And straightaway he ordered: "Chuck this cartridge away." I did so and then without even waiting or looking to see whether he had turned his thumb down I picked it up with my teeth.[54]

Other sources include similar information. "It often seemed as if the Sergeant Himmelstos of Erich Maria Remarque had been reborn," General Gottlob Berger noted in this context.[55] Among the general's papers are various testimonies about the harsh treatment the SS inflicted on its men. The commander of a military school sent Berger the following report:

During the last few days boys from a class which enlisted almost entirely in the SS have come to me and poured their hears out to me. Six of them were in the same squad. All six wanted to be SS officers. Six months later they are not willing to remain in the SS for a single additional day. Not only because their bodies suffered treatment that, in the eyes of those serving in the army, seems unreasonable, but also because they see the suffering of other trainees who, having not received premilitary physical training as they did, are not as strong as they are. Here are some of the stories they told me:

One trainee who volunteered—as did all the others—for the SS of his own free will did not succeed in attaining the same level of achievement that the rest of the platoon did. The sergeant threatened the entire platoon with disciplinary exercises if they did not "deal" with their weak comrade. The sergeant agreed with the men that he would invite the trainee to his room, and upon leaving, they would all attack him. This indeed took place. They beat him with rifle butts and sticks until he bled. The poor man screamed "father, mother!" and they threw him down the stairs. He was seriously hurt.

Another trainee who did not know how to swim received an order to jump from a three-meter diving board. Let us suppose that this is accepted practice, but afterwards he must be helped out of the water. The man jumped and almost drowned. One of our graduates went to pull him out, but the sergeant forbade him to do so. Everyone stood around the pool and watched. When the poor man finally managed to reach the edge of the pool, the sergeant stamped on his fingers and shouted: "Let him drown! I don't want to see him again!" The man began to drown. In violation of orders one of the men helped him out.

A trainee's toe was hurt and it was necessary to remove the nail. The medic said to give the injured man a local anaesthetic, but the sergeant prohibited this. He instead told three of the men to hold him down; the trainee was ordered to sing as the medic removed the nail without anaesthetic. The trainee was sent to perform guard duty immediately thereafter.

This is what the boys told me. Punishment without purpose. The sergeants, the boys say, do everything they can to make the trainees feel like prisoners in a concentration camp instead of feeling like soldiers.[56]

"Correct," Johannes Hassebroeck later noted. "All that was

accepted in the SS. But such demands are accepted in the select units of other armies also. A man only needs courage and desire and strength in order to take it. The SS making you tough on yourself—demanded more. A man was ordered, for example, to shoot the dog he loved, or better—to kill him with a knife. Being tough on yourself means overcoming your weaknesses."[57]

In a famous speech given my Heinrich Himmler in 1943 to officers of the Waffen SS in Posen, he said:

> I can imagine a need to dig an antitank dike and about 10,000 Russian women dying of exhaustion during the course of the work. This is of no interest to me. The only question is whether the dike was completed or not. If someone comes to me and says: I cannot work that way, with all those women and children dropping before my eyes, I will answer him: if you do not work, you are like a murderer, since if the dike is not dug, German soldiers will be killed, sons of German women, members of your nation whose blood is German like yours. . . .
>
> I want to touch here on a very difficult subject with utmost frankness. Let us speak of it once, among us, even though we will never mention it outside. I mean the evacuation of the Jews, the extermination of the Jewish nation. This is connected to one of the subjects that is not easy to speak of. "The Jewish nation will be destroyed," says the Party member. "It is perfectly clear. It is written in our platform." To destroy the Jews. Of course. What's the problem? And then they come, 80 million upright Germans, and each of them has his private Jew. All the others are pigs, of course, and must be destroyed, but this particular Jew is an excellent Jew. What do they know? Not one of them was there, after all, and saw with his own eyes what is happening. Each and every one of you knows how a pile of a hundred human bodies looks, or five hundred, or a thousand. We have faced this, and with only a few exceptions, the result of human weakness, we have remained upright men. This is the essence of our toughness, a heroic page in our history which has not yet been written and perhaps never will be written.[58]

All this demanded and created solidarity among the soldiers; it created the famous comradeship-at-arms.

"It unites them like a magic wand," said an internal memorandum of the organization. The document described the closeness of members of the SS as the essence of the member's experience in the SS; true friendship, like that existing between members of the SS, was meant to wipe out all differences among them. "Among comrades-at-arms there are no differences of class, profession, position, age, property, or education. Only the man himself counts here, his inner faith and his contribution to the general good. . . . In a place where there is no friendship, neither is there character. . . . Brotherhood-at-arms faithfully expresses the spirit of the SS and nothing else expresses this like it. . . . It means that members obey their commanders of their own free will, it gives every member a stake in his life and it gives the SS family its strength. The SS was founded on brotherhood-at-arms and without it it will fall. . . . Comradeship is the soul of the SS. . . . It means solidarity in days of need and solidarity at times of happiness. . . . It means frank conversation: there is someone who listens to you, someone you can trust, there is someone you can put your faith in. . . . No book can teach you the rules of comradeship: you must feel it in your heart, it must be a true experience."[59]

The same memorandum described brotherhood-at-arms in daily life in the following way:

One comrade has problems on his farm. . . . His friends go to help with the harvest. . . . You meet a drunk comrade at a bar. People are staring at him. True comradeship is to take him home, quietly. . . . A comrade is sick . . . his friends come to visit. . . . A poor comrade has become embroiled in a legal dispute: his friends collect money from among themselves in order to get him a good defense lawyer. If men talk about a comrade in his absence and accuse him of something—demand to know what they base their accusation on. If there is no proof—halt the conversation at once. True comradeship means that you defend your friend's honor while he is absent. . . . You have reason to complain about your comrade, you feel that he insulted you:

according to the rules of friendship—speak to him frankly and directly, without intermediaries.[60]

This was often a very personal friendship: SS involvement in the family life of its officers was generally done in the name of the brotherhood reigning among them. They were not to hide anything from one another, and when they had personal troubles, they helped each other. When Hans Loritz, a commandant of Dachau, suspected that his wife was betraying him and decided to surprise her, he took one of his comrades from his unit with him.[61] They helped each other in financial matters, arranged all sorts of grants for each other—to improve accommodations, to buy furniture, and the like. "I owe our old friend to do my best to find him work," wrote one of Günther Tamaschke's friends to the Ministry of Scientific Research: "for this reason I request that you find him some sort of job, despite the cuts in the budget."[62]

They backed each other up if caught in misdeeds. When Jakob Weiseborn, an officer at the Esterwegen concentration camp and afterwards the first commandant of the Flossenbürg camp, was drunk, one of his friends volunteered to guard in his place. Both were censured for this and expelled from their unit.[63] At the highest levels of the SS there were attempts, some years later, to confound the criminal inquiries against a number of the commandants and cover up their actions—but these were exceptional cases. More typical was the effort of SS men to help friends who had gotten into trouble with the civilian authorities. On December 24, 1934, at around six o'clock in the evening, an SS private stood by the ticket window at the train station in the city of Passau. For some reason he needed much time to find the money in his wallet. Those standing in line pushed him. He pushed back and then a policeman appeared demanding that he hurry. He answered disrespectfully, and the policeman dragged him away. One of the eye-witnesses called in the commandant of the Dachau concentration camp, Heinrich Deubel. Deubel arrived immediately and made a scandal. The police had no authority to deal with SS members, he claimed in great excitation (but without any legal basis). Afterwards he threatened the policeman: "We'll see to it that you're sent to us at Dachau. We'll show you what it means to raise a hand against an SS man." In an inquiry Deubel claimed that it was his responsibility as a member of the SS to defend the private.[64]

Albert Sauer, later commandant of Mauthausen, once traveled with some of his friends in a train. They sat in the second-class coach, even though they had purchased third-class tickets. Three elderly women asked them to vacate their places for them. The SS men refused and an argument began, attracting the attention of the conductor. Sauer announced that the conductor had no authority to tell SS men what to do. The women argued that they had bought second-class tickets, and that now they were being forced into the third-class carriage. Sauer suggested that they contribute the difference to the SS aid fund. The conductor, Sauer complained afterwards, did not salute them.[65]

Adam Grünewald, commandant of the Hertogenbusch camp in Holland, got into a dispute with the conductor on a train he was traveling in because he refused to sit in a compartment with a passenger whom he claimed had a "Jewish face." "I have no way of establishing whether the man is Jewish," the conductor defended himself, and Grünewald filed a complaint with the conductor's superiors.[66] All these incidents brought on a great amount of correspondence and are worthy of mention because those involved received full support from their superior officers—all in the spirit of the cohesiveness characteristic of the organization and the ties of friendship among its members.

Each SS member "devoted himself to all the others," Johannes Hassebroeck said. "Even the ties of love between a man and a woman are not stronger than that same friendship that there was among us. This friendship was all. It both gave us strength and held us together, in a convenant of blood. It was worth living for; it was worth dying for. This was what gave us the physical strength and courage to do what others did not dare to do because they were too weak. We knew how to spur each other on while carrying out our missions. Each of us needed the encouragement of his comrades. What we did—we did, of course, for Germany, for the Führer, for the future. But every one of us did what he did for every one of the others."[67]

The SS files indicate that the legendary soldierly comradeship was not always preserved. Personal rivalries, intrigues, and innumerable instances of corruption were all permanent features of the SS. An anonymous letter sent to Heinrich Himmler reflects, for example, rivalry between young and old members: "There are, among the leaders of the organization and its decision-makers, some who joined the party only after it achieved power. They have no tolerance for the movement's senior soldiers. It is no longer an honor to be among the movement's senior soldiers: the young people who joined it only after it gained power are given preference in promotion. Sir: we demand only what is ours by right. We fought for the Führer and the people. We do not now deserve to be attacked."[68] SS men were not permitted to lock their private closets. "This has deep meaning," said one of the organization's publications, but anyone who left his closet open could expect his belongings to be stolen. More than half of the cases heard by the SS courts dealt with this problem.[69] The faith in the brotherhood-at-arms was apparently stronger than the brotherhood itself, but this faith was itself an attraction.

A survey of 260 boys, members of the *Hitlerjugend* (the Nazi party's youth organization) who participated in an ideological seminar organized by their movement, was conducted in 1943. Of them, 53.9 percent said that they wanted to perform their military service in one of the Waffen SS units. The previous year only 11 percent of the participants in the seminar expressed such a desire. Only the air force approached the popularity of the Waffen SS—but did not match it.[70] The more the details of the horror and cruelty of the battles and the number of losses became known, the less enthusiasm the SS aroused. Many were then drafted into the Waffen SS against their will, among them members of the Hitlerjugend. One member of the youth group sent a letter to his father describing how this was done:

Dear Papa:
    Today I experienced the basest thing in my life. At nine in the morning they called the whole camp to report for inspection. Three officers from the Waffen SS and a policeman showed up. They gave us a lecture about the SS. Afterwards there was an order: "Volunteers—step forward!" Only *one* of us volunteered. The officer spoke more se-

verely. You can already imagine how. As a result two more
stepped forward. At this point the real audacity began. They
inspected the ranks one after the other and simply ordered us
to sign up. About 60 of us were forced in this way to sign a
"volunteer form." Everyone was really upset. Some us tried
to get out, some even through the window. But the policeman didn't let anyone out. As you can imagine, everyone
began making excuses. *I did not sign!* They called on me to
report three times. They put me under horrible pressure. I
almost didn't make it. There were some guys who cried.
This afternoon they are going to take us for a medical
examination. Then it will start all over again. Some of those
who did not sign were listed on a piece of paper with the
words "if found fit for combat—draft immediately!" written
on it. The whole camp is up in arms. I'm through with this
place. I've become a different person. . . . They took
even short guys of only five foot five. They aren't allowed
to do that. Even if they throw me in solitary for three days,
I won't sign up.[71]

During the first half of April 1940 it was discovered that
there was Jewish blood in the veins of SS Private Walter
Küchlein's ancestors. The man was forced to leave the organization. Himmler sent him a long letter:

  I can understand your feelings, since anyone who was
once with us, in an organization which demands so many
sacrifices from its members—can never leave it. But in the
end we love this organization precisely because it has always
operated without compromise.
  As for the source of the blood: each of us must prove the
purity of his blood from the conclusion of the Thirty Years'
War. If it is discovered that there is a Jew among his
ancestors, he must resign from the organization. I am less
stringent with the wives of SS members, especially if they
are older and can no longer bear children. I cannot,
therefore, revise my decision, but I can tell you that even
now, when you are outside the organization, I will continue
to consider you an SS man to the end of your days, and I
expect of you that you will continue to preserve your loyalty

to the organization and your willingness to make the sacrifices demanded of you. If you ask me on what basis I allow myself to demand this sacrifice of you, my answer is that we could, of course, allow ourselves to be more flexible with the rules: we live in the era of the Führer, founder of the movement, and I am sure that we would not be tempted to make the exception into a rule. The fear is that those who come after us will see it as a precedent. They are liable to say that what was done in Hitler's day can be done in theirs. This is the danger: what was exceptional in our day might become routine in the coming generations. I believe that you will understand this and be persuaded that even though you can no longer visibly serve in the SS, you may still be part of us in a spiritual way. You may be absolutely sure that if your fate is to lose your life in the war for your country, the SS will support your widow and children as if you were still a member of the organization. Should you receive furlough and want to speak with me, I will be happy to receive you. I wish you all the best,

Heil Hitler,
Yours, Heinrich Himmler.[72]

In many cases the SS waived the need for documents demanded by Himmler's marriage regulations because members of the organization did not succeed in finding them.[73] Sixty percent of the men in the organization were not married at all. All this testifies to the fact that day-to-day life in the SS did not always match the self-image and the mythos that the organization fostered.[74]

There were those who exploited their service in the SS to make useful connections which often helped them improve their financial situation. A secret report compiled in the SS command referred to this phenomenon negatively: "Many officers in the organization see their position as a stepping-stone to better jobs and higher salaries in the private sector and even in government and movement-owned industry. This phenomenon has led to us losing some of the best of our men. In their eagerness to rise ever upwards, to the peak of success, they abandoned us."[75]

The personnel file of Günther Tamaschke contains a copy of

a reprimand signed by Heinrich Himmler: "I heard of your intention to purchase the Nalus and Mansfeld Company, Prague, Czechoslovakia, once owned by Jews. During this war, while millions of our countrymen are sacrificing their lives and blood for our country, you think only of how to take advantage of your position as an SS officer in order to lay your hands on a commercial enterprise you could not gain possession of in any other way. This is shameful behavior. I hereby revoke your membership in the SS."[76]

A survey carried out in 1938 showed that, of 513 officers, only 128 (25 percent) were suitable for their jobs. The survey recommended firing at least 270 of them within two years— more than 50 percent—and replacing them with better officers. During the first years of the organization's existence the SS man could receive no worse punishment than expulsion. The expulsion of the unfit increased the feelings of superiority of those who remained. There were, of course, those who left voluntarily; more than 7000 left the organization in 1937, more than 8000 in 1938.[77] The great majority chose to remain.

3
THEODOR EICKE AND THE DEATH'S HEAD FORMATIONS

AT one of the staff meetings of the Waffen SS the commander of the Death's Head Formations demanded that additional equipment and personnel be made available to him. His superiors answered that he would have to manage with what he had. The commander did not give in. He defended his position vocally and emotionally, scandalizing those present. At one point the man rose from his place, drew his pistol, and threatened that he would kill himself on the spot, at the conference table, if he was not given what he wanted.[1] His superiors quickly promised that they would review his request.

The man's name was Theodor Eicke. In his mind, he and the Nazi movement were one. Its struggles were his personal struggles, its failures his personal failures, and its prestige his personal prestige. This was dearer to him than all else. He aspired at every moment to glorify it. He defended it with unrestrained enthusiasm and pedantic pugnacity. Eicke was as arrogant, impulsive, and uninhibited as his movement was. "A real fighter," members of his family said of him. "At any time, during peace and during war, with his unit and at home, he was always at the front."[2] The Nazi party's newspaper, *Völkischer Beobachter*, described him as "a political soldier with a stormy heart,"[3] and Adolf Hitler considered him "a model of self-sacrifice."[4] He had something of the gladiator in him, the man who fights for glory and money—something of the desperado who lives to fight. "A dangerous man," he said of himself; his opponents said he was insane.[5] His men admired him; they called him "Papa Eicke" in awe, as if he were their father. He was good at developing their pride. "There are no fighters in the SS better than we are," he would boast to them. "There are none more daring and none harder than we are. Germany could not hold on for a single day without us."[6]

Serving under his command was, in his eyes, a great privilege. He often warned his men that whoever did not bring himself up to the high level of achievement the Death's Head Formations demanded, and did not adopt the sense of mission, perseverance, and brotherhood it required, would be transferred to other SS units. He made every effort to ensure that his men realize that transfer out of one of the Death's Head Formations was the most degrading personal failure possible. In one of his routine orders Eicke described what an expelled man could expect: "The man will be demoted in front of his comrades. It is doubtful whether he could stand the shame involved. A man expelled from the Death's Head Formation loses his place in an elite unit and will find himself without a home: his expulsion proves in and of itself that he is not worthy of the faith of others. He will be trusted nowhere. He has almost no chance of finding employment. The SS command and agencies of the organization, including the secret police— the Gestapo—will immediately receive a detailed report of his personality and the circumstances of his expulsion from the Formation. They will open a file on him. This will prevent him from finding any sort of government work, and many industries will also refuse to employ him. He will live in complete social isolation, lacking everything. With his expulsion from the Death's Head Formations, his membership in the party will be revoked automatically; all decorations ever awarded him will be rescinded."[7] Eicke had a tendency to exaggerate: some of these penalties applied only to men expelled from the SS as a whole, not to those transferred from the Death's Head Formations to other units in the organization. Some of the threats were purely the product of his imagination. This was his way of keeping his men on their toes, improving them, and fostering their image. His men believed him and made every effort not to be expelled.

The Death's Head Formations were made up of career men. Most of them were salaried employees serving as guards and administrative personnel in concentration camps. There were also units stationed outside but in the vicinity of concentration camps. These would halt their regular exercises only once every three weeks and spend from a week to ten days guarding in the camps. The first Death's Head unit was set up in 1933 in Dachau, immediately after Eicke received command of the camp. At first there were only a few hundred men in these units. A year after they were set up there were still no more than 2000. Their numbers were, however, doubled in December 1935, and towards the end of 1937 they rose to 7000.[8] In the summer of 1938, when the number of those serving in the Death's Head Formations rose to 10,000, Adolf Hitler signed a secret order establishing that in peacetime the Formations would be assigned "special tasks of a police nature," or in other words, operation of the concentration camps. In case of war, the Führer stated, the Death's Head Formations would reinforce the SS Militarized Formations—what later became the Waffen SS. For this reason they, too, were meant to undergo military training and receive arms and other battle gear.[9] The Death's Head Formations took part in the annexation of Austria and Czechoslovakia; on the eve of World War II about 15,000 men were serving in them, about half of the total membership of the SS.[10] When the war began, 30,000 men from the General SS were brought in to create a dozen new Death's Head Formations. They performed, among other roles, police functions in occupied territory, mass deportations, and executions. Simultaneously, 6500 career members of the Death's Head Formations were sent to the front. They, along with other SS men, formed a combat division under the command of Theodor Eicke—the Death's Head Division, later described as one of the best in the German army.[11]

According to Johannes Hassebroeck, an SS man was not given the opportunity to choose his assignment. "None of us chose to serve in the concentration camps of his own free will," he claimed. "We all considered ourselves first and foremost army men. I certainly did not want it. We had no choice. A man was simply placed in a given unit and that was it. They did not ask us what we wanted."[12] This may well have been the case during the war; the SS archives contain documents testifying that men were sometimes forced to "volunteer" for the organization against their wishes. This is not, however, the way things were done before the war. Those who enlisted in the Death's Head Formations knew well that they would be serving in concentration camps. They were told so explicitly. Members of the Formations volunteered to serve there of their own volition, and even went through exacting acceptance tests meant to select the best candidates. Within a short time after arriving at Dachau, Eicke developed clear ideas about the kind of men he needed. Typically, he began by getting rid of almost everyone he found at Dachau when he arrived—police and SA, most of them 25 or 30 years old. Some of them had even served in World War I. They were adventurers, street rabble of dubious background, and men of questionable mental stability. Eicke looked for more solid types, younger, with a higher degree of motivation and idealism; he could not stand the police or the SA.[13]

According to the criteria of selection he drafted, applicants to the Death's Head Formations had to prove that their desire to serve in the SS was genuine. He demanded "appropriate moral, spiritual, physical, racial, and ideological talents," which would allow them to meet the organization's demands. Until 1937 only a man who met the following conditions was allowed into the Death's Head Formations: single, 16 to 23 years of age, minimum height of 5 feet 8 inches, German citizenship, no police record, and more than 100 years of racial purity. During the first half of the thirties there was no lack of men who met these criteria, so the demands were tightened. From July 1937 onwards, the Death's Head Formations did not accept candidates of more than 22 years of age; 21-year-olds were accepted only on condition that they were "exceptionally" suited for service. Eicke believed in the power of youth. The candidates were required to sign on in advance for at least four years; previously they had signed on for a year at a time.[14]

The conditions of service in the Death's Head Formations were worse than the accepted standards in the Militarized Formations, in the army, and in other government agencies. During the first years of their existence the Death's Head Formations could not promise its men that they would receive a pension upon leaving. The Militarized Formations offered, in contrast, conditions identical to those in the army, including a monthly pension after leaving.[15] As a result, the Death's Head Formations had trouble attracting career officers to their ranks. In 1937, 38 percent of those serving in the Militarized Formations were officers, while in the Death's Head Formations officers were only 25 percent of the total.[16] That same year the Nazi party newspaper published a notice calling for young men to enlist in the police. Theodor Eicke immediately forbade his men to respond to the notice. Every man who tried to do so in secret, he threatened, would be expelled from his formation and would thus lose the chance of being accepted for work by any other public body. "The work conditions offered by the police," Eicke argued, "are no better than the norm in our Formations." This was a lie and his men probably knew it, which is probably why Eicke quickly added that he himself had never bothered to check what he would receive upon retirement and that "young people, who have the great privilege to fight for their country under the Führer's flag, do not even have to give a passing thought to such a marginal subject as the pension they will eventually be offered."[17] Even though, from 1936 onwards, the budget of the Death's Head Formations came from the national treasury, several more years passed before it was decided that the men ought to be paid a monthly pension upon retirement.[18]

Neither were the salaries paid by the Death's Head Formations particularly high. The monthly salary of Second Lieutenant Rolf P. Holtzapfel, for example, came in 1938 to 221.01 marks, and another 13.30 marks as a clothing allowance; his monthly expenses were as follows:

Rent	34.51
Various taxes	24.56
Membership fees in the party and its organizations	7.80
Social security	5.00
Life insurance	4.67
Savings plan	2.50

Cafeteria meals:	breakfast	0.45
	lunch	0.90
	supper and	

tea/coffee	0.95	
cigarettes	0.50	
	2.80 × 30 or 31 =	85.00
Housecleaning		5.00
Clothing		15.75
Laundry		8.00
Shoe repair, tailoring		8.00
Personal needs, haircut, etc.		8.00
Presents		1.50
Newspapers and books		5.00
Writing paper and stamps		3.00

Second Lieutenant Holtzapfel was left at the end of the month with about 16 marks, and this is without going out for even one evening with his girlfriend, without drinking beer with his friends, and without eating anything outside what was served at the canteen on the base.[19] His salary was enough to live away from his parents' house, with possibilities for advancement and a reasonable probability that he would receive help when the time came to set himself up in civilian life after concluding his service. It was not a bad start for a young man from the lower-middle class, but neither was it wonderful. Certainly it was not the salary that induced the deep personal involvement expected of him.

The SS statistical yearbooks indicate that the Death's Head Formations were socially unique in the SS: the social origins of the other men in the organization reflected, beginning in 1937, the class makeup of the German population as a whole.[20] Most of those serving in the Death's Head Formations, however, were born in small towns; Eicke preferred them to those from big cities. He assumed that they were more easily molded in accordance with his needs. The relatively low salaries the Formations offered their men, the fact that they were not required to have even minimal education, and the equal opportunity given to each of them to become an officer, attracted men from the middle and lower levels of the population. One discussion of employment opportunities to be offered to members of the Formations upon their release considered them as artisans, merchants, and farmers. Only a few were meant for the white collar professions or for government jobs.[21] The relatively low social standing which typified those serving in the Death's Head Formations was among the factors which molded the spirit of the unit and formed an egalitarian foundation for the brotherhood-at-arms they fostered.

Eicke's boys, as the soldiers of the Death's Head Formations were called, were younger than other SS men; in 1938 their average age was 20.7 as opposed to 28.7 in the rest of the SS; the largest age group in the Death's Head Formations was 18-year-olds, while in the SS as a whole the largest group was that of the 25-year-olds.[22] Most of those serving in the Death's Head Formations were therefore legal minors. Their service allowed them to live away from home. The large majority of them, 93.5 percent, were single. Only 57.5 percent among those serving in the other units of the organization were single.[23] They were subject to heavier psychological pressures than the men in other units: eleven men in the Death's Head Formations committed suicide in 1938—about 12 percent of the ninety-four SS men who ended their lives in that year. The Death's Head Formations made up, however, only about 4 percent of the SS's personnel. Their suicide rate was, therefore, three times higher than in the rest of the organization's units. The Militarized Formations made up 6 percent of the SS, but accounted for only about 4 percent of the suicides.[24] The Death's Head Formations was a group of young men under heavy mental pressure, strengthening their dependence on each other and making comradeship all the more important.

The fact that they served in the Death's Head Formations of their own volition and that they were accepted only after strenuous tests nourished their self-image. "No one forced them to come here," Eicke stated. "From this point of view they differ from most of the soldiers in, for example, the Wehrmacht. We must appreciate them for this and respect them. Nothing better creates their obedience, devotion, and loyalty than their will to serve among us."[25]

The prisoners in the camps were the enemies of the movement and the state; Eicke treated them as his own personal enemies, although there is no evidence of his having been blatantly sadistic with the prisoners. He was aware of his emotional involvement with his job and tried to create something similar among his subordinates. He did not demand blind, mechanical obedience, but personal devotion to the ideology in the name of which the camps were established, and for which the Death's Head Formations fought. He wanted his men to know why they were serving in the camps, and often overlooked mistreatment of prisoners in violation of order, so long as he believed that those who committed the misdeed did so because of an inner identification with their job. There are data indicating that the ideological identification of those serving in these Formations was deeper than that of those serving in other SS units. Some 43 percent of Death's Head members asked to be accepted into the party; in other SS units only 32 percent made this request.[26] The majority of members of the Death's Head Formations chose not to describe their religious identification as Catholic or Protestant, but rather in the Nazi way—as "believers in God." There were 51.7 percent of those serving in the Death's Head Formations who chose this description, almost three times the rate in other SS units.[27]

Eicke aspired to serve the Third Reich as a general, not as a prison warden. For this reason he took care to speak of the Death's Head Formations as if they were, like the Militarized Formations, a combat unit in every respect. "It is very important that the Death's Head Formations be the best in the SS, not only from a military point of view, but also on an administrative level," he wrote once, as if there was not even any doubt as to the combat superiority of his troops.[28] He took pains with his men's uniforms in order to make them different in little ways from the army's uniforms, and even demanded that it be noted that the unit's band did not play military music, but rather SS music.[29] He told his men that not everyone fit to serve in the army would be accepted automatically by the SS, "and in any case not in the Formations under my command. Only those soldiers who are tested and found to be superior fighters like us will be allowed to join the Death's Head Formations," he once announced. He himself, he added, would personally examine the character and excellence of each soldier requesting to transfer from the army to the Death's Head Formations, and would accept only the best.[30] As a matter of fact he did his best to persuade soldiers from the Wehrmacht to transfer to his troops. He wanted every one of

them he could get. This is why he sent members of his
Formations to army bases, equipped with colorful propaganda
leaflets meant to attract soldiers to the Death's Head Formations. He called these messengers his "headhunters."

The Wehrmacht did not look with favor on this activity.
After a series of incidents Alfred Jodl of the Wehrmacht and
Heinrich Himmler, commander in chief of the SS, reached an
agreement in 1937, according to which soldiers who asked to
see SS publications in order to decide for themselves whether
to transfer would be allowed to do so. This arrangement did not
work well—the SS argued that the army did not live up to its
obligations. Eicke therefore renewed his efforts to attract army
men into his ranks. Since the Wehrmacht had now closed its
camps to his representatives, he ordered his representatives to
befriend soldiers off-base: "Bring them from the bars, bring
them from the sports clubs, bring them from the barber. As far
as I'm concerned, you can bring them from the brothels. Bring
them from every place you meet them," he wrote.[31]

In September 1935 Adolf Hitler publicly honored the
Death's Head Formations and reviewed them in parade. From
here on out Eicke devoted most of his time and attention to
organizing his officers in the concentration camps. He made
great efforts to properly train and equip them, a formation for
each of the six concentration camps under his command. There
came a point at which there could be no doubt that Theodor
Eicke was setting up an army for himself. There was stiff
competition between Eicke's Death's Head Formations on the
one hand and the army and the rest of the SS units on the other.
The SS did not immediately appreciate Eicke's military talents,
and did not soon need his services in that field. The Death's
Head Formations were established in order to run the concentration camps. The SS had set up the Militarized Formations in
order to improve the combat readiness of the army. These from
the start had a clearly combat character. The first years of
service in the Militarized Formations were considered part
of one's mandatory military service. Only in 1939 did Adolf
Hitler decree that service in the Death's Head Formations
would also be considered part of mandatory military service.[32]
The Militarized Formations were more selective that Eicke's
Death's Head Formations. They took only 17-year-olds and

demanded that they be several inches taller than candidates for the Death's Head Formations.[33] In time the Death's Head Formations became less selective. They were forced to ignore various physical disabilities among those asking to enlist; it could no longer insist, as it once had, on healthy teeth. In 1938 they began accepting men with glasses and even lowered the minimum required height to 5 feet 7 inches. Men who had grown up during the period of hunger and shortages that followed the World War I were not in perfect physical shape. When World War II broke out, the Death's Head Formations were forbidden to take men under the age of 30; they published enlistment announcements targeted at 17-year-olds only one time thereafter, and the minimum height demanded was now lowered to 5 feet 6 inches.[34]

The superior quality Eicke attributed to his troops, in all its distortion and exaggeration, derived not only from the combat missions he wished to assign his men, but also from the role they were meant to play in the concentration camps, he claimed. The camps, Eicke explained, were the most important means available to the Nazi movement in its fight against its enemies. A heavy responsibility weighed on those serving in the camps. The fact that the Führer assigned the Death's Head Formations to operate the camps testified to the fact that he saw them as a chosen elite in the SS, or in other words, an elite of the elite in every respect: racial, ideological, and operational. The question-and-answer guide book for the Death's Head men included the following lines:

Question: Our comrades at the front are fighting to defend our country from the enemy threatening it from outside. From whom are we defending it?

Answer: We are defending our fatherland from treason, espionage, sabotage, defamation, rape, and murder.[35]

Eicke told his men that they had reason to be proud of the job they were doing in the concentration camps. The image of the Death's Head men in the eyes of their commandant was not, however, their image in the eyes of others. Their arrogance gave rise to hostility and jealousy. Their opponents often described them as nothing but simple jailers who were not at a high enough level to be combat soldiers. This was why, they said, they had been assigned to the dirty work. From time to time they also spread stories about the horrors of the concentration camps within the ranks of the SS, as if self-righteously saying that men who respect themselves as fighters do not participate in such deeds. The struggle over the image of the Death's Head Formations in the eyes of the SS made the Death's Head men identify all the more deeply with their work.[36]

Theodor Eicke had a large part in crystalizing this identification. He demanded that his officers maintain close—and, in comparison with the army, fairly friendly—contact with their men. "A soldier is but a carbon copy of his commanding officer, for better or worse," he would say.[37] He eliminated the separate dining rooms for officers and NCOs and ruled that at lunch at least one officer should sit at each table. "I attribute huge importance to this," he declared.[38] A Death's Head soldier's subordination to his officer had a more functional and less personal nature than in the army. "We did not have personal servants who shined our boots, nor drivers who carried the bags when our wives went to market," Johannes Hassebroeck said.[39] Every Death's Head man, without regard for his rank, was always required to prove his total loyalty and devotion to the Nazi ideology and to the Führer. The inevitable result was a fundamental sense of equality among officers and enlisted men. This feeling was reinforced by the fact that, unlike in the army, the social origins of each man had no bearing on his chances of climbing the ranks. Eicke instructed his men to address one another in the familiar, friendly second person, *du*, even when talking to their superiors. Such familiarity was unthinkable in the army.[40] In order to prevent personal dependence among his men, Eicke forbade them to borrow money from one another.[41] On his orders a special box for requests, questions, and complaints was placed in each camp, so that his men could apply to him directly and not through their commanders. His responses to these requests, in the routine orders he issued from time to time, reflect something of the daily life in his Formations: "All those serving in the Death's Head Formations and their families have the right to free medical care. They are forbidden to go to private doctors except in case of emergency. . . . Single men must have a savings account in a bank and these must be open at all times to inspection by their officers. . . . The unit canteens are not to sell on credit exceeding 70 marks per man. . . . Formation men would do best not to throw away the SS newspaper after reading it, but rather send it home to their relatives and friends in order to strengthen the link between the organization and the civilian population. . . . More than 750 beer glasses, coffee cups, and teaspoons have disappeared from Formation canteens in a short period of time. I have ordered the purchase of replacements, but for the last time: if they disappear again—their cost will be deducted from the Christmas bonuses of the various units. . . ."[42]

Eicke from time to time berated those of his men who applied to him anonymously: "If you don't have the courage to identify yourself—you do not belong among us," he wrote in one of his routine orders to one of the soldiers who sent him an unsigned note through one of his wooden boxes.[43] He spoke with his men with a sort of clubbishness and intimacy, as if he expected that everything he said, even in writing, would remain in the family. "The number of automobile accidents in which Death's Head Formation vehicles are involved has reached horrifying proportions," he once wrote. "The valuable lives of SS men are being thrown away for nothing, and vehicles purchased with great effort and which cannot be replaced for five years have become wrecks. It seems that most drivers know how to start a car, but they have no idea how to drive carefully and in accordance with traffic laws. It is hard to believe how many weak-headed drivers there are. All they have in their heads is the desire to exceed the speed limit. Every time something happens, they blame the other driver. In most cases the accidents are caused by nothing more than horrible carelessness. In one case a driver simply fell asleep at the wheel. This phenomenon must cease!"[44]

Eicke's routine orders also openly detailed suicides. "Sergeant Hoffmann Richard," he wrote dryly, "was killed on January 1, 1937, from self-inflicted gun shots. Motive—jealousy."[45] Eicke wrote in a similar way and without emotion about another subject which was generally not discussed in public: "The military hospital in Berlin now holds several

Formation members who have become infected with venereal diseases. This was caused by their not having taken precautions. The irresponsibility among us in this area is alarming!"[46]

In each of his routine orders Eicke listed the disciplinary actions taken against members of the Formations. "Second Lieutenant Birzle Wilhelm," he noted, for example, "has been demoted and expelled from the Formation for corruption and fraud."[47] Of the 200 members of the Death's Head Formations expelled during the space of six months in 1937, close to half of them were allowed to continue serving in other SS units, an indication of the stricter discipline in the Death's Head Formations.[48] Publication of the punishments, with the names of the violators, including officers, was meant as a deterrent, but also reflected the special atmosphere the Formations fostered. Eicke demanded that his men live up to strict military standards of behavior at all times. For this reason he forbade them to wear civilian clothes even while on furlough. He also put much emphasis on small external details, such as the form of the Nazi salute. "I demand that a bow never accompany the Hitler-style salute, even to a lady. We did not bend during the period of struggle and we will not bend now. Our soldiers greet their commanding officers with a properly stiff arm, stretched at a diagonal upwards. A limp arm is an insult. Men of the Formations never take off their hats as a greeting: we will not allow such bourgeois rules of etiquette to corrupt our way of life."[49] His habit was to accompany most of the orders he issued with ideological explanations of this type, since discipline, and so punishment, in the Death's Head Formations was meant to be part of a system of education. Eicke expected his men to obey his orders without question, but said that it did not matter to him if, while doing so, they let out a healthy curse, if they thought the order was unnecessary.[50] He warned his officers not to be too harsh on their men, since those who did not meet their demands would in any case be expelled; the others should not be humiliated or frightened. They should be educated, through personal example, so that they behave better in the future.[51] Eicke announced that he would, therefore, personally examine every disciplinary action taken in his Formations for absence without leave, desertion, drunkenness, or disobedience. It would seem that punishment for more serious violations was not in the scope of his authority, but rather the responsibility of the SS courts; in any case the violations he noted were more common than all others.[52] He took care to keep up direct contact with his men. He often visited them in the camps, spoke with them out of earshot of their immediate commanding officers, and sometimes sat and drank in their company into the small hours of the night. In the framework of the SS's struggle against religion Eicke pressured the men in the Death's Head Formations to cut their ties with the organized churches. When he heard of God-fearing parents who expelled their sons from home, he wrote to the officers of these men: "There are among us people who have, for all intents and purposes, been left without families. The Formation is all they have left in their lives. We must make sure that the Formation is a home for them and their commanders friends."[53] In 1937 Eicke announced that any of his men could spend their vacations in his house, with his family, "by prior arrangement." Amalie Müller, who managed Eicke's household for years, did not remember that he ever actually hosted one of his men,[54] but the very fact that the invitation was publicized must have reinforced the pride of the Death's Head Formations; it was a gesture unmatched in the SS.

Theodor Eicke was among the architects of the SS creed and one of the organization's mythic figures. He did not excel as an ideologist or theorist; his strength was in molding the SS mentality in daily life. By the time he began his work in Dachau this mentality was already part of him. The pride of the unit and brotherhood-at-arms, Eicke stated, were the guarantees of the Formations' invincibility; they are what makes its men into aware and directed political soldiers. Few identified with the SS system of values to the extent he did; he made his personal mark on the Death's Head troops and concentration camps the same way he afterwards left his mark on the division he led during World War II.

Eicke was born on October 17, 1892, in the small village of Hampoint in Alsace, the son of the director of the local train station.[55] His relatives remembered his father as a tall, powerful man, meticulous and serious. They said that he gave his children a strict upbringing.[56] When Eicke reached the age of 10 his father was 53 years old, a devout Protestant and enthusiastic German patriot. His mother was Catholic and spent much time with her relatives in Paris. Eicke studied in the village school for eleven years. At the age of 17 he ended his studies, enlisted in the army, and served as a paymaster for nearly ten years. His relatives said that he was eager to leave his father's house, where he was treated like a boy. He had ten brothers and sisters, all of them older than he. It seems that the Eicke children suffered from an internal conflict between their father's German patriotism and their mother's francophilism. Some of Eicke's siblings followed their mother, linked their fate with that of France, and even fought in its army during World War I. His relatives said that he had not been a happy child. Upon enlisting, however, he suddenly became a man, as he already was in his own eyes.

At that same time he was already in love with the young woman he later married, a few weeks after he turned 21. She was his sister-in-law's sister; her parents were not excited about the prospects for marrying another one of their daughters into the Eicke family. Neither were his parents happy with the match. His relatives said that this was also one of the reasons he left his father's house. Having decided to be independent, he could either have looked for an artisan who would employ him and teach him his trade, or enlist in the army. He may have deluded himself with the thought that he would succeed in penetrating the officer class and advance to a rank with social standing greater than that of his father, the train station director; lacking a high school diploma, he had little chance of doing so. In any case, the army fired his imagination, as he later related. He was attracted, like others, by heroic adventure, the chance to excel through patriotism. He loved army life, but his military record did not testify to excellence. When he was discharged, when the army was disbanded at the end of the First World War, he was 26 years old, father of a two-year-old daughter; he had no immediate plans. Success did not come. For long months he studied at the Ilmenau technical school. He wanted to be an engineer. The lack of a high school diploma caused him difficulty here as well. It may be that he failed, or it may be, as he later claimed, that he was forced to end his studies because his wife's parents refused to help him finance them. One of his friends helped him find a place in the local police force, but he was fired by the time six months were out. He enrolled instead in the police school, finished it successfully, but still had trouble finding work. He made no fewer than five attempts to find work as a police officer, in various cities, and each time he was rejected "because I was not a member of the ruling party," as he argued. He was hired on a trial basis several times, but was repeatedly laid off. He would later claim that he was the victim of "Red Terror." Had he been a police officer, his economic future would have been secure; he would have worn a uniform, carried a weapon, and enjoyed a certain measure of power—as in the army and, later, in the SS.

It is hard to know with certainty when Eicke became a Nazi. Documents he wrote himself say that his political views were always an inseparable part of his personality. In a letter to Heinrich Himmler he claimed that as far back as 1920 he tore down Communist and Social Democratic posters. This he claimed, led to his arrest and was the reason for his dismissal from the police force. It could, of course, be true that Eicke was actually the "old fighter" he said he was. It could also be that his views crystalized gradually during the period after World War I, since he joined the Nazi party only in 1928. He had not previously belonged to any political organization. His views could therefore not have been the cause of his failure to find a job with the police force. Most probably his superiors simply noticed that he was eccentric. Whatever the reasons for his failure, Eicke himself never doubted that his superiors in the police force punished him for his political opinions. "He could never forget that he failed in his attempt to become a policeman, and to the end of his days spoke of those who rejected him as traitors to the fatherland," recalled Amalie Müller, his housekeeper.[57]

When he joined the Nazi party in December 1928, he did so, Müller said, because he identified with what she still described in 1975 as "the party's proud nationalist views." Eicke told her, she said, that he had decided to join the party under the influence of a speech by Adolf Hitler. He enlisted in the SA at the same time. He was then employed full-time and on a regular basis by I.G. Farben, the huge chemical concern, in Ludwigshafen. One of his brothers had previously worked there and had helped him find the job. He first worked in one of the factory's offices and afterwards joined its security unit. He later argued, in the overblown style so characteristic of him, that he was put in charge of the plant's "Intelligence and Counter-Intelligence Unit." His salary was 550 marks per month, and there is no indication that he was in danger of losing his job. Even during the days of the great unemployment at the beginning of the thirties he kept his place there, and could no doubt have remained in the factory as long as he wanted had he not been arrested in 1932 because of his activity in the SS. Eicke was not, therefore, one of those who joined the movement as a result of financial difficulties. On the contrary, his activity in the movement cost him economically, since his arrest led to his dismissal from work.

Less than two years after he joined the SA Eicke became SS member number 2921. The SS had just come under the command of Heinrich Himmler and had begun developing its self-image as an elite organization, in competition with both the SA and the army. Eicke explained many years later that the transfer from the SA to the SS was for him an act of setting himself apart from the masses. From that point onward he was part of a select minority. His SS activity was on a volunteer basis at first. He devoted all his free time to the organization, afternoons and evenings, weekends and holidays. Eicke showed himself to be a talented SS man: he succeeded in a short period of time in establishing new units of the organization in all of Ludwigshafen and its environs. His superiors promoted him from the rank of lieutenant colonel to colonel and in 1931 he was put in command of a formation. His ten years of service in the army, including four years of war, did not advance him with the speed with which he was promoted in the SS. Eicke was extremely proud of his rank. An SS formation was not an army unit, just as a factory guard was not a police officer, but as soon as he accepted the fact that he was fated to have to satisfy himself with substitutes, he took to the SS with great enthusiasm and soon discovered that his activity in the organization gave his life meaning.

Eicke was a quarrelsome man and the list of his enemies became longer from year to year. He despised them with an inner fury that sometimes bordered on hysteria. No sooner had he joined the movement than he fell out with the head of the party's district branch in Ludwigshafen, the *Gauleiter* (District Party Chief) Josef Bürckel. This man became his foremost nemesis. Eicke once related that the tension between them was the result of an incident in which Bürckel supported the local police. The police forbade SS members to march through the streets of the city while wearing their black shirts; in protest, they marched shirtless. The competition between the SS and the SA also had a part in the dispute between Eicke and Bürckel. Bürckel was proud of his membership in the SA; Eicke had nothing but contempt for it. The dispute between the two also reflected local power struggles and there seem also to have been personal motives for their mutual hatred. Bürckel was younger than Eicke and better-educated. He was a teacher and newspaper editor. He joined the party a few years before Eicke and had a more senior position. In 1930, while Eicke was still working as an anonymous guard for I.G. Farben, Bürckel was a member of the Reichstag.[58] He would later conduct a slander campaign against Eicke, accusing him of, among other things, cowardice and corruption. "Everyone knows that he is syphilitic and completely mad," the gauleiter wrote to his men.[59]

In March 1932 Eicke was arrested and accused of terrorism. The police found several dozen homemade bombs in his possession. This was the period of growing political violence in Germany, and the authorities were helpless in the face of it. Eicke was sentenced to two years in prison, but like many of his friends he succeeded—without much difficulty—in evading the penalty. Friends helped him get a postponement for health reasons on the day the prison term was to begin. Eicke took advantage of the extension in order to get out of Germany and arrived, after a series of adventures, in Italy. During the following months he was one of a number of other SS men, among them escaped criminals, enjoying the protection of the Fascist government of Benito Mussolini. Many years later, *Il Duce* was to pat himself on the back. He had never had any doubt that those SS men would be useful some day, he said when Theodor Eicke was presented to him in a general's uniform. Himmler gave Eicke command of the SS exiles in Italy and Eicke tried, as expected, to give this appointment political significance. On October 28, 1932, he decided to celebrate the tenth anniversary of Mussolini's march on Rome. He ordered his men to put on their uniforms and he paraded them directly to the German-speaking area of the Bolzano district. The locals, however, wanted to be annexed to Austria and saw no reason to celebrate the victory of Italian fascism. The Austrian Nazi party, which supported the aspirations of the German minority in Italy, was put in an awkward position. Himmler had to work hard to bring the incident to a peaceful conclusion. His man among the exiles in Italy was, it is true, loyal to his organization, but was not blessed with a nose for politics. Himmler was to learn that over and over again in the coming years.

Eicke devoted a large part of his time in Italy to the continuation, by mail, of his personal war with Bürckel. He claimed that the gauleiter had turned him in to the police and brought about his exile. Bürckel had in the meantime taken advantage of Eicke's absence to remove him from his formation command. In response, Eicke sent Himmler an eighteen-page letter. He wrote in great fury and burning anger. He described his opponent, "the pig from Ludwigshafen," as an enemy of the entire Nazi movement. Eicke saw his struggle for his rank as the struggle of the entire movement. "Bürckel is a traitor," Eicke wrote. "He should be shot." He threatened that upon returning he would blow Bürckel up with bombs he had hidden before his arrest. "I have not changed at all during my absence," he declared. "I am fundamentally and incomparably ruthless, like I always have been. I have always acted like a man and have even paid for my actions like a man. Now I will defend my honor like a man."[60]

Eicke came home in March 1933. He was now 41 years old, father of a daughter and son. It seems that he did not immediately comprehend the meaning of the changes which had taken place in Germany during his absence. The Nazi movement—which had once busied itself mostly with local fights and show parades—was now the ruling party. It was no longer interested in considering the personal whims of an SS officer. When Eicke tried to lead a putsch against Gauleiter Bürckel he was hospitalized in a mental institution; Bürckel was now a man of great power in his district. Before returning to Ludwigshafen Eicke promised Himmler that he would not try to reassume control of his SS formation. When he broke his promise, Himmler decided he needed to be taught a lesson. He approved his forced hospitalization and at one point even expelled him from the SS. Eicke spent his time in the hospital writing long letters to Himmler sternly demanding, then requesting, finally pleading for his release. The doctors ruled that he was in perfect health. Eicke now faced an economic problem as well. His family, he argued, had been left penniless. "My problem does not result from my so-called illness, since I am not sick, but from the fact that I have no work," he stated, and added pathetically, "I do not ask for mercy. I ask for justice. Only give me what I have aspired for during my long years of struggle: bread and freedom."[61]

Himmler did not rush to answer him, but treated him fairly. He ordered that Eicke's family be paid a monthly allowance and, in a letter he sent to the psychiatrist who examined Eicke from time to time, he wrote that he was willing to find him employment, "but on condition that he no longer make trouble." Himmler asked the psychiatrist, Werner Heide, to influence Eicke to restrain himself and not repeat the actions which led to his hospitalization.[62] Himmler respected Eicke as one of the senior figures in the the movement's struggle, but wished to keep him away from the political arena, where he was a hindrance. Eicke was released during the second half of 1933 and was transferred directly from the mental hospital to the Dachau concentration camp, where he replaced Hilmar Wäckerle as its commandant.

"The Nazi movement," Eicke would tell his men, "achieved what it has achieved at the price of heavy sacrifices and only after a long, hard struggle. It must do everything it can to protect its gains."[63] Eicke himself had experienced many failures over the course of the long and frustrating struggle that ended only with his appointment as commandant of Dachau. He would in the future do everything he could to preserve his attainments. From the day he arrived at the camp he also worked at broadening the scope of his authority; as years passed his power increased until he became one of the SS's leading figures. As commandant of a concentration camp he was at first in command only of those Death's Head units sent

to the camp once every three weeks for a week at a time, in
rotation. Eicke demanded command of all the Death's Head
Formations. When he became the head of the concentration
camp administration in 1934 he based his acceptance of the
appointment on the condition that he receive command of the
Death's Head Formations, and on the removal of these units
from the SS regional command. His demands were accepted.
He always took care to emphasize his double role: director of
the central camps authority and commander of the Death's
Head Formations. This was a powerful position. Reinhard
Heydrich, head of the security service (*Sicherheitsdienst*, or
SD), tried to keep Eicke in his place. He asked that the camps
be put under his control. He also spread rumors about the
disgraceful conditions in the camps and about the torture and
murder of prisoners, in violation of orders, as well as about
administrative improprieties, financial corruption, and the like.
He demanded from time to time the establishment of an
investigatory commission to look into these charges. Eicke
succeeded in warding off his enemy time after time. This was
no easy task—Heydrich was a tough opponent.

After being appointed director of the central camps authority
and commander of the Death's Head Formations, Eicke displayed no small organizational talent, although he did not
properly understand the development needs of the camps,
failing to foresee their growth or appreciate their economic
value. He once, for example, argued with Oswald Pohl, his
superior, when the latter suggested setting up a women's
concentration camp with space for 100,000 prisoners. Eicke
answered that 2000 places would suffice. His opinion was
accepted in the end, and led to the horrible overcrowding and
lack of facilities in Ravensbrück and other camps.[64] Likewise,
Eicke did not examine the administrative talents of his men so
long as they were, in his opinion, devoted to their jobs as
representatives of the movement. The result was, at best,
failure, but often criminal neglect and corruption, too. Eicke
took more interest in the political role of the camps as
instruments for protecting the movement and increasing its
political power than in their routine management. When
Buchenwald was established, it was originally intended to
receive the name of the mountain on which it stood, Ettersberg.

Eicke wrote Himmler that cultural circles in nearby Weimar were likely to object, since Ettersberg was one of Johann von Goethe's best-loved spots. The mountains' name figures in the poet's work, so better to name the camp after the forest, Eicke suggested, so as not to anger the Weimar cultural establishment.[65] He called the camps his life's work. "When I first arrived at Dachau," he wrote, "there were no weapons there and no men who knew how to use them. I found nothing but neglect and filth. The camp staff was forced to wear their personal clothes because uniforms were not even available. Their pay amounted to 230 marks a month. There was nothing but good will and devotion to the movement's ideals."[66]

Eicke had a powerful figure and a dark countenance, all brazenness and self-confidence. The documents he left behind, however, reflect a constant fear that someone, somewhere, was trying to do him in, discriminate against him, deprive him of what he deserved, call his honor into question. He was always looking over his shoulder in expectation of being hit and was always on alert to defend himself. In this sense he really did find his proper place in the Nazi movement—there were many others like him among its members. The movement itself carefully fostered the myth of the imaginary enemy plotting against it and against every individual German. It described its struggle for rule as a defensive battle against that same enemy. Eicke identified his struggles against his persecutors with the struggles of the movement; it seems he also identified his personal aspirations with it.

In November 1933 Eicke sent a letter to the chief of the Bavarian police about one of his men, Max Kögel, who had applied for a job in the police force and had been rejected because he had once been bankrupt. The letter reflected the mentality of the entire movement.

. . . in 1926, that is, almost nine years ago [sic], Kögel was sentenced to nine months in prison. The German law to be administered from now onwards does not, like Roman law, base itself on dry legalities, but will endeavor to bring the violator to mend his ways. If this is not possible, it will endeavor to prevent him from doing any more harm. In Kögel's case, a man was caught breaking the law, but this was a result of his financial straits and not in any way of greed. It is only proper to ask if he must pay for this deed for the rest of his life after having already endured his legal punishment. We, the men of the National Socialist movement, must also consider who is guilty in the Kögel episode: he himself or, perhaps, the corrupt ways of November [the reference is to the Weimar Republic, established in November 1918]. After a careful examination, we can state that it is that same cursed politics of liberal-Marxist tendencies that is, alone, guilty. What I cannot understand is that members of the National Socialist movement, even members of the SS, now lend their support to that filthy government inasmuch as now, years later, they still persecute this man and unceasingly demand his crucifixion.

The undersigned knows the power of public opinion from personal experience. When he was sentenced to two years in prison there were people, and among them some who today define themselves as part of the National Socialist movement, who ostracized his anguished wife and were not ashamed even to condemn her publicly as a criminal's wife. If the Führer had not taken control of Germany, I would have been considered a criminal until the end of my days and would never have found government work. I therefore ask that the Kögel episode be forgotten once and for all. He is an honest man; as a discharged soldier and one of the chief fighters for Adolf Hitler, he was found worthy of serving as an SS officer. His achievements and loyalty speak for themselves. Were he not honest and loyal, I would have already expelled him. The evaluation of his superiors in the SS is therefore sufficient to shut the mouths of gossiping women, even if they dress themselves in the black robes of a public prosecutor.[67]

Eicke, like many others, joined the SS for reasons similar to those which drew him in his youth to the army. The organization represented in his eyes everything the army had represented in the past, and even more. As a member of the SS he reached a position he had aspired to but had not achieved in the army or in the police force.

Eicke tried again and again to find a place for himself in

authoritarian, "manly" frameworks requiring total submission, but also offering a large measure of personal power to their members: the army, the police, the SA, the SS. He imposed iron discipline on his men, and horrible terror on the prisoners in the concentration camps. At the same time he was obedient, ready to submit to his superiors to the point of servility. Like many of the concentration camp commandants, he needed both power and obedience. The SS granted the former and demanded the latter. It seems that he knew himself well, and so described himself simultaneously as a "man of unparalleled cruelty," and a "martyr." "My men are dearer to me than my wife and family," he once stated, and added: "The man-boys, full of power and fighting courage, give me something I do not find at home. They are fond of me and their fondness is everything to me."[68] One of the senior members of his unit, Johannes Hassebroeck, later confirmed this. "We really were fond of him," he recalled. "Eicke was more than a commander. He was a true friend and we were his friends in the way that only real men can be. Today it is hard to recreate that feeling. Eicke was dynamic, the source of the special brotherhood-in-arms which joined each of us with all the others and all of us as one with Eicke. Anyone who today examines SS literature will find that it speaks of the superiority of male youth, of the covenant of warriors, and there are also descriptions of the ideal man, blond and strong as the SS described itself. That seems like the romantic chatter of adolescent boys. But what we felt then was something very deep. Eicke was a symbol of identification with it. Together with that we felt a very personal closeness to him. Each of us needed Eicke, and there was something in his appearance, his behavior, in the way he worded his orders, that told us that he also needed us. It was a very deep and complex relationship."[69]

"I recognize my weaknesses and shortcomings very well," Eicke wrote in one of his letters to Himmler, "but I also recognize loyalty to the truth, something that no intrigue can call into question . . . my officers know this just as well as I do."[70] Somewhat melodramatic expressions of self-pity were also characteristic of his sudden explosions of anger. "Only an idiot would trust these cowardly dogs who are afraid to die and whose only dream in the war is that they remain alive," he once wrote in Adolf Hitler's guest book.[71] He was speaking of the men of the Wehrmacht; the Death's Head Formations, he meant to say, are not afraid to die. On paper Eicke was subordinate, like all SS officers, to the central office, as the organization's command was called. But he saw the units he commanded during the war as a private army, just as he saw the formation he commanded during his early days in the SS, in the concentration camps and in the Death's Head Formations, as his own territory. His war was, to a large extent, a private one, uncoordinated with the general command, and at times directly violating its orders: Rudolf Höss testified that he had not hesitated to steal equipment his unit needed from other units.[72] He once wrote to one of his superiors: "It is so easy to undermine a man like me, far away at the front."[73] For him, everything was measured in personal terms; in time he agreed to accept only the authority of Adolf Hitler and Heinrich Himmler themselves. Himmler treated him tolerantly, but was forced on occasion to ask him to hold himself back. "The Death's Head Formations are subordinate to the SS leadership and their commander does not enjoy any special privileges," he wrote Eicke.[74] He said that he had no intention of allowing the division to be a private club and asked Eicke from the depths of his heart to stop driving the entire SS crazy. "It seems to me that something has gone wrong lately with your nerves," Himmler wrote. "Perhaps you should consult a good doctor."[75] This may have been a reminder of his period of incarceration in Professor Heide's clinic. Himmler nevertheless valued Eicke's loyalty and his talents as an officer.

The trust both Himmler and Hitler himself placed in Eicke was founded, among other things, on his part in the execution of Ernst Röhm, leader of the SA, on July 1, 1934. Eicke and his men were sent to escort SS General Josef ("Sepp") Dietrich and two platoons of Hitler's bodyguards to the spa at Bad Wiessee on the shore of Lake Teger, south of Munich, in order to arrest the head of the SA. It is doubtful whether Eicke was aware of the details of the intrigues which brought about the arrest of Röhm and his men. In all likelihood he had no trouble believing the accusations that Röhm had been plotting to topple Hitler's regime. The day after the drama later known as the "Night of the Long Knives," Hitler decided to do away with Röhm in the Stadelheim Prison in Munich. He hoped, however, that Röhm would save

Prisoners at work, Dachau.

Richard Baer, commandant of Auschwitz.

Registration of prisoners, Dachau.

Franz Ziereis (right), commandant of Mauthausen, with Heinrich Himmler in the camp.

(Standing, at right) Martin Weiss, commandant of Dachau, at his trial.

Prisoners at daily roll call, Dachau.

Rudolf Höss, commandant of Auschwitz, at his trial.

Amon Göth, commandant of Plascow.

Theodor Eicke, commander of Death's Head Formations, behind
Heinrich Himmler.

Les fers aux pieds le bourreau est tenu sous bonne garde.

Joseph Kramer, commandant of Bergen-Belsen, in British military prison.

Karl Koch, commandant of Buchenwald, with his wife, Ilse Koch.

Prisoners at work, Dachau.

him the unpleasantness and would commit suicide. Himmler, who received orders from Hitler in this regard, passed them on by telephone to Theodor Eicke, who was already waiting for them in the southern district headquarters of the SS in Munich. From the evidence presented at the 1956 trial of Sepp Dietrich and of Eicke's assistant, Michael Lippert, it seems that Eicke went to the prison with an extra pistol loaded with one bullet. His assistant accompanied him to the jail. A third man, Heinrich Schmauser, was apparently with them, and served as a sort of liaison officer. Upon arriving at the prison they explained to its warden, Robert Koch, their reason for coming. Koch hesitated. He argued that he could not turn Röhm over to Eicke without express orders from his superiors and without Eicke presenting the "necessary documents." Eicke replied, as he usually did, with an explosion of anger, and told the warden that he would be accused of disobeying an express order from the Führer if he refused to give Eicke access to Röhm. Koch telephoned the Bavarian Minister of Justice, Hans Frank, in order to receive instructions. While he was explaining the matter, Eicke grabbed the telephone and barked into it that Frank did not have authority to interfere since he, Eicke, was acting on orders he had received from the Führer himself. Frank satisfied himself with that and ordered the warden not to hold Eicke and his companions back.

The three were brought to cell 474. They found the deposed leader of the SA sprawled on his bunk, naked from the waist up, dripping sweat, dreary, and depressed. "You gambled with your life and you lost!" Eicke declared dramatically after a few seconds of awkward silence. "The Führer grants you one last opportunity to avoid the punishment you deserve." He placed the spare pistol on the table and turned to go out. At the door he announced, "You have ten minutes to get it done." Eicke closed the door after him and waited in the corridor, together with his companions. After fifteen minutes had passed without a sound, Eicke ordered Lippert to draw his pistol. He opened the cell door, stood facing Röhm, addressed him as chief of staff of the SA, and called, as if on stage: "Ready!" Afterwards he ordered Lippert to aim his pistol carefully and the two of them fired simultaneously. Röhm collapsed on the cell floor, murmuring: "My Führer, my Führer." Eicke approached the wounded man and remarked: "You should have thought of that before. Now it is too late." One of the SS men, Lippert or Eicke, aimed his pistol at Röhm's heart and finished him off.[76]

Forty years later, and twenty years after the trial in Munich, Amalie Müller said that Eicke himself had told her that he had not shot Röhm. Immediately after returning to Dachau from Munich, he told her, she said, that at the last minute he could not bring himself to pull the trigger. The housekeeper remembered that Eicke always spoke of the incident as the most terrible experience he had ever undergone.[77] He did, of course, win a handsome reward for his willingness to murder in the service of the Führer: a week later his appointment was confirmed as head of the central camps administration and commander of the guard units which later became the Death's Head Formations. Within four days he had been promoted to gruppenführer. There were only two higher ranks in the SS. Hitler and Himmler did not forget Eicke's part in the Röhm episode—it opened the movement to him, strengthened his position in the SS, and deepened his personal involvement in the struggle.

His acquaintances described him as a patriarchal man, a strict father, and a jealous husband.[78] He clearly enjoyed the social status he was able to give his family. Within a few years he had adopted a luxurious life style and at one point ordered himself a family coat of arms, on the pattern of the squires who served medieval knights.[79] In 1937 his name was even included among those of the members of the suspended Reichstag. In 1943, Adolf Hitler awarded him the "oakleaf," the Third Reich's highest decoration, together with a check for 50,000 marks. He had good reason to be pleased with his life, since there had been a time when it had seemed that all his hopes were false ones, not only as a student and a failed police officer, but also as a member of the SS. In Berlin, Eicke lived at first in a five-room apartment which had once belonged to a Jewish family. He later built himself a house in a luxurious suburb, Fronau. In his free time he painted large landscapes in oils. His wife frequently hosted SS officers at sumptuous receptions and dinners. Theodor Eicke was a sort of Nazi grand seigneur, the product of a new bourgeoisie raised up by the Third Reich from the ruins of the republic. Those who knew him said that he loved good meals and red wine, and that he at times could display a fatherly humor.[80] Among the documents reflecting the Third Reich mentality that Eicke found appealing is a letter sent to him during the war by one of Himmler's assistants. The salutation is "Dear Theo" and it contains the following paragraph:

> I today interrogated a German who was taken prisoner by the Poles and succeeded in returning. He told me much of the atrocities and horrible tortures he underwent, together with 6000 other Germans. There were among them a few Jewish immigrants and these did not stop saying that they had no greater wish than to return to the resort, as they called it, at Dachau, because life there, compared with life in the Polish camp, was, they said, paradise. Himmler laughed from the depths of his heart when he read that; I thought you would also enjoy hearing that Jews give you such high marks.[81]

On February 26, 1943, Eicke was told that communications with the armored unit of his son-in-law, Karl Leiner, had been cut off. Eicke had just been released from a military hospital after having been confined for several months for wounds received in battle with the Russians. When he received this report he was not at full strength and his judgment as a commander had also, apparently, been affected. Even though there was no actual reason to worry, and in opposition to the advice of his assistants, Eicke decided to take a special plane to search for his son-in-law. Soon after taking off the plane was hit by Soviet artillery and crashed over enemy lines. Eicke was killed on the spot. "When I think of that today," Leiner said many years later, "I cannot free myself of the thought that the sudden impulse to search after our unit was at base suicidal, most likely unconscious, deriving perhaps, who knows, from the death of his son Hermann." SS officer Hermann Eicke had been killed about two years previously; his death put Eicke in a state of shock from which he never recovered, according to his son-in-law. He said that Eicke often told him that when he was informed of his son's death, he felt as if he had been killed himself.[82]

Karl Leiner had been, in his youth, a local boxing champion.

Theodor Eicke, who was then already a senior SS officer, saw his picture in an illustrated magazine. Eicke was so enthusiastic about Leiner's physique that he summoned him to appear before him, with the help of the magazine's staff. Like Himmler, he had a great weakness for strong young men with light hair and Aryan appearance. Rudolf Höss noted in his memoirs that Eicke tended to prefer the advice of young, muscular officers.[83]

EICKE enlisted Leiner and later gave him his daughter's hand. The marriage was not successful. They divorced and Eicke's daughter remarried, to a police officer in her city. She refused to speak to me about her father. He caused much ruin, she informed me, but I cherish his memory. Karl Leiner was very proud of his acquaintance with a general to whom Hitler had given such honor. He also maintained close contact with the elderly housekeeper, Amalie Müller. The two willingly responded to all my questions. The time has come for someone to clear our Theo's name, they said. Frau Müller displayed a remarkable memory for names and details. Some of them could be confirmed with documents in Eicke's SS file. She had in her possession some notes and papers of Eicke's, which she showed me and read into a tape recorder. My conversation with the two of them lasted for many hours, in Müller's house, after which she cooked me lunch. I learned from her that Eicke had been domineering at home, as well.

4
WHERE CIRCUMSTANCES LED

THE concentration camp commandants were parts of the same machine, colleagues in the same bureaucracy of oppression, terror, and murder, accomplices in a crime. There were those born in small villages and those from large cities, some from the north and some from the south, some Protestant and some Catholic. Hans Hüttig, commandant of the Flossenbürg camp, was 30 years older than Richard Baer, commandant of Auschwitz. Paul Werner Hoppe went to elementary school in an established bourgeois atmosphere at the same time that his future father-in-law, Hermann Baranowski, was fighting in World War I. Hans Aumeier, commandant of the Vaivara camp, was the son of a manual laborer; Karl Künstler, the second commandant of Flossenbürg, was the son of a barber; and the father of Amon Göth, commandant of the Plascow camp in Cracow, was a well-to-do publisher. Göth studied at the University of Vienna. Max Kögel, the second commandant of Majdanek in Lublin, had only six years of education at a village school. They joined the Nazi party at widely different times. The last to enlist in the SS did so fifteen years after the first one. The order in which they joined the party and the SS did not, however, correspond to their ages: Wilhelm Gideon, one of the commandants of the Gross Rosen camp in Silesia, was only a year older than the first commandant of Dachau, Hilmar Wäckerle. Gideon, however, joined the party only in 1937, while Wäckerle had

belonged to it since 1922. Heinrich Deubel, also of Dachau, and
Egon Zill, of Flossenbürg, enlisted in the SS in the same year, but
Deubel was 16 years older. Friedrich Hartjenstein, of Auschwitz,
was Zill's age, but joined the SS fifteen years after him.

There were among them men of different types: bureaucrats,
opportunists, sadists, and criminals. The great majority of
them were political soldiers.

Soon after receiving command of the concentration camp
administration, in the first half of 1942, Oswald Pohl issued a
list of promotions and new appointments. He dismissed six
commandants and appointed twelve, all of them with previous
experience in the camps. Five of them had been born before
1900 and had participated in World War I; seven were from the
SS's younger generation. The latter had not been old enough to
take part in the war, and grew up in a different world. Not all
of them were successful at their assignments. Some of them
received their appointments only because the SS did not know
what to do with them.

During the second half of the thirties, for example, the SS
leadership was in a dilemma over what to do with one of the
organization's oldest and most loyal members, Hans Helwig,
an official in the Ministry of Justice in the state of Baden, then
55 years old. Everyone respected him for being one of the first
members of the "fighting family"; in the twenties he had
already been one of the movement's enthusiastic supporters
and had represented it for a few months in the Reichstag in
Berlin. But Helwig was too old and too stupid to serve in the
SS; his service file testifies to his also having failed as the
second commandant of Sachsenhausen. Most other commandants were successful, irrespective of their ages. As with many
of his fellow commandants, Helwig's period of service in the
concentration camps appears in his service file as but one
chapter in his life and service.[1]

Helwig was the son of a forest ranger in Hemsbach, a small
town of less than 2000 residents, 15 miles north of Heidelberg,
Baden. He had fourteen siblings, all older than he. After eight
years in elementary school, he decided to become a bricklayer.
His apprenticeship lasted four years, during which he studied at
a vocational school. It would seem that he did not like his
chosen profession very much—at the age of 19 he decided to

sign up for a two-year stint in the army. He remained in the army for eighteen years, serving almost continuously as a master sergeant in an infantry unit. In 1914 he left the army and began working as a court clerk in his city. The war broke out a few months later. Helwig returned to his battalion and went to the trenches with it, in the east and the west. When he returned home he was 37 years old, married, and the father of a two-year-old boy. He had no professional experience.

There was a new social and political situation in Baden which he neither wanted nor understood. Formerly ruled by a grand duke within the German Empire, Baden was now part of the German Republic, and the Social Democratic party was in power. Part of it, including the city in which Helwig had lived for many years while in the army, was still under occupation by the French army. Baden was deep in an economic crisis. Many factories decided to remove themselves from the French border, transferring themselves eastwards into the German Republic and leaving recession and unemployment in their wake. The Belgian and French invasion of the Ruhr area in 1923 made the situation even worse. Helwig, still in shock from the humiliating defeat after so many years in the army, detested the new situation, even though it did not affect him directly. He resumed his work in the court and after a while was made a minor official in the Ministry of Justice. Since he lacked a high school diploma he did not have any chance of advancing in the ministry, just as he could not be an officer in the army. It was not long before he was in trouble, apparently for political reasons. Helwig was an admirer of Adolf Hitler. The government of Baden was not tolerant of those of its employees who associated themselves with the extreme right. When, at the ministry, Helwig spoke favorably of the conspirators behind the Beer Hall Putsch of 1923, he was suspended indefinitely from his job, although he was not fired. Helwig was by that time a member of the SA. Prior to that he had joined the German Alliance for Defense and Deterrence (*Deutschvölkischer Schutz und Trutzbund*)—an umbrella organization of various extreme right, nationalist, and anti-Semitic associations and clubs established in Germany after the war.

By 1921 the alliance had about 140,000 members and 500 branches throughout Germany. They demanded the establishment of a new regime, headed by a strong leader with dictatorial powers who would liberate Germany from Jewish capitalism and restore its racial purity. All members of the alliance were required to prove their Aryan descent; its symbol was the swastika. The alliance organized meetings and ideological seminars of all types, hikes for young people, and German ceremonies, all to the taste of the lower middle class. Once a year the alliance organized a nationwide gathering, "Germany Day"; among the participants were the leaders of the small Nazi party, including Adolf Hitler. In the wake of the assassination of German Foreign Minister Walther Rathenau in June 1922, the alliance was outlawed. Most of its members then joined Hitler's party.[2]

Helwig, suspended from work, had the leisure for activity in the SA, to which he now devoted most of his time. Helwig did not join the Nazi party in protest against his economic difficulties. On the contrary, he faced the danger of losing his job as a result of his association with the party. His was a true expression of identity with the party's principles. From time to time he was involved in street fights with its opponents; during one of these he was beaten by a police officer and suffered serious head wounds. In 1925, when the Nazi party began to reorganize itself after Hitler's release from prison, Helwig was one of the founders of the Nazi party branch in his city and was elected on its ticket to the city council, where he eventually joined Heinrich Himmler's faction. He sided with Himmler in his fight with Gauleiter Robert Wagner, and in 1929 left the SA for the SS, then put under Himmler's command. Helwig was already 48 years old and could not be of much use to the movement. Gauleiter Wagner warned his superiors about him. "The man is corrupt and foolish," Wagner wrote, "and in conversation with his friends he has threatened that, if it turns out that most of the high party posts are given to men who served in the army as officers, he will organize a 'sergeants' rebellion' and take them into the Communist party, in order to 'to fight from the outside' for their place in the party."[3] The possibility that Helwig said something of this sort should not be dismissed. Years out of the army, he still thought of himself as a sergeant and was very eager to advance in the party. His superiors thought he was not very smart. The main problem was that he did not understand when things were explained to him, they said, and he talked too much. Later on the secret police would report that Helwig boasted of the atrocities being committed at Sachsenhausen to foreigners in a beer hall. Wagner tried to prevent Helwig's election to the Reichstag, but Himmler succeeded in obtaining Hitler's personal endorsement of Helwig.

Helwig was one of the seven Nazi delegates from Baden, the rest of whom were younger and better-educated than he. Among them were a journalist, a lawyer, a former officer, and a medical assistant. Helwig's term lasted for only a few months. The only reference to his parliamentary activity in the surviving records is his participation in a roll call vote. Wagner had meanwhile become the strongman in Baden. He succeeded in toppling the government and setting up another in its place. Helwig was deposed from the Reichstag and transferred to the Landtag, the local parliament, which soon ceased to function.

Helwig's long military career at first impressed his commanders in the SS. Thinking they could learn from his experience, they put him in command of a battalion and, later, a regiment. All this was evening and weekend activity on a voluntary basis. A few months after the Nazis came to power, Helwig was appointed commander of the prison in Bruchsal, perhaps as a result of his work in the Ministry of Justice, but most likely because he needed a job. He did not like it. It demanded a mental effort that Helwig could not handle; he suffered a nervous breakdown and decided to retire. He then discovered that his pension, after thirty-three years of service, was very low, 202 marks and 53 pfennigs a month. His service file indicates financial difficulties as well as a fierce desire to do something else for the movement. "As soon as I left the Bruchsal Prison I recovered, both physically and mentally," he wrote, but a job still had to be found for him. All he had to offer was twenty years of political loyalty. His superiors in the SS now had mixed feelings about him. They still respected him as one of the first members of the movement, but the more the SS became part of the state security apparatus, the less it needed burdensome old men like Helwig.

At one point a superior of his wrote a personal letter to Heinrich Himmler and described the Helwig problem in these words: "We have for more than a year been doing our best to find Helwig respectable employment appropriate to his talents, as he deserves in light of his past activity in the movement. All our efforts thus far had failed. Several people in the movement have promised to help, but have not done anything. They are all words but no action. Helwig has the party's Gold Medal and that in and of itself justifies assistance. For this reason we permit ourselves to ask if there is a possibility of employing him in the police administration, making him, for example, responsible for supplies and equipment, or to appoint him commandant of one of the concentration camps, or any other job appropriate to his talents." To prevent any misunderstanding, the writer added the following sentence: "H is not suited to serve as an SS officer." This, for all intents and purposes, said: "We want to help him, but we don't want him here." It would seem that the writer thought that Helwig's past as an army master sergeant and warden of Bruchsal Prison, as well as his long connection with Himmler, would help him. He was not mistaken—Himmler responded at once and appointed Helwig commandant of the women's concentration camp at Lichtenburg, near Leipzig. Lichtenburg was one of the first camps, like Dachau, Sachsenhausen, and Buchenwald. It operated until May 1939, when its inmates were transferred to the new women's camp at Ravensbrück.

Theodor Eicke was not enthusiastic about Helwig's becoming one of his men. He tried to get rid of him. At one point he was forced to appoint him commandant of Sachsenhausen in place of Karl Koch. A few weeks later he also confirmed that the movement had no member of deeper loyalty than Helwig, and that he was worthy of promotion. Eight months after that, however, he demanded his removal. Helwig implicated himself—as well as Eicke—in an incident which reflects the unique double standard between the standing orders by which the concentration camps were supposedly run and the arbitrary regime which actually prevailed. The matter involved a prisoner, Johannes Winiarz, who was vasectomized by the camp doctor. The problem was that the operation was performed without prior approval of a judge, as was required; the prisoner did not have the opportunity to petition the court in order to appeal the decision to operate on him. The incident led to a

lengthy correspondence between the Minister of Justice, Franz
Gürtner, and SS Commander in Chief Himmler. "It is not the
fate of the criminal which interests me," Gürtner wrote
Himmler, "but the failure to comply with the law." Himmler
turned to Eicke and Eicke to Helwig. Helwig, Eicke explained
in a long letter to Himmler, had apparently confused his orders.
He thought that he did not need a judge's approval and that it
was sufficient for an internal camp committee to have ordered
the prisoner's sterilization. It had not been an easy period in the
camp, Eicke wrote. "A large shipment of prisoners had
suddenly arrived, and it was hard to control the situation."
Eicke was angry at Helwig for not having prevented the story
from leaking out of the camp to the minister's office, and
decided to get rid of him. "Helwig will turn 57 this year,"
Eicke wrote to Himmler. "He is a totally decrepit man, both
mentally and physically, and is no longer able to fulfill his
position as camp commandant. Extending his appointment will
lead to further political complications and will also lead to the
deterioration of the situation in the camp, including a weaken-
ing of discipline among the prisoners."

Helwig was deeply hurt when he heard that he was being
removed from his command. "It will destroy me," he wrote. "I
have nowhere to go. Here I thought I had received what I
deserve, after so many years of service to the movement. My
wife is as shocked as I am. My financial state is very bad. I
recently took out a mortgage to fund the purchase of my house
and now I will not be able to make the payments, since my
pension is only 140 marks a month." The Helwigs now had
two children. Himmler promised to raise Helwig's pension by
another hundred marks a month. Helwig replied that this was
not enough. Eicke did not give in. "Under no circumstances
should such a position be used to solve someone's personal
problems," he argued, and found a line in his budget that
allowed him to give Helwig a one-time severance payment of
5000 marks, if only he would go. So in August 1938, Helwig
returned to Hemsbach, his home town, but his problem
continued to bother the SS long thereafter. His service file
thickened. They tried to find him financial support and tried to
find him work. In the end he was detailed to the Todt
organization, a public company involved in defense construc-

tion projects, fortifications, roads, and the like. It seems that here, on the eastern front, he finally found his place. Among other things, he helped set up a base to supply fuel and which also served as a camp for Soviet prisoners. Towards the end of the war, now an SS general of 63, he served as a liaison officer between Heinrich Himmler's headquarters and the headquarters of the army's northern command. He died in Hemsbach, in August 1952, before they could put him on trial.

Helwig was an idealist and opportunist at one and the same time, as were many other concentration camp commandants. In 1942 he still visited the Protestant church regularly, contrary to SS ideology. His name had previously been engraved on the Hemsbach church bells. He apologized, explaining that it was a local custom when he was asked about this, and quickly announced that he did not belong to the church but "believed in God," according to the accepted SS formula. Some time later he was seen in uniform at a church memorial ceremony. He went there, he explained, only because the church had given him a loan of 5000 marks that he needed to buy his house.

Helwig could have done another job, had one been offered to him. He wanted to do something. He wholeheartedly identified with his movement, and was an old hand in the army and at war. His work at Bruchsal Prison prepared him for his job at the Lichtenburg camp, and Lichtenburg prepared him for Sachsenhausen.

THE personnel file of Heinrich Deubel, another Dachau commandant, also overflows with correspondence, this time aimed at ensuring his status as a customs worker on unpaid leave, assigned to the SS.[4] Deubel was among the movement's most senior men, one of the first 200 members of the SS. He had previously been active among extreme rightist, nationalist, anti-Semitic, and paramilitary organizations. He saw himself, however, as a civil servant, like his father the mailman. As a senior SS man, devoted and loyal, he felt a deep commitment to the organization's ideological goals. When, however, he was asked to decide between continuing to serve in the SS and preserving his privileges as a civil servant, he announced that he could not give up his tenure at the customs service.

"Starting in 1920," he wrote, "that is, for fifteen years now, I have been a customs worker. Prior to that I served in the army for twelve years, and spent another five years at the front [actually, he spent most of the war in a British prisoner-of-war camp]. If I resign from the customs service, I will renounce my right to receive a pension for fifteen, twelve, and five more years, a total of thirty-two years, which are about 67 percent of my salary today. I hope that the day is not far off when the SS will also set up a pension fund of its own. In the meantime, I cannot leave the customs service."

EDUARD Weiter had never displayed any special interest in politics.[5] He did not join the Nazi party until 1937, more than six months after he began serving in the SS. There does not seem to have been an ideological reason for him to join the organization; he had never been a volunteer. He had previously served for many years as a paymaster in the army and in the police force. When he was appointed, at the end of 1943, to be the last commandant of Dachau, he saw it as a purely administrative task, not substantially different from what he had done before.

Weiter was born in July 1889 in Eschwege, a small industrial city about 45 miles south of the city of Kassel in the state of Hesse. His father made horsewhips. Weiter completed elementary school and in the six following years worked as a salesman in a book store. For three of those years, he simultaneously studied at a commercial school. At the age of 20 he volunteered for the army. He had meant to serve for two years, but stayed for ten. He went with his unit to the French, Russian, and Balkan fronts. Afterwards he became battalion paymaster and finally regimental paymaster. In the meantime he married and had two children. The defeat of the German army and its disbandment did not seriously affect Weiter's professional development, since in October 1920 he began serving as a paymaster in the Bavarian state police. The social and political upheavals Germany experienced, including the Nazi revolution, did not change his life. He had a steady job and continued with it for thirteen years. In March 1936 the Bavarian police forced became part of the army. A few months thereafter, at the age of 47, Weiter was eligible for retirement, and he went to work at the Waffen SS administration as a paymaster. He simply transferred from one army to another, in each case filling an administrative position. His superiors gave him warm recommendations, praised his organizational ability, his honesty, and his diligence. His service file describes him as a strong man of soldierly bearing. This was an advantage in the SS, but even there he continued as an office worker and dealt with money and administrative matters.

As late as 1936 he wrote that he had no clear political identity. He nevertheless began gathering evidence testifying that he had never numbered among the opponents of the Nazi movement, and he joined the party. When his superiors wanted to praise him, they were uncertain how to handle his ideological apathy. He has a military background, they wrote cautiously. He is an experienced bureaucrat, they wrote, eminently correct, who makes every effort to integrate himself into the SS family and win its approval. In time he won favor with Oswald Pohl, the administrator of the concentration camp system. During World War II Weiter continued to deal with various administrative and financial matters of the Waffen SS. At one point he was also put in charge of the administration of the Dachau concentration camp.

He still had no connection with the prisoners, but it was a good way to gradually get used to what was going on in the camp. At the end of 1943, when he was 54 years old, he was appointed commandant of the camp. After the war, survivors of Dachau said that Weiter minimized his involvement with prisoners. He was rarely seen in the camp, spending most of his time in his office, behind his desk. He made only small changes in Dachau. The camp deteriorated, among other reasons because of the overcrowding, which became more severe as prisoners evacuated from camps in the east were sent there. Weiter made no attempt to ease the congestion. During the last days of the war, not long before the camp was liberated, he spoke with some inmate leaders in an attempt to ensure that they would testify in his favor after the war, indicating the extent of his calculating, cold self-distancing from the SS. Weiter died a few days before the camp was liberated. The circumstances are unclear. According to one version, he was shot to death by one of his colleagues, an SS officer of deeper emotional and ideological involvement.[6]

* * *

ARTHUR Rödel, on the other hand, was probably a sadist. There is evidence of atrocities he ordered or even performed with his own hands; the impression is that he enjoyed an erotic thrill from them. Just before midnight on January 1, 1939, he forced several thousand inmates at Buchenwald to line up for inspections, chose five men from among them, ordered them stripped and tied to special beating posts, and had them whipped in rhythm as the prisoner orchestra played. It lasted almost until morning.[7]

Rödel was born in May 1898 in Munich.[8] His father was a messenger in one of the banks, and his mother ran a small news and tobacco stand. When Rödel was 10 she was forced to close it; Rödel was brought up to believe that this was because she could not compete with the owner of the neighboring stand, a Jew. They were devout Catholics and had three other children, a boy and two girls. Upon finishing elementary school Rödel decided to be a blacksmith. While still an apprentice he joined a paramilitary nationalist organization and, when the war broke out, he rushed to report to the enlistment office. He was then 16 years old. The army refused to take him. Rödel wanted very much to be a soldier, so he doctored his papers and claimed to be 18. He spent the next four years in combat units on the front. He was wounded in battle at least once, and required lengthy hospitalization.

At the end of the war he was 20. The social, political, economic, and psychological crisis Germany suffered after the war embittered him, as it did other former soldiers. He lacked work experience and became involved with a 34-year-old woman. Her parents—and his—forced him to marry her; four months later a baby girl was born. They were to have no more children. Just before the wedding Rödel was accepted for a job at the post office. Because of his limited education there was no opportunity for him to advance in the civil service, but he was at least promised tenure. This he could see as an improvement in his status, civil servant instead of blacksmith. He continued, like Helwig, to be active in the extreme right, and like him ran into problems with his superiors at work. In 1920 Rödel joined the Bund Oberland, an organization of discharged soldiers who refused to accept that they had been defeated and that the war had ended. They searched for—and found—new battlefields. Rödel went to join the gang wars between Germans and Poles in Upper Silesia. His relatives would later testify that Rödel's marriage had not been a happy one.[9] He preferred being at the front, with his friends in the Oberland. The post office warned him that he must return to work; his wife also demanded that he return. He came back, reluctantly, a few days before they planned to fire him. Some time later he was caught distributing nationalist literature at his window in the post office. He was reprimanded. When his superiors discovered that he had personally participated in the attempted Beer Hall Putsch, he was fired. He was now 26 years old, burdened by a wife 13 years older than he whom he did not love, and a daughter. He was also unemployed. Having been one of the movement's supporters for the last five years, one of the senior members of the fighting family, it was only natural for him to go to the Brown House, the Nazi party headquarters. Rödel knew someone there who gave him work in the mimeograph room, and from then on he was a party employee. In 1928 he joined the SS as a volunteer, and in 1934 began working for the organization as a full-time salaried worker.

He first served in one of the Death's Head Formations, the "Elbe." The formation from time to time sent some of its men to patrol around the women's concentration camp at Lichtenburg. This did not require direct contact with the prisoners. Rödel hoped to advance in the Death's Head Formations, but Theodor Eicke ordered his transfer to the Sachsenburg camp, also among the first camps, though later closed. Rödel did not want to transfer; he saw it as a demotion. He obeyed unwillingly and resentfully. His superiors did not appreciate his military talents and did not consider promoting him. He is a good man, loyal Nazi, and good comrade, they wrote of him, but this is not enough. He is naive, they said, appropriate perhaps for a low-level position at a concentration camp. Like Helwig, he later became a problem for Eicke, causing great unpleasantness. One day a foreign visitor appeared. There is no way of knowing who he was—perhaps a diplomat, or an International Red Cross representative, or a journalist; at that time there were still foreigners who were permitted to visit the camps. The man asked questions, and Rödel answered, apparently without properly disguising the truth about the camp. "We had to make a great effort to correct the misunderstanding," Eicke complained afterwards and demanded Rödel's removal. If he were allowed to stay in the camp, Eicke wrote, he was liable to cause great damage to the country's external relations.

Rödel tried to improve the quality of his work, and as he was transferred from camp to camp he learned more, accustomed himself to and became part of the daily routine. Most of the testimonies about his cruelty, including the mass flogging of New Year's night, 1939, come from Buchenwald. At Buchenwald, Rödel was deputy to Karl Koch, who allowed his men to do as they pleased. But even then Rödel's superiors did not rush to promote him. He does not deserve it, they wrote again and again in their evaluations of him. This frustrated him. Only in 1942, when he was 44 years old, was he appointed commandant of the Gross Rosen camp in Silesia. At that time they were being less strict about the quality of the staff at the camps. The good officers were needed at the front. "Rödel was a cruel, corrupt, and drunken man," said Johannes Hassebroeck, who knew him.[10] Towards the end of the war Rödel found himself in the Nazi occupation police in the Ukraine; with the collapse of the Third Reich he committed suicide, apparently with a hand grenade.

The movement gave him work, but he was not drawn to it out of unemployment. Like Helwig, his activity in the movement led to the loss of his civil service job. His identification with the movement preceded its ability to help him. He was also one of its first soldiers, a military man who served in the camps unwillingly. He, like Helwig, could have done something else had it been offered, and perhaps he would not then have found an outlet for his sadism—or he might have found a different outlet.

Rödel was not the only sadist among the concentration camp commandants. Egon Zill tied prisoners to trees and ordered his dog to attack their genitals.[11] Karl Fritsch would strangle male and female prisoners with his own hands, after having ordered them stripped.[12] Karl Chmielewski ordered prisoners drowned in pails of water during inspection.[13] The cruelty of Karl Koch and his wife was legendary.[14] All of these, however, also identified with their movement, and most of them did so years before it gained power. They might have ended up at the camps even if they had not already been sadists, and could have gotten used to the atrocities gradually, step by step, as other camp commandants did.

EGON Zill was 8 years old when World War I broke out.[15] The war was the central experience of his childhood. His father was drafted immediately, was gone from home for the entire war, and returned severely wounded. Before the war he had worked in a brewery in Plauen, a city not far from Leipzig in north Germany. Zill was born there. He had a younger brother who died at the age of 8 months and a little sister. When he finished elementary school it was decided he would be a baker. He worked for three years as an apprentice and then received a certificate. A few days later he joined the SA and the Nazi party; by then he was 17 years old. This was not an expression of personal protest, nor a response to economic difficulty. The SA in any case could not help him at that point, but the movement exuded comradeship and youth and an ideal of loyalty, in a foggy way—the movement's ideology was still in formation. It would seem, then, that the "politicization" of Zill began as an attraction to the friendship of young men like himself, at the beginning of their adult lives as self-employed craftsmen. Through them he met his future wife, a black-smith's daughter. His personnel file preserves a form she filled out. Under the heading "leisure activities and hobbies" she listed the initials of the Nazi party. Zill remained loyal to the party even when it stopped functioning during Hitler's imprisonment, and returned to its ranks immediately upon its reorganization in 1925. In time an SS formation was established in Plauen, and Zill joined it at once. Only 534 men in all of Germany joined the SS before he did.

Zill was unemployed for a time in 1927, and then found work as a guard in a local curtain factory; his future wife also worked there. He remained at this job for seven years. Millions of other Germans were unemployed and he was better off than they were. Even after the Nazis came to power he did not rush to leave work. Only in May 1934 did he go to work for the SS full-time. He was stationed in a small concentration camp near

Chemniz, halfway between Plauen, where he lived, and Dresden. He would later claim that the SS "drafted" him.[16] The truth is that he had good reasons to join the organization of his own volition. He supported the movement in difficult times, for almost ten years, without asking for any compensation and without receiving any promises. That was true dedication. Now that the movement had the power to improve his lot, Zill naturally preferred to be an SS officer instead of a guard at a curtain factory; the SS was more attractive to him, and also paid more. He was then planning to marry; his fiancée was already pregnant.

Zill remained in the camps for nine years. In 1943 he was transferred to the eastern front. He, like Arthur Rödel, first served in the Elbe guard unit and patrolled the area around the Lichtenburg camp. Until 1943 he served in different capacities in Dachau, Lichtenburg, Ravensbrück, and Hinzert, and finally as commandant at the Natzweiler and Flossenbürg camps. In this way he advanced along with the camps from the start, followed the growing brutality, and became part of it. Each stage prepared him for the one after. He identified with his role as a commandant. Like Eicke, he issued a series of daily orders to his men that were a combination of severe discipline and ideological piety. Both Zill and Eicke limited the routine cruelty with clear orders concerning what was permitted and what forbidden. "We sit here on enemy territory [France]," he once wrote. "We must take care always to preserve a soldierly, pressed appearance and disciplined behavior in order to win the favor of the population."[17] He apparently believed in this. As an old fighter who believed in his movement's slogans, he once suggested separating out from among the inmates of the concentration camps those who had turned from opponents to supporters of the regime as a result of the education they had received there, and allowing them to go to the front to prove their loyalty to the Third Reich. If they lived, they would receive freedom in exchange for their combat service.

Alongside strict obedience to the standing orders of the concentration camps, Zill allowed, ordered, and personally carried out bloodcurdling atrocities. In one case he ordered that a group of naked Soviet POWs be paraded in front of him. He watched them for a long time while he amused himself with his riding whip, exploiting to the end his absolute power over their bodies, turning over in his mind who would live and who die. He then chose one of them and shot him to death himself. He frequently tortured and abused prisoners. His service file reveals that at one point he caught a venereal disease. He may have been a sadist who drew erotic pleasure from his abuse of prisoners, which he often carried out after he had ordered them stripped naked. In any case, he also served in the camps out of conviction.

He was a short man; behind his back he was called "little Zill." After the war he took on a false name, but, correct as always, when he became a father he took care to see that the baby was registered under his real name, even though the mother was not his wife. This led to his discovery, arrest, and trial. A court in Munich first sentenced him to life in prison, but later accepted his appeal and reduced this to fifteen years. That was in 1955. Zill died in 1974, at home in the city of Dachau, a mile or so from the concentration camp in which he had once worked.

KARL Fritsch also frequently tortured prisoners to death, often while they were naked. Apparently he, too, derived erotic pleasure from such deeds. It was not sadism, however, which brought him to the camps. His motives were, in part, very practical, and he also identified with the movement's ideology.

Fritsch was born in Nassegrub, a small village in Bohemia, in July 1903.[18] His father installed ceramic stoves for home heating. His work required much travel in Czechoslovakia, Austria, Germany, and Italy, and he liked to take his family with him. Fritsch, the eldest of the six children, was frequently forced to switch schools. He never received a formal education and had difficulty reading and writing to the end of his days. He would later tell his wife that he had never really had a home or real friends; he had been a quiet child, very sensitive and attached to his mother. When the war broke out his father was drafted immediately and was away from home until the end of the war. Fritsch was 15 when his father returned, defeated. After the war his father opened a musical instruments store. Fritsch displayed a measure of musical talent. He played several instruments and dreamed of conducting an orchestra, but his family moved to Vienna and Fritsch became an apprentice shingler. This did not satisfy him; at the age of 20 he decided to be a sailor and joined a transport company that shipped cargoes along the Danube. At this point, his widow said, he dreamed of being a ship's captain. He remained on the Danube for ten years, until just after the Nazi came to power. In December 1928 he married. His wife was the daughter of a soda manufacturer from Regensburg, Bavaria. In the summer of 1930 he joined the Nazi party and three months later the SS, as a volunteer.

"It happened very suddenly," his widow recalled. "He would go to party meetings with his friends, most of them sailors like him. Afterwards they would debate all night. Once or twice they also traveled specially to Nuremberg to hear Adolf Hitler. At some point it caught him, it seems. He became very enthusiastic. I didn't understand what exactly was happening to him, but I saw that it was happening under the influence of his friends. Looking back, it seems that he discovered a new kind of friendship; it was very powerful. That friendship eventually became everything to him." At first, the SS in Regensburg had only seven members, five of whom were unemployed. Fritsch's wife cooked for them, and she and her husband also lent them a little money. "They were like brothers," his widow said. At that time he still worked on the Danube; he had four days off every two weeks. More than anything else, his widow said, Fritsch dreamed of normal family life in a house of his own. More than once he told her, she said, that if they had children, he would do everything to ensure that they enjoyed a childhood happier than his, and that they should be brought up in the real home he had lacked as a child. When the Nazis came to power, in January 1933, his wife was pregnant. Her husband had discovered, meanwhile, that his chances of becoming a captain were not good. "One day," his widow recalled, "he came home and asked me what I thought: was it worth joining the Death's Head Formations of the SS on a full-time basis. He explained to me that it was a unit that combined army with police work. We would have to move to another city, Dachau, and we would live in a little house, so that when the baby was born he would no longer work on the river and we would live solid lives, with regular work hours. He asked me if I wanted that. I saw that he wanted it. He was a little disappointed with his work on the Danube. He was very enthusiastic about the new political situation and wanted to become part of it; after all, he had supported the movement for years. And it would be great to work with friends from the SS, he said, and both of us wanted a normal family life, before the baby was born. I said that he should decide, and he decided. If I had said no, he would have stayed on the Danube."

The baby, Gertrud, was born in August 1933; a son and another daughter were born later. The Death's Head Formations paid more than the shipping company and made the family's future secure. "He said that, if he were killed, I would receive 280 marks a month. I was angry that he even went so far as to find out about that. Nothing will happen to you, I told him." His enlistment in the Death's Head Formations was the right decision under the circumstances, whether or not he was a sadist. He first worked a few months in the Bavarian police auxiliaries, after which he was seconded to the Dachau guard unit, where he stayed for seven years. In the meantime he was given various courses, military and ideological. By the time he was appointed deputy commandant of Auschwitz, in 1940, he had gained much experience. The situation in the camps had become more brutal from year to year, and Fritsch was there. It is not clear at what stage he discovered that the camps allowed him an outlet for his cruelty; it is not impossible that this also developed bit by bit. In August 1942 Fritsch was transferred to the Flossenbürg camp. His superiors wrote that he was diligent and energetic, but tended to exceed his authority from time to time: they may have been referring to atrocities he committed. One day Fritsch ordered some prisoners to be lined up. He intended to choose ten of them to be starved to death as punishment for an escape attempt by one of the prisoners. An eye-witness said afterwards that Fritsch paced back and forth in front of the prisoners, very slowly, serenely, a small smile at the corner of his mouth. He looked them over one after the other, pointing at one, then at another—a camp commandant at the peak of his power, deciding who would live and who would die. The ability to choose them in this way, slowly, as he liked, expressed absolute control over all of them.

His widow said that he was a man of poor health, and as the years went by, very irritable. He once came down with typhoid fever and never completely recovered. In Auschwitz, the widow said, he suffered from insomnia and nightmares. He would often wake up suddenly with horrible cries. In Auschwitz and until he died, she said, he no longer achieved sexual satisfaction with her. After a while they separated. He was sent to the front. In his letters—in which there were still spelling errors—he described in minute detail the atrocities committed by soldiers of the Red army, as well as the firebombing of Dresden; Fritsch was killed in the battle of Berlin.[19]

FANNY Fritsch was 67 years old when I visited her in her apartment in Regensburg; she was a small woman who lived in her memories. It was not hard for her to explain to herself the atrocities attributed to her husband: she decided that they had never occurred. Her husband, she said, was "the best man in the world" and never harmed a soul.

Rudolf Höss wrote in his memoirs that it was Fritsch who began killing Soviet POWs in Auschwitz with gas, before the extermination of the Jews began. Could it be that he was there and did not take part in what happened, I asked his wife? No, no, the woman said: what they say about Auschwitz, about the extermination of the Jews, and all that—is a lie. Simply a lie. The fact is, she said, after the war, when her Karl was no longer alive, some prisoners released from the camp visited her and even helped her manage with the children. They would not have done that if what others said about her husband was true. Her sister, Frau Fritsch said, had always told her that Karl was degenerate, but her sister had been a Communist. She often thought about the past. She had among her friends a number of other SS widows. All of them told her she was right.

I had the impression that she did not know the details of her husband's sadism. He always wanted to leave Auschwitz, she claimed—it was not for him, he told her (his personnel file contains no evidence of a request for a transfer). The things she told me about his health and sexual frustration (she spoke of this at her own initiative) lent weight to her argument that he was a victim of circumstances. She had a few letters he wrote her, including descriptions of wartime atrocities. In one of them he described Soviet tanks running over children. In his last letter he wrote that he had remained faithful to her and to Germany. "It is important to me that the children know that," he wrote. His widow tried to educate them to his example, she said.

———

THE worst of them all was Karl Koch. His life and death mix cruelty with passion and corruption, including undercover investigations, threats, forgeries, anonymous letters, liquidation of witnesses and a secret trial, all against the background of the intrigues at the top of the SS. There is also sex—Koch became one of the symbols of the atrocities of the concentration camps, partly owing to the deeds of his wife, the "monster of Buchenwald."

Ilse Koch was his second wife. They met in 1934, when he was commandant of the Sachsenburg camp. She was his professional secretary, a party member, younger than he by ten years and attractive. "She loved men in uniform," her biographer, Arthur L. Smith, wrote.[20] She had been in love once before, with an SS man. Frau Koch spent much time with her husband in the camps, even before they married. He presented her to his colleagues, but they could not live that way for long without marrying—the SS expected its men to live ordered lives. They married at midnight, in an oak grove, by torchlight, without a minister, she in white, he in dress uniform, all in accordance with SS ritual. Immediately afterwards he was promoted to lieutenant colonel and was sent to set up the Buchenwald concentration camp.

Buchenwald became the personal kingdom of Koch and his wife, and they were its absolute rulers. There they built their opulent house and there they gave birth to their three children. Their youngest daughter died of pneumonia when she was three and a half months old. To the extent that it is possible to reconstruct it, it seems that Koch and his wife did not live together happily. He found other women in nearby Weimar; she betrayed him with several officers in the camp, among them Hermann Florstedt, later commandant of Majdanek. There are reports that she liked to walk through the camp in what was considered provocative dress. This frequently caused prisoners to turn to look at her, in which case she would demand that they receive twenty-five lashes for their presumption. She would tour the camp on horseback. The verdict of a West German court against her describes how she beat prisoners with her own hands, or, in dozens of cases, with her riding whip. There were prisoners who were beaten by her husband at her request, and others beaten by SS men at her orders, even though she had no formal authority in the camp. There were prisoners beaten and kicked to death at her instigation. The suffering of prisoners brought her pleasure, the court ruled; a psychiatrist who examined her diagnosed sexual aggression.[21]

After the war there were accusations that Frau Koch would single out prisoners with tattoos, order them killed, and have them skinned. The skin was processed in a way developed specially for this purpose at Buchenwald, and made into lampshades, wallets, book bindings, and so on. There is evidence that, alongside the medical experiments and the grisly tortures that were a matter of course at Buchenwald, such articles actually were produced from human skin. It began, apparently, as part of a criminological research project on the link between crime and tattoos pursued by a member of the camp's staff. An evaluation based on laboratory tests and submitted at one of the trials confirmed that the objects were in fact made of human skin. Evidence was also heard about the chemical processing of the skin developed in the camp laboratories.[22] Franz Ziereis, commandant of the Mauthausen camp, claimed after the war that Karl Chmielewski also manufactured such articles from the skin of prisoners at his camp. According to Ziereis, there was an order from Berlin expressly forbidding this.[23] Given the status Ilse Koch enjoyed in the camp, there is good reason to believe that she knew of such things; there was testimony that she had a human-skin lampshade in her house. It has never been proven beyond all doubt, however, that she was behind the project. Those charges against her which were proven show sadistic cruelty, a trait shared by her husband; he was also a thief.

The interrogation and trial of Karl Koch stood at the center of a scandal which rocked the SS. The war was already lost, the Reich was on the brink of collapse, but the SS continued to emphasize honesty and good administration through internal self-evaluation and determination to root out all corruption. It is not clear what brought about the investigation. Someone may have informed on Koch—his dishonesty was well-known. However it began, the first pieces of information came into the hands of Prince Josias Georg Wilhelm Adolf zu Waldeck-Pyrmont, an SS general and chief of police in the district which included the city of Weimar and the Buchenwald camp. The prince was much admired for being the first of the royal family to join Himmler's SS, in 1929. Waldeck opened an investigation, and when enough evidence had been gathered he summoned Koch, told him of the suspicion he was under, disarmed him and arrested him.[24] This was in the winter of 1941. Himmler was furious. Within twenty-four hours he had Koch released and then ordered that no senior SS officers were to be arrested without his express permission. At the same time, however, he removed Koch from Buchenwald and transferred him to Majdanek. The incident became the subject of debate among the SS leadership. There were those who demanded an investigation, and others who tried to cover up the facts. Oswald Pohl, Koch's immediate superior, wrote him: "My dear friend, if there is a prosecutor who tries to set the hangman on your innocent soul, I will do my best to stand in his way." Koch made copies of the letter and distributed it among his friends.[25]

As the first commandant of Majdanek, Koch concentrated on setting up the camp's infrastructure, but he had no luck there, either. On the night of April 14, 1942, eighty-six Soviet prisoners of war succeeded in escaping from the camp. Himmler suspended Koch and ordered an investigation. He was accused of criminal negligence. Koch answered that the escape was unavoidable. "We have here few guards, most of them Lithuanians not fluent in German, or unit SS men," he explained. "The local headquarters is manned by reserve soldiers untrained in concentration camp work. . . . Because of the war, there is no possibility of replacing them. There are today two guards at the gate; one of them is deaf in one ear and the second does not know how to read and write. We have no alarm system. In an emergency we have to shoot in the air in order to summon help, but the sound of the shots is often carried off by the wind. Because of the overcrowding in the camp, there are only a few guards there at night. All the others sleep forty-five minutes away."[26] The investigators accepted Koch's version of events and recommended that the investigation be closed.

At this point no one really knew what to do with him. He was transferred to Berlin and made a liaison officer between the SS and the post office. Himmler wrote that he was a tired and lazy man, and contemplated sending him to the front. In the meantime, Prince Waldeck was continuing his investigation. He acted very carefully—at least two members of the concentration camp administration, Richard Glücks and Oswald Pohl, had threatened that if he did not put a stop to his investigation harm would come to him. Waldeck assumed that they feared the discovery of corruption in the entire concentration camp administration. It was a reasonable assumption. Much money passed through this closed system, without any real oversight, and in secrecy. Waldeck questioned members of the camp's staff as well as a number of prisoners and handed over his findings to Himmler. Himmler allowed him to continue the investigation, but limited it to the circumstances surrounding the personal enrichment of Koch and his wife. At that point the war had already turned, and many Germans were suffering from shortages of necessities. Koch, however, had lived a luxurious life in his camp. At a certain point the inquiry was transferred to Berlin and put in the hands of an investigating magistrate, an SS man named Konrad Morgen, an expert in uncovering corruption and fraud. Morgen's inquiry was frequently quoted at the Nuremberg trials and at the trials that followed it. Not all the material was preserved, but Morgen helped reconstruct it after the war; some of it was made available to researchers only recently.[27]

Morgen went to Buchenwald, settled into the camp, and began to snoop. Everyone knew why he had come, and they feared him. Koch was no longer there and Morgen was working under Himmler's protection. At first he heard only snatches and hints. Afterwards he was told of two prisoners who had worked together with members of the camp staff and sold meat on the black market in Weimar. Morgen asked to interview the two of them. The camp doctor, Werner Hoven, one of Ilse Koch's lovers and an accomplice in her husband's misdeeds, told him that the two were sick and that he could not speak with them. Morgen said he would wait until they recovered, and then he was told that they had died. Morgen asked to see their medical files. The entries there were very detailed, too detailed, Morgen thought. Their temperatures had been taken and their blood pressure checked almost every hour, and everything had been done to save their lives. "Only millionaires get such treatment," Morgen later noted. It aroused his suspicions. Some time later he learned that the two had been murdered by injecting typhus into their bodies. It was not the only instance of this kind. Morgen decided to find out why this was happening and ordered the doctor's arrest.

The large-scale corruption in the camp began, the doctor related, when the Jews began arriving in 1938. Some of them had brought large sums of money. Koch ordered it stolen from them, sometimes under the guise of promising that the money would buy their release from the camp, sometimes by force and without explanation. Many prisoners knew of this: Morgen discovered that those who could have known had all died, and those who were still alive did not know. He therefore suspected that those who had known about the theft had been silenced. He began examining the files of the dead men. He discovered that all of them had died in the camp's internal prison. Morgen surmised that the stories of their illnesses had been put together only after their deaths. This led him to have the houses of several staff members, among them Koch's closest assistants, searched. The search uncovered large quantities of gold taken, apparently, from the teeth of prisoners killed in the camp. Jewelry, other valuables, and much cash were also found. Morgen was shocked. There were those who took the trouble to warn him, for his own good, that at this point Himmler wanted to finish off the matter quietly and send Koch to the front. Morgen, however, was not deterred, and laid his findings out before Himmler. To his surprise, he was told to conclude the investigation and bring charges against Koch.

Morgen ordered Koch to return from Majdanek to Buchenwald. His wife was still there, in their house. Koch returned late at night, but instead of reporting to headquarters, where Morgen awaited him, he went home. Morgen and one of his assistants went to arrest him. "It was a dark night," Morgen later recalled, "and the weather was stormy. When we arrived at Koch's house we did not see his car. We thought he might be preparing an ambush for us. We drew our pistols. I kicked at the door with my boots. At first nothing happened. Suddenly, the door opened and Koch stood there, totally calm, in a sweater. He asked what the matter was, as if he did not know why we had come. I told him he was under arrest. He was cool as ice, and did not answer. He asked for a moment to speak with his wife. We refused. We told him to take a coat and we brought him to prison."[28] His wife was arrested the next day. She reacted with hysterical screams and threats, Morgen said. From there on out they were treated as criminals in every respect and, it seems, given no favorable treatment. Some of their men were also arrested. Two months passed before the trial opened. A relative took care of the children in the meantime.

Koch was charged with the theft of 200,000 marks. He was also accused of the murder of three prisoners who might have testified about his activities, two in Buchenwald and one in Lublin, all "involving damage to state security in wartime." Thirty-two witnesses, staff members and prisoners, appeared at the closed trial. It was not publicized, but many in the SS knew about it. Pohl continued his attempts to halt the trial, but to no avail. Koch was found guilty and sentenced to death; his wife was acquitted. He was sent to the Weimar Prison. When they came to take him to Buchenwald he tried to resist with force, but his guards overcame him. On the last night of his life, in a prison cell at Buchenwald, he raved like a madman. The next day he was taken to the courtyard, stood against a wall, and shot. His body was burned in the camp crematory. It was the first week of April 1945. A few days later the camp was liberated by the U.S. army; a few weeks later Germany surrendered.

Ilse Koch, his widow, settled after the war in Ludwigsburg, living with the relatives who had cared for her children. Someone recognized her on the street after the world had learned of her barbarity in the camp. She was arrested, and two years later, in 1947, an American court-martial held her sensational trial at Dachau. During the trial it was suddenly discovered that, despite her having been in prison for more than two years, she was expecting a baby. It is not clear whether the father was an American or German prison guard or another prisoner. Frau Koch refused to reveal his identity. When the time came, she gave birth to a son, Uwe.

The court-martial sentenced her to life imprisonment, but General Lucius Clay, commander in chief of the U.S. forces in Europe, commuted her sentence to four years. Clay was known for his efforts to conciliate the Germans and integrate them into a democratic state under American influence. Ilse Koch's impending release wakened a public outcry in the United States. The Senate set up a special committee to investigate the matter, in the wake of which Koch was tried again before a German court. This time she was not accused of manufacturing items from human skin. She was sentenced to life in prison for a series of murders and brutal acts against prisoners. Her attorney, Alfred Seidel, submitted many requests for pardons. In one of them he hinted that she had been the victim of the American Jewish lobby's vengeance.[29] All her petitions were rejected and she was forgotten. She made headlines only twice thereafter. The first time was when her son, then 19 years old, discovered his identity and began visiting her in prison. He told his story to *The New York Times*.[30] In September 1967 she was heard of again—she committed suicide.

Karl Koch's biography is composed of the same elements that make up the stories of the other camp commandants of his generation; he also could have found himself working in the camps even if he had not been a criminal and a sadist.[31] His father had been an official in the municipal marriage department in Darmstadt, in central Germany. His father, at 57, married his mother, 34, two months after Koch was born. His father died when he was 8 years old. His mother later remarried. His stepfather had three sons from a previous marriage, all older than Koch. Koch went through elementary school and at the age of 15 was sent to the office of a nearby industrial concern, where he worked as a messenger boy and apprentice in the bookkeeping department. He studied commerce at the same time.

He did not finish his studies and did not advance in the office, since two years later, a few days after he turned 17, World War I broke out. Koch immediately volunteered for the army, but his mother intervened and the army refused to take him. He was too young, his mother argued, and his three stepbrothers had already enlisted. Koch did not give up. It seems that he was very eager to leave his parents' house. From time to time he reported to the army and each time his mother demanded that he be sent home. He was not taken until March 1916. He served as a rifleman in a number of battles on the western front and was wounded twice. Towards the end of the war he was sent to scout out enemy lines and fell prisoner to the British. He was in a POW camp until 1919. When he returned he was 22 years old, and had had a difficult life. Like millions of other Germans at this time, he stood before a new beginning. He had no real professional experience, no plans, and no reason to feel secure about his future. He was lucky enough not to be unemployed—he worked first as a supervisor, then as a bookkeeper, and soon found himself a fairly comfortable position as a bank clerk. At this point his life seemed to be going well. In 1924 he married and two years later had a son. The economic crisis Germany was suffering hit Koch directly—the bank in which he worked collapsed and was closed down, and Koch was unemployed. At the same time he was undergoing a personal crisis. His marriage began to fall apart. His wife petitioned for divorce. The court found that the two had lived apart for several months and that Koch had been involved with another woman (not Ilse Koch). The divorce was granted in May 1931. Koch joined the Nazi party not long thereafter, and a few months later the SS as well. He now dealt in insurance, but had much time to put into the movement as the local Party branch's honorary treasurer. He also served as a volunteer in the SS. The movement did not forget him. As soon as the Nazis gained power, they sent Koch, then 36 and divorced—and thus free of family obligations—to organize the Auxiliary Police in Kassel. The Auxiliary Police, mostly SA and SS men, were later enlisted in the Death's Head Formations on a permanent basis. Thus Koch arrived at the concentration camps. He was one of Eicke's first loyalists.

Over the next eight years he was part of the development of the camps. As they became more brutal, Koch was promoted. From Sachsenburg he went to Esterwegen and from there to Lichtenburg, to Dachau, and to the Gestapo prison on Columbia Street in Berlin. In 1936 he was sent to establish the Sachsenhausen camp, and then set up Buchenwald. His superiors had a high opinion of him. A hard man, they wrote of him, but not too harsh, open, calm-minded, goal-directed. He worked untiringly, displayed dexterity and organizational ability. It took him only a few weeks to prepare the camps he set up for thousands of prisoners. He was praised for this: "His achievements are higher than average: he does everything for the National Socialist ideal." At that point, it was true.

HERMANN Florstedt was also a criminal. He had tangled with the law several times before joining the SS.[32] His personnel file contains information about various crimes in his past, including assault and disorderly conduct in public (fights in the streets and in beer halls). In 1934 he was investigated for his part in a clash which led to the death of one of the participants. He was about to be charged with manslaughter, but his commanders in the SS got him out of it. He was later accused of insulting a public employee while on duty—Florstedt threatened to slander him in the pages of *Der Stürmer* and was reprimanded for this. A dispute with one of his friends led the two into a pistol duel, prevented at the last minute. A police officer arrested him for drunkenness and disorderly conduct, and he tried to prevent the officer from arresting another of his friends, also drunk. Another incident, involving a debt he did not pay, went as far as the deputy Führer himself. Florstedt was an alcoholic and brutalized the prisoners at his camp, especially the children, with great cruelty. At Buchenwald he was Ilse Koch's lover. He was transferred to Majdanek to supervise the extermination of the Jews, but at about that time it was discovered that he was an accomplice in Karl Koch's frauds. He, like Koch, was interrogated, and it seems that he was also put on trial in the SS and executed.

Adam Grünewald, commandant of the Hertogenbusch camp in Holland, was sentenced to 15 years in prison (but was pardoned);[33] Chmielewski, another commandant of Hertogenbusch, was found guilty of stealing diamonds. He ended his career in the SS as a prisoner at Dachau.[34] There were others like them. The SS did not want people of this sort, just as it did not want apathetic types like Eduard Weiter. It did not, however, succeed in purging them all; defeat came too quickly. The ideal SS man was neither apathetic nor sadistic, but the SS tended at times to turn a blind eye to the shortcomings and weaknesses of its men, especially if they were political soldiers of the type the organization wanted. That was the case with Amon Göth.

AMON Leopold Göth was born in December 1908, the only son of a Vienna publisher who specialized in military history and professional literature for army men. Theirs was a well-off Catholic family. Göth later told his wife that his parents had neglected him as a child and that he had turned his back on the bourgeois social values they hoped to educate him in.[35] His father, Göth related, was often away from home on business trips in Europe and the United States. His mother managed the printing plant and left the housework and child care to her sister-in-law, Göth's Aunt Kathy. For as long as he could remember, Göth said later, they impressed him with a sense of obligation and responsibility to prepare himself to take over the business his parents had founded and diligently developed so that he could some day inherit it.

Göth was six years old when World War I broke out. His father, apparently, was not drafted. Years later Göth told his wife that his father had evaded his obligation to the fatherland. Göth was a tall young man—six feet four inches, according to his personnel file—and of athletic build. He was fond of outdoor sports and hikes, and took part in escapades and adventures that did not please his parents. They tried to give him more delicate tastes. When he finished his elementary education they sent him to high school; he passed his matriculation exams but then decided to study agriculture, which did not make his parents any happier. They wanted a publisher and intellectual, not a farmer. Göth knew, of course, that one day he would inherit his father's business. For this reason he made no great effort to finish his studies, and left them after a few semesters. From this point onward his papers describe him as a publisher.

In 1925, when he was a 17-year-old student, he first joined the Nazi party's youth movement. A classmate who had joined before took him along to a meeting. The movement captured his heart. It knew how to appreciate his physical strength and athletic ability, and fostered friendship and youthful rebellion. Göth, his widow said, needed to belong. His identification with the movement deepened as the years went by. In 1930, five years after he first joined the Nazis, Göth became a member of the SS, a volunteer at age 22. His widow said that this was a natural continuation of his membership in the youth movement. What drew him to the movement drew him even more strongly to the SS; more than anything else he was attracted by the comradeship it promised. At one point he also tangled with the law, another indication of the depth of the devotion he felt towards the movement. It seems that he was involved in its terrorist activity. The police found firearms and explosives in his possession, but before they managed to arrest him Göth fled over the Austrian border, to Nazi Germany. That was in the first half of 1933. Göth spent the following months going illegally back and forth between Germany and Austria, smuggling weapons, money, and information. He seems to have played a role in the murder of Chancellor Engelbert Dollfuss in July 1934. He was arrested in Austria but again succeeded in escaping, and settled in Munich. During the following years he tried to develop his publishing business. His parents were worried—they put pressure on him to make a normal life for himself and even found him a wife. Göth married her unwillingly; within a few months they were divorced. His father had a general leaning towards liberal views, but was not a political man. Many years later—he died in 1960—he told Göth's widow that he had not properly understood what motivated his son and did not take his political activity seriously; Göth senior did not take Nazism seriously, either. The whole thing looked to him like teenage adventurism.

Göth, combative by nature, had problems in the SS as well.

At one point he was even expelled, but later overcame his opponent and was allowed to return. It was a very local dispute; had he been defeated, he might never have gone to Plascow.

In October 1938, soon after the Nazi invasion and annexation of Austria, Göth returned home to Vienna and married again. In July 1939 a baby girl was born, but she died seven months later. A few days after that Göth decided to leave his wife and join his friends in occupied Poland. The Göths had two more children, but there is reason to believe that his second marriage also did not succeed and that the failure of the marriage and the death of the baby influenced his sudden decision to leave for Poland. In Cracow he met Ruth Kalder, a former actress and a secretary in the Wehrmacht. The army then employed a number of local Jews in a workshop which produced uniforms and military boots. "My role as a beautiful secretary," Ruth Kalder Göth said many years later in an interview, "was to win Göth's heart so that he would continue to supply these workers even when the Jews of the city were sent to the concentration camp under his command." Her mission was a success. "He was an impressive man, tall, strong, the dream of any secretary," she said.[36] They fell in love, lived together as husband and wife, and had a baby. Göth did not divorce his second wife until May 1945; his third wife took his name and brought up their child, but they did not have time to marry officially.

After arriving in Poland he first dealt with the administrative and financial aspects of the mass deportations. It was office work. He then worked with Odilio Globocnik, formerly Gauleiter of Vienna and now chief of police of Lublin, also involved with the extermination of the Jews. Göth gained an on-the-spot knowledge of the different ways of exterminating a civilian population and, in time, began to do it himself. When he fell out with Globocnik, he was transferred to Cracow. His new superior was Julian Scherner, an old friend. Scherner offered him a choice between an administrative job and setting up a new forced-labor camp. Göth, his widow said, preferred the opportunity to establish a little kingdom of his own, where he would be his own boss. He saw it as a challenge and an adventure, his widow said. According to her, he did not really

know what he had taken on, but this, of course, is unlikely.
From the beginning of 1943 Göth knew very well what was
going on in Poland. Close to 50,000 of Cracow's Jews had
already been deported, and most of them had been murdered.
Göth knew that as well.

He served as commandant of the camp between February
1943 and September 1944. Four weeks after his appointment
he supervised the destruction of the Cracow ghetto on March
13, 1943. Some 4000 were killed that day. Six months later, in
September, he oversaw the destruction of the Tarnow ghetto.
Thousands of people were killed in this action as well.

Survivors of the camp tell of his horrible brutality. At least
once he set his dog, Rolf, on a prisoner, killing him. One
incident supports the supposition that he had found an outlet for
sadistic urges: he ordered a group of prisoners between 17 and
20 years of age lined up before him, all of them naked, paced
before them and examined them carefully and slowly. Then he
chose several of them and shot them to death himself.[37]

In the autumn of 1944 Göth was arrested in connection with
an investigation of corruption in the camps, the same investigation by Morgen that brought about the execution of Karl
Koch and Hermann Florstedt. Göth was also suspected of
embezzlement, but before he could be put on trial the war
ended. The Americans who captured him turned him over to
the Poles, who hanged him, not far from his camp. It was a
lightning trial that lasted only two weeks—Göth was convicted
of the murders of tens of thousands of people. During his trial
Göth displayed provocative indifference. He accepted responsibility for what had happened at Plascow. He had been given
authority and permission to do everything he had done, he said,
and acted in accordance with orders he had received. He was
at peace with himself to the end, his widow said, a political
soldier.

————————

IN the late 1970s, Ruth Göth, a secretary in the Goethe Institute in Munich, lived in an apartment house that had seen
better days. She received me wearing a Chinese gown. Vel-
vet curtains in dark green, covered with dust, and heavy

furniture gave her apartment an atmosphere of dimness. She sat on the couch, her legs crossed diagonally, and smoked cigarettes through a long holder, her small finger pointing upwards, coquettishly. It was all staged; Frau Göth, once an actress, exuded a sort of Weimarish nihilism. "Ah, Plascow," she said in veiled, slightly throaty tone of voice, "yes, yes Plascow." She paused and then said suddenly, "They will tell you that I had a horse there and that I was a whore. It's true, I slept with many officers, but only until I found Göth, and he bought me a horse. Ah, yes, Göth—what a dream man."

I had the impression that she was enjoying every moment. The signs of the cancer from which she suffered were already evident. After the war she followed Göth's trial through moviehouse newsreels. He wrote her a few letters from prison, in pencil. They expressed no regret. "It was a beautiful time," his widow said. "We enjoyed being together. My Göth was the king, and I was the queen. Who wouldn't have traded places with us?" She was only sorry that it had all ended, she said.

———

A short time before the Third Reich collapsed, Franz Xaver Ziereis and his wife decided that, at the last minute, they would kill themselves, so that their children would not bear the burden of their imprisonment or execution; the two of them knew what awaited them. They missed their chance: "The Americans came and took me when you weren't home," Ziereis wrote to his wife. "I left the submachine gun under a tree, by the river, instead of using it. I must have lost my head." The American soldiers shot him and seriously wounded him, but managed to take down a long confession—not completely accurate—which included the sentence: "It was forbidden to beat prisoners, on orders from Berlin; I beat them in violation of orders out of pure sadism." He now understood, he said, that Hitler, Himmler, and Pohl, his superior officer, had brought disaster upon the German people. He died of his wounds 24 hours later, on Thursday, May 24, 1945.[38]

"It is hard to take measure of him," his superiors wrote of

him at the beginning of his career. "He is introverted, and the impression is that he is not totally frank, is always watching you behind your back, following you, as if he was craftily planning an ambush."[39] They did, however, value his military experience. "In this he has great strength," they wrote.

Ziereis was born in August 1905 in Munich. He had two sisters, one older than he, and a young brother who became a locomotive engineer. His father drove a horse-drawn cart. He was killed in the war when Ziereis was 11 years old. There is no way of being sure how this affected Ziereis, but he often mentioned it. Perhaps it laid the foundation for the sternness he developed over the years. Ziereis spent eight years in elementary school and then, at the age of 15, it was decided that he would train himself as a merchant. He began as an apprentice and messenger boy in a department store. In the evenings he studied commerce. This lasted until he was 17 years old. He had trouble finding work in his field. He went to work as a laborer in a carpentry shop, which he found disappointing. From time to time he was unemployed. Germany was still recovering from its defeat, and the masses of soldiers who had returned from the front demanded—and often received—preference in receiving work. Ziereis, like others then just entering the adult world, had stiff competition. For this reason, he decided in 1924 to enlist in the army, a logical decision under the circumstances. He signed on for 12 years. Lacking a high school diploma, he had no real chance of ever becoming an officer; he remained a master sergeant, but his military service saved him from the hardship and unemployment which would, in a few years' time, be the lot of millions of other Germans. The army sent him to a management school, which increased his chances of finding work when he was released.

A few months before completing his term of duty, he married. His eldest son was born almost two years before the wedding, when his future wife was only 18 years old, a juvenile 11 years younger than he. Whenever Ziereis mentioned his children in official documents he would use the words "my legal children." When he was discharged he was 31 years old, with a wife and children, and without civilian professional experience. The political situation had changed in the meantime, and the Nazis were preparing to celebrate three years in power. They were popular and it seemed that they were the future. Ziereis now claimed, like many others, that he had always supported the movement. Even though his military service had limited his ability to be politically active, he had, he claimed, helped set up some SA and SS units. He may have told the truth, or he may have simply touched up his biography in accordance with the demands of the times. Either way, he was offered a job in the Death's Head Formations, with the rank of first lieutenant and opportunities for advancement. Ziereis accepted the offer without hesitation. He had no reason to refuse. He joined the SS and the party and simultaneously left the church. From his point of view, he had gone from one army to another.

He was at first given assignments of a military nature. His superiors praised him particularly for his abilities as a training instructor. "He does it exceptionally well," Eicke wrote. His job did not immediately bring him into direct contact with the concentration camps, but he visited and became acquainted with them—he saw this as part of his service. In 1937 he was seriously wounded in his knee during a training exercise and needed lengthy hospitalization. Less than two years later he was wounded again in the same knee, also during an exercise. His doctors told him that he would be handicapped for life. He had just been appointed commandant of the Mauthausen.

World War II broke out within a few weeks. Had he not been wounded, he might have been sent to the front as a relatively young man with a military background. His superiors were happy that he would remain at their disposal in the camp. "He does a fine job," Richard Glücks wrote of him in 1944. "To his credit the camp progressed from a very modest beginning to what it is today." When he arrived at Mauthausen there were about 3000 prisoners; under his direction it held 72,000 at its height. Conditions in the camp deteriorated and the level of brutality rose in step with unthinkable atrocities. There was also mass extermination at one point, using gas and other methods. Ziereis fit well into the camp and was frequently promoted. At the end of the war he was a colonel. The impression is that, even as a concentration camp commandant, he saw himself as a military man rather than as a political soldier. This was also true of several other commandants. (One of them, Friedrich Hartjenstein, commandant of the extermination facility at Auschwitz, never even joined the Nazi party,[40] and from this point of view was hardly an ideal SS man.) After the war Ziereis claimed that he had asked to go to the front and had not been allowed to. His personnel file contains no record of such a request. Given his physical limitations, there was no chance of such a request getting a positive response.

HANS Loritz fought in World War I, and that was the central experience of his life. He also went through much before joining the SS; his personnel file reflects a personal and deep identification with the SS.

He was born in the city of Augsburg in Bavaria, in December 1895.[41] His father was a police officer. After eight years of elementary education it was decided that he would be a baker, as his grandfather had been. He began in the usual way. He worked for four years as an apprentice in a bakery, and afterwards became a journeyman, working in various establishments in Innsbruck, Vienna, Budapest, and Berlin, where he was in August 1914. As soon as the war broke out he went home and volunteered for the Bavarian infantry. By the time he earned the rank of sergeant, in 1917, he had participated in a series of battles ("all the battles," he later claimed). He was wounded four times. In addition, he suffered gas poisoning that was to bother him for the rest of his life. In 1917 Loritz became one of Germany's first combat pilots. His personnel file reveals that he made no less than twenty-eight flights over French lines. Once or twice, he related, he was forced to make crash landings, and in July 1918 his plane was hit, burst into flames, and went down in a forest on French territory. Loritz was seriously injured—several of his ribs were broken. French farmers who found him mistreated him before turning him over to the authorities. These were not quick to give him medical treatment; instead, they interrogated and imprisoned him. Several days passed before a representative of the International Red Cross discovered where he was being held. The Red Cross representative was successful in having Loritz transferred to a hospital and then to a POW camp. When he recovered he tried to escape, but was caught and put in a long stretch of solitary confinement. He was then sent to do hard labor at another camp on the Somme River. The war had ended in the meantime, but Loritz was not allowed to return home. He was not released until September 1920, about two years after the end of the war. He was then 25 years old. He had served four years at the front and spent another two in the hospital and POW camps. Given this war experience, he was unlikely to be the same man who set out for the war, an apprentice baker of 19. He had suffered more than many other soldiers, and the humiliating defeat no doubt affected him more than it did others. Either way, by the time he reached the concentration camps he was well-versed in atrocities. He had almost certainly experienced greater brutality than what he saw when he first arrived at a concentration camp. From this point of view he was an ideal candidate for the Death's Head Formations.

Upon returning home, with all Germany facing a new beginning, he did not return to the craft he had learned. Instead, he joined the Augsburg police force, like his father. In 1922 he married, and five months later a son was born. At some point, apparently at the beginning of the thirties, Loritz was employed by the Augsburg municipality, but it is unclear what his job was. He was never unemployed, not even when he joined the party and volunteered for the SS in 1930. It seems that he did not do so as a personal protest, but because of his political, ideological, and emotional identification with the movement. After the Nazis came to power he was seconded by the Augsburg municipality for work in the SS on a permanent basis. At this point he also became an honorary member of the city council. His personnel file is laden with correspondence concerning his status as a municipal employee on unpaid leave. Loritz never relinquished his position in the city administration, thus retaining his eligibility for retirement compensation and a pension. At one point it was necessary to have the deputy Führer, Rudolf Hess, write a letter to the mayor of Augsburg in order to extend his leave. Other documents in his file also reflect a somewhat exploitative but deep relationship with the SS and the party.

In August 1932 Loritz fell out with his neighbors, a

company which manufactured felt hats for men. Loritz would drive his car on a road which the company claimed was a private one, closed to traffic. The company went to the police and also demanded payment for use of the road from Loritz. He refused to pay, arguing that the road was a public one. One day, before the Nazis had won power, Loritz sent a letter to the company on Nazi party stationery and wrote: "I do not use this road for my own enjoyment. It saves me time and this time I devote to voluntary work in the Nazi movement and the SS. I am an officer in the organization. Not long ago I spoke of this matter with several party members and they were extremely surprised. Among other things, they noted that it is not fitting, to say the least, for a man like you, who belongs on the nationalist side, to cause problems for a man like me, who serves Germany proudly. They were especially outraged by the fact that you are demanding that I pay for the use of the road. There were those who suggested publicizing the matter in the party newspaper, since you are attacking not only me but the entire national interest. At present, I refuse to do so, and prefer to wait and see what you do now, since as a businessman you certainly know how to appreciate the damage which might be caused by such publicity." The owner of the factory sent a copy of the letter to SS headquarters and complained of Loritz's using official stationery for his personal needs. Loritz was reprimanded. The files of SS officers are filled with such incidents. The attempts to pursue personal interests, often coupled with threats, reflects the attachment of SS men to their movement and the support they gave one another—brother-hood-at-arms, after all, was one of the reasons they joined the organization in the first place. When Loritz joined the SS his relations with his wife were deteriorating; the couple eventually divorced, thus giving him a personal reason to leave home. He later remarried.

In 1933 Loritz was appointed commander of the guard unit at the Dachau concentration camp; he still had no direct contact with the prisoners. He once wrote to Himmler describing his daily routine:

Before I arrived at the camp there were officers from Austria who did not succeed in controlling the people. Some of them were openly laughed at. Everyone did what they wanted. When the supply room gave out brooms, pails, and cleaning materials, they went to sell them in Dachau. The staff quarters were filthy, with garbage and remains of food in every corner. The toilets were completely stopped up, wash basins served as latrines, and it stank to heaven. Huge cooking pots were used for bathing. The new tables and benches were used as firewood. The men slept every day until nine or ten in the morning. Their commander told them that, since they were Austrian, they had no chance of advancing in the SS—the Germans would hold them back. I called the men and told them that from this day onward this would stop. We began putting things in order. They didn't accept me immediately, but in time they learned to obey and accepted even my punishments. We took about a hundred prisoners from the camp to do a thorough cleaning.[42]

Theodor Eicke endorsed this. It was making order out of chaos, Loritz later said.

The application to Himmler came as part of a long-running dispute. It seems that one member of the camp staff made off with the money from the canteen. The question was who would cover the loss, a total of 225 marks. The episode reflected the competition between the concentration camp commandants and the commanders of the Death's Head troops stationed outside the camps. The camp commandant was, for a while, the commander of the local troops as well. After the two roles were separated, conflicts of interest and friction often arose between them. When Loritz was recommended for promotion, it was noted, among other justifications, that it was necessary because the commander of the local formation was of higher rank and that even if Loritz were promoted, he would not outrank the other commander. The investigation of the canteen theft led Loritz to request to be under Eicke's direct command in one of the camps. Himmler rejected the request at first and told him to make peace with his opponent. Loritz replied that the gas poisoning he had suffered in the war still bothered him, making him unfit for combat duty. In fact he wrote to Himmler from the hospital where he was undergoing routine treatment. The work in the camps was easier physically, he wrote, and his experience as a police officer would help him. He also had personal reasons for wanting the transfer, and Eicke knew him and wanted him under his command, he added. It seems that one of Loritz's friends in Himmler's office succeeded in arranging the matter. Loritz became the commandant of the Esterwegen camp. This camp was filled with problems, Eicke wrote, since all the prisoners were criminals. Loritz, Eicke stated, established iron discipline in the camp, a model for all others. Former prisoners would later say that he imposed a reign of terror on them.[43] When Esterwegen was closed, Loritz was appointed commandant of Dachau, which he also administered with savagery. Rudolf Höss, commandant of Auschwitz, even claimed that Himmler had ordered Loritz out of Dachau in the wake of reports of atrocities he committed there.[44] At the beginning of 1940, Himmler visited Sachsenhausen and, according to Höss, found serious shortcomings in the discipline of the staff. He ordered the replacement of the commandant, Walter Eisfeld, with a stronger man. Loritz was brought over from Dachau.

Loritz's personnel file contains evidence that he violated disciplinary regulations more than once, and there is also some indication that he was accused of murder, but his superiors trusted him. He is the right man for Sachsenhausen, they stated, among other reasons because the camp's location near Berlin means that there are often outside visitors, including foreign guests. This demands an intelligent commandant who knows how to talk with them. Loritz, Eicke wrote, does this better than others. At least once, in 1942, Loritz was chosen to carry out a delicate mission of a decidedly political nature: the Gestapo discovered that the mother-in-law of a general, Eugen Ritter von Schubert, a woman named Gollwitzer, secretly listened to foreign radio broadcasts. Himmler ordered her banished from her estate and sent to a distant resort. A measure of tact was needed, and Loritz was able to carry out the mission. (In his personnel file there is a typically lengthy exchange of letters, designed to prove that these were not private journeys.) Towards the end of the war he was stationed in Norway, overseeing the labor camps the Nazis had set up there, another testimony to their trust in him. Loritz was captured by the Allies and sent to a prison camp. In January 1946 he killed himself.

* * *

BY the time Hermann Baranowski was made commandant of one of the camps, he had twenty years of service in the Imperial Navy behind him. This experience established more than his attitude towards the prisoners in the camps. It also formed the background to his relations with his staff, his superiors, his family, and himself. "His domineering manner is truly pathological," Theodor Eicke stated.[45] His personnel file is quite instructive on the relations between SS men and headquarters.

Barnowski was born in June 1884 in the city of Schwerin in northeastern Germany. His father, who worked in the local brewery, died a few weeks before Baranowski turned eight. His father had been Catholic, and his mother was Protestant. Until he began describing himself as "a believer in God," Baranowski called himself a Protestant. It is not clear whether his mother remarried, but their financial situation allowed him to study one year in secondary school. When he was 16, Baranowski decided to leave his mother's house and his school and enlist in the navy. He signed on in advance for twelve years of service. His superiors in the SS noted that Baranowski could function only when his superiors kept him under their thumbs. He needed discipline and obedience, they said. Theodor Eicke thought this characteristic was a result of his long naval service, but it may be that the opposite was true: he may have been attracted to the navy because of this need in his character, in order to impose severe discipline on himself. This also could have drawn him later to join the SS. In any case, Baranowski could not expect a shining career in the navy; without a high school diploma he had only the slightest of chances of ever becoming an officer, which was his dream. But upon leaving his mother's house he turned instantly from a boy to a man, at least in his own eyes. The sea promised adventure, challenge, and mystery that set his imagination on fire. He received a uniform and was trained to use firearms; he also received some of the prestige of the Kaiser's fleet.

The ships were run with alienating and harsh discipline, often violent. The conditions worsened with the declining rank and social standing of the seaman. A parliamentary committee that investigated the condition of sailors in the navy found that they were often cruelly mistreated and humiliated. Baranowski began as a deckboy and rose slowly through the ranks. When he became a chief petty officer he attained almost unlimited power to treat simpler and younger sailors as he had been treated when he had been one of them. At the same time, he was subject to the arbitrariness of the officers. Something of the same harsh and rank-conscious discipline developed in the SS as well—a concentration camp commandant had almost unlimited power to mistreat his prisoners and even to decide which of them would live and which die. On the other hand, he, too, was completely subject to his superiors.

Baranowski adjusted well to the navy and seems to have been happy there, since he extended his service past the twelve original years of obligation. At the end of his first term of duty he married. A year later he had a son, and two years after that a daughter. World War I broke out fourteen years after he enlisted in the navy. Baranowski was attached to a submarine crew and served on combat duty until the end of the war. He remained in the service after the war, until September 1920, "when the army was forced to dismantle itself," as he wrote bitterly.[46] He had just been awarded, nevertheless, the rank of second lieutenant. He was now 36 years old; he might have chosen to extend his service in the navy had he been able to.

He did not find his place in civilian life easily. After twenty years on the sea he found himself foreign to the routines and frameworks of life on land. For the first time in his life there was no one telling him what to do. For a while he did nothing. He lived at first in Kiel, a port on the Baltic Sea, and found himself employment in a local metal-working factory. He did not like the job, and before the year was out he moved to Hamburg and became a salesman for a food products company. This brought him no more satisfaction than the previous job had, but he held it for close to ten years and was never unemployed. The humiliating defeat at the end of World War I certainly affected him more than it did other Germans, who had not, like him, seen their future in the military; it forced a new, unhappy life on him. Baranowski, however, never showed an interest in politics. He did not understand it or trust it. Neither did he join one of the veterans' organizations. He could not long ignore the rising crisis, though. In September

1930 the Nazi party organized a large public gathering in Hamburg. One of Baranowski's friends suggested that he accompany him, and Baranowski went, more out of curiosity than out of identification, and mostly because he had no other plans for that evening. The main speaker at the gathering was Adolf Hitler. Baranowski was enthralled by his speech and joined the movement on the spot.

In his speeches, Hitler knew how to identify the elements of Germany's crisis since its defeat with the personal problems of each member of his audience. His promise to save Germany was also a promise to save Baranowski from the reality of little hope. From that day onward Baranowski tried to assist the organization in its propaganda efforts, and some months later volunteered for the SS. The organization, like the party, promised a new beginning in a tough military framework of the type Baranowski missed. He was 46 years old when he joined the SS, and it renewed his youth. When he enlisted he was undergoing a difficult personal crisis: a few months previously he had lost his son, Ernst, who died of cancer at the age of 19. Baranowski's service in the SS may have helped him overcome his grief at his son's death, just as his enlistment in the fleet had, perhaps, helped him long ago to overcome his grief at the death of his father.

Baranowski served the SS in a volunteer capacity for more than two years, devoting his time to it after work and on weekends. A few weeks before the Nazis gained power Baranowski became a full-time salaried employee of the SS. His uniform now granted him national prestige and he received the SS rank equivalent to a lieutenant colonel in the army. At first his superiors were impressed with his military experience and praised the discipline he knew how to impose on his men in the General SS while "preparing them for an emergency." The early praise did not, however, continue. Later evaluations generally called his achievements "mediocre" and noted that they were "appropriate to his age." One day Baranowski got into a fight with one of his fellow officers, and this led to his transfer from the General SS to the Death's Head units. Eicke agreed only reluctantly to accept him—he did not like to take men who had had problems in the General SS. It seems, however, that his experience in the navy, his rank, his age, and

his rigid personality, as reflected in the evaluations in his
personnel file, persuaded Eicke to accept him. He appointed
Baranowski commandant of the Lichtenburg concentration
camp. Within less than eight months he found himself regret-
ting his decision and demanded his dismissal. Baranowski,
Eicke wrote, had functioned for twenty years under the strong
arm of his superiors. The moment he was given a free hand he
lost control of himself. Eicke described him as a "stiff-necked
seagoer" who was driven mad by ambition. He asked for his
transfer to Dachau, as deputy commandant of the camp. This
was meant to remove him from direct command over SS men
and place him under the unbending commandant of the camp,
Hans Loritz.

Baranowski strenuously protested what justifiably seemed to
him a disciplinary transfer to an inferior position. At one point
he even asked to be discharged from his service in the SS. The
incident gave rise to a long correspondence, preserved in his
personnel file. It all began, it seems, with a complaint
Baranowski sent to Eicke. An SS officer, he claimed, had
insulted him in the presence of other officers. The man said
that the concentration camps did not, in practice, function in
accordance with their standing orders, which were constantly
violated, including those which dealt with the treatment of
prisoners. Baranowski quoted the other officer as saying that
the camp commandants are nothing but jailers in SS uniform.
"We are not jailers," Baranowski replied, and demanded that
the officer be put on trial.[47] It may have been the continuation
of a previous quarrel. In any case, Eicke rejected the complaint. By this time he had already reached the conclusion that
Baranowski tended to fall out with his colleagues. For this
reason he ordered his transfer to Dachau. Baranowski claimed
that the order stained his honor. Eicke replied, in writing, that
the honor of an SS man is in his loyalty and willingness to obey
every order, and that the order could therefore not damage his
honor. He could leave the organization, but if he wanted to
prevent his expulsion, he should first obey orders and accept
the position at Dachau. Baranowski wrote to Himmler. An aide
rejected his application. Baranowski did not give up, and
demanded that Himmler himself look into the matter. Himmler
answered him: "An SS officer never sees his assignment to any

position as a personal insult, whatever the position might be," supporting Eicke as expected. With no other choice, reprimanded, humiliated, and frustrated, Baranowski accepted the assignment at Dachau, and became assistant commandant for prisoner affairs. He treated the prisoners with great cruelty.

During his two years at Dachau, Baranowski learned to be what was expected of him. Eicke decided that his service in Dachau, under the tough hand of commandant Hans Loritz, had good results. "Baranowski now obeys orders. There are no complaints against him." When, in March 1938, there was need for a strong man to replace Hans Helwig, he chose Baranowski. "He is still not an easy man," Eicke wrote, "but I now have reason to believe that he will do good work." In time, Eicke did indeed describe Baranowski as an excellent camp commandant of great dexterity and understanding. Sachsenhausen, with 9000 prisoners, was then the largest concentration camp. Baronwski ran it until his death in February 1940. The death notice his family published said he died of a long illness. Years later the family attorney revealed that there had been suspicion that Baranowski had been poisoned by one of the prisoners, but the matter was never investigated. Baranowski was a cruel man, his attorney said, and even mistreated his wife, his daughter, and his son-in-law, Paul Werner Hoppe, commandant of the Stutthof camp.[48]

PAUL Werner Hoppe received all his officer training in the SS; he knew no other system of values. He grew with the concentration camps from the very beginning.

Hoppe was born in Berlin in February 1910; his father was an architect.[49] He died when Hoppe, his only child, was two and a half years old. Upon being orphaned, Hoppe was sent to live with relatives of his mother's and remained there until 1919. After the war he returned to Berlin, to the house of his late father's brother, also an architect. His uncle and aunt had no children of their own; in addition to him, they adopted a girl. It was a good home, of the established middle class. Hoppe was sent to the gymnasium and in 1929 passed his matriculation examinations with middling marks; he excelled in Latin, mathematics, and sport. Upon finishing his studies

Hoppe left Berlin and traveled, working as an apprentice to gardeners—he liked nature. In 1931 he returned to Berlin and began studying landscape design at the university. He joined the student cell of the Nazi party.

It is difficult to say for sure why he chose this particular student organization. Hoppe himself later wrote that he did so because he agreed with the political ideology of the movement, and this might have been the case. His political activity caused a break with his uncle. Hoppe sneeringly referred to him as a "democrat." His uncle eventually demanded that he leave his house and cut off Hoppe's financial support, which forced Hoppe to end his studies. He later resumed them, after receiving aid from the Nazi student organization, thus deepening his involvement in the movement. Immediately after the Nazis gained power Hoppe joined the party and, in October 1934, submitted an application for membership in the SS, meaning to become an officer in the organization. In the meanwhile, he completed his studies and became a certified landscape designer. He could still, at this stage, have chosen another way of life, but he preferred the SS. He identified with the organization ideologically and emotionally. The SS had by that time become a powerful organization. The Nazis began to construct the Third Reich. Hoppe believed in them and wanted to take part in their work. He passed through all the stages of service in the SS, from one rank to the next: candidate, private, NCO, cadet, and officer. This process lasted two years and he met all the demands. His personnel file notes:

The candidate Paul Werner Hoppe is blessed with an outstanding revolutionary personality. He has a tendency to rush forward and pull his comrades after him. The level of friendship he displays outside the framework of the formation is greater than average; he excels at cleanliness and order. On this basis, he has been recommended for officers school. [February 1935]

Examinee Hoppe displays readiness and great ability to deal with practical undertakings. He finds the correct solutions quickly, and knows how to present them confidently. He stands out in the formation. His thinking is very ordered, though limited to everyday matters. When he is asked to go into theoretical questions, he tends to display unwillingness and contempt. His thought is routine, and he has difficulty with abstractions. His character is unstained, but he is very unpolished. He tends to get carried away. [April 1935]

Cadet Hoppe is blessed with a positive personality and is worthy of serving as an officer. He received average marks in most subjects—"almost good." In tactics and fundamentals of the movement's ideology he received only "satisfactory," but there can be no doubt that he will succeed in the final examinations, so it is recommended that he be allowed to take the examinations. [September 1935]

Hoppe is quiet a man who knows how to get what he wants. He knows what he wants. Like all Berliners, he is self-confident, although unpolished. At times he must be held back a bit, but he fits into the SS well and has a good soldierly appearance. His general knowledge is good, all in all. Fit to be an officer. [January 1936]

Second Lieutenant Hoppe dealt well with the difficulties of his job as a shooting instructor (machine guns), knew how to establish his authority as a commander, even with men more senior and older than he. He excels at personal relations. He makes a constant effort to improve his achievements and has already attained good tactical ability. He is well-liked by his comrades in the formation. Fit to be a commander. [July 1936]

Hoppe obeys the orders of his superiors diligently and successfully. He is a subdued man and not boastful, and so is well-liked by his comrades and his superiors. He could be an excellent officer in the SS. [July 1937]

First Lieutenant Hoppe is an excellent officer who behaves flawlessly with his superiors, comrades, and subordinates. He displays a good grasp of the material and organizational ability that earned him a reputation in the formation. [July 1938]

Captain Hoppe served as deputy formation commander in the Death's Head Upper Bavaria Formation. In the course of

his work he saw close up the needs within and without
concentration camps. Likewise, he served as adjutant to SS
General Theodor Eicke when Eicke served as administrator
of concentration camps. In this role he learned from close up
the problems involved in running the concentration camps. It
seems to be, therefore, that he is most appropriate for service
as a concentration camp commandant. He is known to me
personally as an exceptionally talented man, an officer
whose understanding is much greater than average and who
has won the admiration of his superiors. He is a serious man.
I recommend his promotion to major. Because of his battle
wounds he is no longer fit for service at the front. [March
1942][50]

Hoppe knew the concentration camps before he served in
them himself. As a shooting instructor he did not come into
direct contact with prisoners, but as he advanced in rank, he
became more involved in the camps, step by step.

At the end of 1938 Hoppe married the daughter of Hermann
Baranowski, commandant of Sachsenhausen, who at that time
had already succeeded in regaining the confidence of Theodor
Eicke, his superior officer. The marriage was not a happy
one.[51] For this reason, Hoppe spent much time in his unit, with
his friends. His marriage did, however, advance his career in
the SS family. Two senior camp commandants served as ushers
at the wedding. A short time thereafter Hoppe was called on to
be Eicke's adjutant. From here on out Hoppe dealt with the
general management and development of the camps. Sitting
behind his desk in Berlin, he did not come into direct and daily
contact with the routine atrocities of the camps, but frequently
accompanied Eicke on tours of the camps and was well-
acquainted with what was going on in them.

He and Eicke worked well together. Their personnel files
give evidence of a deep personal relationship of the type often
formed between SS men. Hoppe was 18 years younger than
Eicke, from a comfortable urban background, had a university
education, and was in essence what Eicke had dreamed of
being in his youth but had never achieved. Hoppe was
simultaneously both submissive and stern and felt completely
obligated by the SS's ideology and values. He was the ideal

officer that the SS strove to produce. "Papa" Eicke, on the other hand, was the old fighter that Hoppe had been taught to admire, an ideal father figure of the type he had lacked in his childhood, a commander who inspired fear, a friend who inspired loyalty. When World War II broke out, Eicke took his adjutant to the front; Hoppe was then 29 years old.

Hoppe might not have come to serve in the concentration camps themselves had he not been wounded in battle, and then hurt again in an automobile accident in France. His personnel file indicates that he became commandant of the Stutthof camp near Danzig because he was no longer of use at the front. That was July 1942. He accepted command of the camp without question. After so many years of service in the SS he could not even conceive of refusing. He had, of course, worked with the concentration camp system before, and had no moral difficulty in accepting what he saw at Stutthof. His toughness and loyalty to the organization had grown during his service on the front.

A few months after becoming commandant of the camp Hoppe was summoned by the head of the system of concentration camps, Richard Glücks, to Berlin. Large transports of Jewish prisoners from Lithuania had recently arrived in Stutthof. Glücks told him in a general way that Hitler had ordered the Final Solution of the Jewish problem. There are grounds for believing that Hoppe already knew of this—the extermination of the Jews had already begun by that time. A few weeks later Hoppe was summoned to Berlin once more, and this time Glücks ordered him to gas those Jewish prisoners in his camp who were not fit to work. The gas, Zyklon B, he was told, would be sent by Glücks's office to the camp doctor. Hoppe returned to the camp and ordered his men to make the necessary preparations for carrying out the orders he had received. After the war, the Bochum District Court in West Germany had difficulty establishing if Hoppe had only given the order or whether he had also taken part in the details of its execution.[52] In the meantime, Rudolf Höss, formerly commandant of Auschwitz and experienced in the use of gas, came to Stutthof to offer advice and assistance. The gas chambers at Stutthof had, up until then, been used to execute Polish partisans sentenced to death.

The extermination of Jewish prisoners at Stutthof began in September or October 1944 and lasted for several weeks. The Jews were brought to a room in another camp facility, as if for a medical examination. SS men in white coats would line them up along the wall, in pairs, as if to measure their height. As they stood with their backs to the wall a slit would be opened in the wall behind them, through which a single pistol shot would be fired into the backs of their heads. It is not clear how long this method was in use. At his trial, Hoppe claimed that he had ordered it halted, since it was not in accordance with the orders he had received from Berlin. He also claimed then that he did not remember how many prisoners in his camp had been murdered. The court estimated that there had been several hundred. Since it was not proven that Hoppe himself participated in the murders he was convicted only of being an accessory to murder. Testimony about mistreatment of prisoners was also heard at his trial. Among other things, prisoners at Stutthof were tortured with jets of cold and hot water and were injected with gasoline. Hoppe was there.

He did what he was told in full awareness of what he was doing. Even after the war and after his release from prison he did not cease to remain loyal to the ideals of the SS, as his son learned when he tried, unsuccessfully, to get him to talk about his past. In the words of Hoppe's attorney, "He was very sorry for the great suffering the war caused." The attorney, Dr. Gerhard Täuber from Bochum, asked him more than once about his involvement in the crimes of the SS and what his motives were. Hoppe evaded his questions as he evaded those of his son: "You will never be able to understand it. Everything was so different in my day."[53] Hoppe was sentenced to nine years in prison. He was released in 1962 and died in July 1974.

SURVIVORS of the Neuengamme camp described Max Pauly as a cruel man. "The system was cruel," his attorney responded.[54] Both they and he were right. Pauly carefully obeyed the orders defining what was permitted and what forbidden at his camp. The authority he held allowed for a large measure of brutality, but it would seem that he did not exceed it. The concentration camps administration saw him as an ideal. Neuengamme, about 20 miles from Hamburg on the road to Berlin, and Max Johann Friedrich Pauly, its commandant, *were* the system.

He was born in June 1907 in Wesselburen, a small city about 50 miles south of the Danish border, the eldest son of the owner of a household goods store.[55] Upon completing elementary school he was sent to be an apprentice in a local hardware store, and at the age of 18 became a sales clerk. After his father's death he took over his store and joined the Nazi party and the SA. When he was asked about this at his trial he said: "In 1928 my father died. We faced serious financial problems. We had all tried to overcome our problems. I joined the party as the result of our financial difficulties." Pauly, however, could not expect any improvement in his circumstances as a result of his membership in the party. On the contrary, he related that "reactionary elements"—political opponents—organized a consumer's boycott of his store and made his economic troubles even more serious. There were those who still boycotted him in 1935, two years after the Nazis came to power. Pauly had previously been sentenced to four months in prison for damaging an election campaign wagon belonging to the Social Democratic party. The incident demonstrated the depth of his identity with the movement and his willingness to make sacrifices in order to strengthen it; his long absence from the store could not have helped business. Pauly, then, joined the party and the SA out of political, ideological, and, most likely, emotional identification with them. His political opinions undoubtedly crystallized into this form of protest under the influence of the economic crisis. His personnel file indicates, however, that he did not suffer such great difficulty. In February 1930 he married the daughter of a local cattle merchant, and his father-in-law helped him rent the store from his mother. "From then on I had my own business," he later wrote with some pride. At about that time, in May 1930, he left the SA for the SS. At his trial he argued that he had been ordered to do so. "But you joined the SS of your own free will, is that not right?" he was asked. "No," Pauly answered. "SS General Matthiessen placed me in the organization."

Question: Pauly, try to think logically. This happened years before the Nazi Party came into power. Matthies-

	sen was a civilian like all other civilians. How could he order you to do something?
Pauly:	Yes, he could.
Question:	And if you had refused?
Pauly:	They would have put me on trial.
Question:	What sort of trial?
Pauly:	A trial in the movement.
Question:	Did you not at that time believe in the principles the SS espoused?
Pauly:	Yes, I believed in them.
Question:	And that is what motivated you to join the organization, is it not?
Pauly:	I already told you that they told me to join.[56]

Whether he lied or believed what he said, he was in error. In 1930 the SS was still a volunteer organization, and candidates competed among themselves for the privilege of serving in it. Not all were accepted. No one enlisted in the SS unless he wanted to. Pauly, who was then a married man with his own business, may have believed that his place was among the best men, in an elite organization, and not among the rabble that made up the SA. He was among the founders of the local chapter of the SS. The organization awarded him the rank of captain and in 1934 promoted him to major—not a bad start given that he had never served in the army. During the next six years he served on a volunteer, part-time basis. He left the church, another indication of his identification with the organization, but still spent most of his time in his store. There is no evidence that the SS ever gave him financial assistance.

In 1936, when he was already the father of two children, he was offered a full-time paying position with the SS. He handed the store over to his brother and accepted the offer—eight years after joining the movement, six years after volunteering for the SS, three years after the Nazis came to power, it was a reasonable offer from his point of view. He saw himself as part of the movement and the movement was now Germany.

The movement trained and molded him gradually, according to its needs. He was first sent to a police course and then to officers school at Dachau. In 1933 his superiors described him as a stubborn young man who had trouble adjusting to the demands the organization made. They still complained of this two years later, but thought he could be changed. In 1939 they still thought he needed to work on himself in order to develop his self-confidence. Pauly tried to conform to the demands of his superiors, and they praised him for this. He is adjusting, they wrote, he is developing self-confidence, he is a talented officer. He was seconded to the Danzig police force. His unit was responsible for maintaining routine security, guarding roadblocks, and making standard identity checks of passersby. When the war broke out he was assigned to make arrests among the Polish nationals in the city. More than 1500 of them were arrested on the night of August 31, 1939. They were brought to a new camp, Stutthof. Pauly first handled technical and administrative matters, and according to his superiors he did this well. Life in Danzig quickly returned to normal, they wrote in his personnel file, and Pauly played a role in that. As long as Stutthof served as a detention camp for Polish nationals it remained under the control of the police and the General SS, not the camps administration. It did not officially become a concentration camp until 1942. He asked to be sent to the front, Pauly later claimed. His personnel file contains no reference to such a request. The SS had no reason to transfer him. He had no military experience, and they were satisfied with his work in the police force and at Stutthof. He made extensive visits to other concentration camps in connection with his work. In September he was appointed commandant of the Neuengamme camp. When, during his trial, he was asked if he had been sent to Neuengamme as a result of his success in Stutthof, he answered: "Yes, because I had organizational ability."[57]

He said that he was most involved with managing the industrial enterprises at the camp. Beginning in the winter of 1942, the SS tried to increase the industrial output of camp prisoners. This involved an attempt to bring down the mortality rate among them. Several survivors testified that, with Pauly's arrival, conditions at the camp improved. Random terror was almost completely halted, they said. The daily reality was still, however, very violent. Pauly carried out lashings to which he had sentenced prisoners and shot them to death as well; many were tortured and there were medical experiments on children. It seems, however, that Pauly adhered to orders more than others did. One of his officers was put on trial and sentenced to death for committing an atrocity without permission. Pauly passed judgment against about 200 of his men; about 20 of these were tried for illegal mistreatment of prisoners. He worked according to the book.

At a certain point he lost control of the situation. Beginning in 1945, tens of thousands of prisoners hastily evacuated from camps in the east began flowing into his camp. The overcrowding reached catastrophic dimensions. Among them were prisoners of Danish nationality. In Berlin, the Danish ambassador made a somewhat pathetic demand of one of the heads of the SS that Pauly be replaced with a more effective commandant; he was, of course, ignored.[58] Pauly himself had other worries. In August 1944 his wife died and left him with their five children, aged 6 through 11. Pauly was taken prisoner at the end of the war, tried before an American military court and sentenced to death; he was executed in October 1946. His attorney took an unusual line of defense for such cases—he told the court that the defendant was a small man with a small store in a small town who had suddenly been handed a uniform and high rank without ever having been a soldier. He had been given a management position in a large industrial enterprise and unlimited power over the fate of thousands of human beings. It was no wonder that the system corrupted him, his attorney said.

It was not that simple. Pauly believed in the movement and identified with its ideals years before it gave him power. He had supported the existence of the camps well before going to work in them. He fit into them better and better as he underwent training, as he rose in rank, and as the years went by and the war went on. His personnel file contains a letter he once sent to one of the heads of the SS, an acquaintance of his. "I have a wide scope for activity here," he wrote. "The extent of my authority and responsibility is much greater than it was at Stutthof. I am being made good use of and am happy about this. Otherwise I would not feel satisfaction inside."[59] It would seem that his judges did not know of this letter. For this reason they asked him many times why he had not refused to carry out various orders he had received. He could not even have conceived of such an idea. Pauly was full of unshakable faith in the Nazi movement. To the end he believed Germany would win the war. At the last moment, he thought, it would use an atom bomb.[60]

JOHANNES Hassebroeck, one of the commandants of the Gross Rosen camp in Holland, almost broke at the beginning of his SS career. His personnel file gives evidence of the effort demanded of him until he succeeded in meeting the demands of the organization and integrating himself into it, and the gradual process of his molding and toughening, step by step.[61]

Hassebroeck was born in 1910 in the city of Halle, on the Saale River, north of Leipzig in Saxony. His father, a guard in the local jail, had three other children; one died at the age of 1 year, when Hassebroeck was 3. When he wrote his autobiography he noted proudly that when he finished elementary school he received a scholarship to continue his studies for two years. The scholarship was awarded for his talent and diligence, he wrote. He dreamed of studying agriculture and living in the country, perhaps running some sort of farm; sometimes he played with the idea of enlisting in the standing army and becoming an officer. Both possibilities reflected the political conservatism impressed on him in his youth. Hassebroeck had not yet celebrated his fourth birthday when World War I broke out. His father was drafted immediately and returned four years later. Upon his return he joined the *Stahlhelm*, the largest of the barely legal paramilitary veterans' organizations. Its 100,000 members were inclined from the first to vengeful nationalistic conservatism, and soon began lending more and more support to the Nazi party. The father sent his son to the *Bismarckbund*, a right-wing, conservative, paramilitary youth movement. The young Hassebroeck did not succeed in enlisting in the "army of the hundred thousand," the reduced force that the Allies had permitted Weimar Germany to maintain. Given the agricultural crisis, there was also no chance of finding work as a certified agriculturalist. Disappointed, and with evident reluctance, Hassebroeck, now 16, became an apprentice in a factory. In time he became a clerk in the bookkeeping department. At first he continued his association with the Bismarckbund. At the age of 19 he left it to serve in the SA; less than a year later he joined the Nazi party. This was a natural extension of the conserva-

tive, patriotic education he had received in his father's house
and in the Bismarckbund. "Like his father, he saw communism
as a real danger and was determined to fight it," a West
German court later ruled.[62]

In 1931, two years after he first joined the Nazi movement,
Hassebroeck lost his job. "Now I had to go look for work, like
millions of other Germans, day by day, week by week, month
by month. It was horribly frustrating and depressing. In the end
I tried selling magazine subscriptions, from house to house.
Just to do something and not to sit idle all day," he later said.
All in all he was unemployed for three years. Unemployment
deepened his faith in the Nazi movement. "I had believed in
the party before," he said, "but now, for the first time, I saw
on the basis of my personal experience that it was right. My
attachment with the movement became stronger. I also now
had much time to work for the party."[63] Alongside his activity
in the SS he volunteered to work as a counselor in the
Hitlerjugend. The party later certified that, during the period of
the struggle for power, Hassebroeck put forth exceptional
efforts to assist it. He sometimes took part in fistfights with its
opponents. Twice he received head wounds and required
hospitalization, for two weeks each time. Hassebroeck continued to do "all sorts of things" during the year until the Nazis
came to power. At the beginning of 1934 the party arranged
him a job as the secretary of the Saxon Fishermen's
Association—there was no better job at the time. Within a few
months, however, the association transferred its activities to
Berlin and Hassebroeck was once again left without work. The
party placed him in the Ministry of Finance. He later said that
he had toyed with the idea of enlisting in the police force. One
of his friends, who worked in the party's security service,
suggested that Hassebroeck join the General SS first. It would
be easier to get into the police from there, and he would
probably get a better job. Hassebroeck accepted the offer in
June 1934, about four weeks before the great purge of the SA.
"It might seem that I joined the SS for opportunistic reasons,
because I knew they were planning to liquidate the SA. This is
not correct. I was full of pride when they accepted me into the
SA. The party's elite units were already very selective in their
choice of new members. Only the best could be accepted. I saw

my membership in the SS as a great challenge."[64] This was undoubtedly true. It seems, nevertheless, that he enlisted in the SS more or less by chance and for practical reasons. Had the Saxon Fishermen's Association not moved to Berlin, he might have continued to work for it, a loyal Nazi like many others, without any direct involvement in terror. He might not have joined the SS had he not been told that his membership would help him find work with the police. He ended up at a concentration camp in the same sort of circumstantial way, as a result of being wounded in battle.

Hassebroeck began his SS career in an administrative position, in one of the organization's offices. About a year later SS psychologists determined that he was not fit to serve as an officer. They praised his good intentions and his friendly behavior, but said he was completely lacking in inner strength, drive, and self-confidence. "He tends to accept the views of others," they said of him. "This characteristic indicates a weakness in his personality and unbalance. He is not tough enough, neither in his attitude towards himself nor in his relations with others. He tends to softness and submission."[65] They recommended, for these reasons, that he be discharged from the organization. Hassebroeck appealed this recommendation. He had aspirations to serve as an SS officer. His superiors reluctantly allowed him to become a member of the first officers course the SS opened in Braunschweig. He failed, as his superiors predicted from the start. They again ruled that he did not meet the requirements of the SS. Hassebroeck appealed again and somehow won another chance. He was sent to the second class, beginning again from the start like a child who had been held back a grade. This time he was more successful—his grades ranged from "satisfactory" to "good," but not "very good," as were those of most of the other cadets in the course. Hassebroeck was allowed to remain in the SS for a trial period. His superiors did not see a bright future for him, but were always impressed with his strong will to serve the organization. Hassebroeck was then 26 years old; after a series of further training programs he was assigned to one of the Death's Head Formations.

Hassebroeck's unit was stationed by the Esterwegen camp.

His superiors wrote in his personnel file that there was a certain improvement in the level of his performance, but they were still unsatisfied. He had still not learned sufficient tenacity and self-confidence. There were, however, some among them who now saw for the first time "some chance" that he would be a good officer, despite the weaknesses in his personality. His formation devoted most of its time to training with light weapons, like army infantry units; once every week or ten days several of its men were sent to perform guard duty at Esterwegen. Part of their work was accompanying the prisoners as they set out to work at dawn and at their return in the evening. Even if they never entered the camp, as he would later claim, it is unlikely that Hassebroeck did not know what was happening there. It prepared him for the assignment he was given a few years later.

The Esterwegen camp was closed in 1936 and Hassebroeck was transferred to a different formation, not far from the Sachsenhausen camp. He continued to have only an indirect connection with the camp itself, but heard, as he had before, about the conditions and brutal treatment of prisoners there. At this point, however, his superiors still did not have him in mind for service in the concentration camps. They sent him for training in the army, and when the war broke out he was sent to the front. Hassebroeck was then 29 years old. His superiors continued to follow the gradual development of his personality. In 1937 they found that he had developed "a certain measure of self-confidence and firmness of decision." His ideological identity had also crystallized over the years, step by step. For example, on a form he filled out in 1934 he listed his faith as Protestant. In 1935 Hassebroeck left the same question unanswered; in 1936 he wrote that he had no religion. In 1937 he brought himself to write the Nazi formula that he was "a believer in God." He fought on the western and eastern fronts and won several citations. The horrors of the war made an impression on his personality: in 1940 his superiors noted for the first time that Hassebroeck had developed "tenacity and the ability to succeed at a task." In 1942 he was promoted to captain.

In the summer of 1942, Hassebroeck fell ill, affecting his combat fitness. Some time later he was wounded in his right leg and was hospitalized for an extended period in several hospitals, first in Riga, then in Munich, and finally in Berlin. While there he ran, apparently by accident, into Richard Glücks, then responsible for the overall operation of the concentration camps. According to Hassebroeck, he was "very surprised" when Glücks had him transferred to work in the camps. "When we spoke I told him explicitly that I wanted to return to my unit at the front immediately," Hassebroeck later claimed. The judges who heard his case after the war concluded that he in the end "acceded" to the offer to work in the concentration camp system.[66] The state of his health would not in any case allow him to return to the front for a year. So, in August 1942, he found himself in one of Sachsenhausen's branch camps; in October 1943 he was given command of the Gross Rosen concentration camp. As with the entire system of camps, Hassebroeck's camp soon reached monstrous proportions: when Hassebroeck arrived, there were approximately 3000 prisoners; when he left there were some 80,000. According to him, most of them were criminals and homosexuals. By the end of the war some 100,000 of his prisoners had died. Close to the end of the war Glücks noted that Hassebroeck was among the outstanding concentration camp commandants: "He exudes self-confidence and toughness," he wrote in Hassebroeck's personnel file.

This was a process that most of the other commandants underwent as well. Hassebroeck was not a sadist. The Gross Rosen trial unfolds a series of horrendous acts that occurred in the camp, but most of them conformed with the norm and did not exceed what was allowed by the standing orders and regulations. It seems that Hassebroeck hardened at the front. He had been ready for a military life from his youth. Others passed, as he did, from military service to service in the camps; there were others who went in the opposite direction, from the camps to the front. Each served an average of five years in the SS before being stationed in one of the camps. "We were all military men," Hassebroeck said years later, "but it was a very special kind of army. A political army. Our service was an overwhelming emotional experience of enormous strength. We believed not only in the same values and ideals—we believed

in each other. It was that faith that gave us the spiritual and
physical power to do our duty."[67]

———————

JOHANNES Hassebroeck was 65 years old when I visited
him in his home in Braunschweig, a retired businessman. It
was in March 1975. On the morning of our conversation his
granddaughter's bicycle had been stolen from his front door.
"The police are helpless and the public prosecutor's office is
still opening cases against people like me, who only did
their duty, instead of defending the citizenry from crime,"
Hassebroeck said. "That's why I'll tell you that I sometimes
miss those days, before the war. Are you surprised? Go out
to the street, ask people. Not those lazy youngsters. Ask
people like me, who did something for their country. They'll
tell you the same thing."

Hassebroeck was arrested at the end of the war, first by
the Czechs, then by the Americans, and finally by the British, who put him on trial. "You should have heard the witnesses," he said. "One swore that he saw how I led people
to the left, and the next one said I had led them to the right.
One swore that we used one kind of gun to execute them,
and the second swore we had used a different kind. The
[British] court sentenced me to death.

"What do you think happened then? They put me in
prison for life. Then they commuted the sentence to fifteen
years, but in 1954 they released me already. I moved to
Braunschweig, and worked as a sales agent. I didn't receive
a pension, because those who served in the SS don't get
one, but I didn't do badly. Years passed. One day they again
needed someone who would take responsibility on himself.
In a pretty sudden way, in 1967, they came and arrested me.
This time it was German police. They arrested me and immediately let me out on bail. So why did they arrest me?
Years passed until the case came to trial. What they didn't
say about me at that trial, what they didn't say! Once again
they brought witnesses who remembered everything.
Twenty-five years had passed since the things they described
happened—but they remembered everything. Do you know

what happened? The District Court in Braunschweig acquitted me. The prosecution appealed: no, they won't give up. They laid out the whole story one more time. The judges of the Supreme Court behaved as if they had never heard of Adolf Hitler and the SS and the war and the concentration camps before. They had to be told everything, again and again, and what do you think happened? The Supreme Court acquitted me. If you think that's all, you're wrong. Today, so they tell me, in 1975, there is still an investigation going on. What can I do, that's the way they work, without order, without method. But they don't catch the real criminals."

My impression was that he believed what he said. I showed him his personnel file. Was he aware of the gradual toughening he underwent? "Nonsense," Hassebroeck answered, insulted. "I was always a strong SS man."

———————

IN the morning hours of December 20, 1960, an official of the West German general prosecutor's office came with two police officers to a lone sawmill in the heart of a forest, about 15 miles southeast of Hamburg. At a distance of about 200 yards from the place they had parked their car they made out the figure of a man, bent over his work. A heavy fog made it hard to see, but when they approached him they identified him without any problem. They had brought his photograph with them. "Hands up!" the official called. The two police officers pulled out their pistols, but the surprised sawmill worker did not resist as they handcuffed him. "My name is Karl Neumann," he told them.[68] He had documents which proved his identity. The officers drove him to his house in the nearby village. His wife identified herself by her real name. The captured forester claimed that he was not her husband. The officers searched the house. They found much evidence. Afterwards, they ordered him to roll up his pants and found the scar on his right thigh. The prisoner suddenly stood up straight and declared, somewhat solemnly, "I am Richard Baer. I was an officer. I asked you to treat me accordingly." He meant the handcuffs.

This ended a long pursuit of the last commandant of Auschwitz. The authorities had published his picture. Someone

identified him and turned him in. He was found out fifteen
years after he bought his false identity and forged papers and
built himself a new life as a quiet and introverted forester who
never spoke of his past. The Americans had arrested him twice
after the war, but did not discover his identity and freed him.
He was now to be the central defendant at the Auschwitz trial
at the District Court in Frankfurt. During his stay at Auschwitz
he had been responsible for the extermination of Jews.[69]
During the preliminary interrogation he claimed in his defense
that the extermination was not within the bounds of his
responsibility. He said this to, among others, the Israeli
attorney Ervin Shimron, who questioned him while gathering
evidence against Adolf Eichmann.[70]

Baer was born in a small Bavarian village, Floss, not far
from the Czechoslovakian border.[71] Upon concluding his
elementary education ("average achievement"), he was sent to
learn the trade of a baker. He worked as an apprentice and at
the age of 17 left to travel through several German cities, going
from bakery to bakery, as was customary. He was not
politically involved. After returning home he settled in a city
not far from the village where he was born and worked as a
salaried baker. He was never unemployed. It seems that he was
caught up by Nazi propaganda like millions of other Germans,
believing that its direction was the right one. He joined the
party in 1930 and soon after the SS began operating in his city,
he joined it as well. He was then 21 years old, still single. The
SS most likely attracted him for the same reasons that it
attracted others. Two years later the Nazis were already in
power and he was offered full-time employment in the SS. He
had no reason to refuse. He joined the "auxiliary police" and
after a while was transferred to the guard unit at Dachau, where
he served under Theodor Eicke. From Dachau he was transferred to the Gestapo prison on Columbia Street in Berlin, and
from there to the Brandenburg Death's Head Formation, which
was stationed near Sachsenhausen. Then he was sent to the
Thüringen Formation near Buchenwald. He still did not serve
in the camps, but only in the area outside them. Most of his
time was spent in military training. He was thus acquainted
with the camps before he became directly involved in them,
and even saw himself already as part of the system in which

they operated. He sometimes led prisoners to work. He was also trained for other assignments. In 1939 he was described as "hesitant." His achievements, they said, approached average. A year later they found that Baer was making an effort to develop self-confidence and was taking on a measure of "toughness on himself." A year later they certified that he had confidence in himself, and after another year, that his attainments were much higher than average. Thus the young baker gradually integrated himself into the SS system of values, accompanying its development from year to year, from camp to camp, first in Buchenwald and then in Neuengamme.

In the summer of 1940, when he was still single, Baer was sent to the front. He could have ended his career in the SS, and his life, as a combat soldier, had he not been wounded. He was treated in the officers hospital in the Neuengamme camp. While he was still recovering, he was attached to the camp staff and received the position of deputy commandant. He now bore responsibility for what happened there, but was still not involved in the daily atrocities. In November 1942 he was transferred to Berlin and appointed deputy to Oswald Pohl, director of the concentration camp system. He toured the different camps, saw everything, knew everything, including details of the project to exterminate the Jews. He was revealed as a very ambitious man. He may even have plotted to topple Pohl, but in the meantime decided to strengthen his position by becoming commandant of one of the important camps. He chose Auschwitz, and when the commandant of the camp, Arthur Liebehenschel, was caught in an illicit love affair, he took advantage of the situation to get rid of him. His handling of the episode also reflects his loyalty to SS values: "I am aware of the honor of life under the flag and the right to die for it," he once wrote. He ran Auschwitz between May 1944 and January 1945. Evidence given by survivors of the camp indicates that he also worked according to the book, carefully differentiating between the permitted and the forbidden; he drafted some of the orders himself, while still stationed in Berlin. Extermination of the Jews and the "selection" which preceded each operation of the gas chambers—Baer was present at several—were within the bounds of the permitted.

While at Auschwitz he had to deal with a very personal

problem as well. The woman he had married in 1942 had not
borne him children. This bothered him not only because he
wanted to be a father, but also because he feared that without
children his advancement in the ranks would be halted. His
wife underwent fertility treatments and finally became pregnant. A document in his personnel file establishes that, during
one of the bombardments of Hamburg, his wife went into
shock, lost the baby, and never again became pregnant. Baer
died in 1961 in the Frankfurt Prison, not long before his trial
was to open. His attorney asked him before his death how he
could have done what he did. Baer answered that it had not
happened all at once, but gradually. "Once, during a furlough
in Hamburg," he related, "I saw a little girl in the street,
flaming like a torch. She had been hit by a phosphorous bomb
dropped by British planes. She burned to death in front of my
eyes. That happened before I came to Auschwitz. You can get
used to everything."[72]

MAX Kögel learned "to get used to everything" many years
before he joined the SS.

Kögel was born in October 1895 in Füssen, a Bavarian town
50 miles southwest of Munich.[73] He was the fourth son of a
Catholic carpenter employed by a furniture factory. Just before
his sixth birthday, Kögel's mother died while giving birth to
her fifth child. Six years later, when Kögel was 12, his father
also died, of an illness. Kögel was cared for by a farm family
who took him out of school and sent him to be a shepherd on
the slopes of the Alps. From time to time he carried the bags
of tourists and mountain-climbers and sometimes also guided
them along the mountain paths. Some years later he signed up
for a tour guide course, but as soon as he began his studies the
war broke out.

Kögel, then 18 years old, immediately volunteered for the
army. Within three months he found himself at the front, in an
infantry unit of the Bavarian army. His personnel file shows
that he was wounded three times, and twice required hospitalization and lengthy treatment. One wound was from the
horrible battle at Verdun, and the second from an accident; an
ammunition bunker exploded while he was nearby, killing
more than 100 men. At the end of the war Kögel returned to

Bavaria. At first he worked as a customs officer in Garmisch, a ski town near the Austrian border. In time he succeeded in opening his own souvenir shop and at first it did well, but four years later he was forced to close it. Years later, when he listed the events in his life he noted only that he sold his store at a great loss. He hid the fact that he had been given a suspended sentence for bankruptcy and fraud. During the following years he traveled between Vienna and Zurich as a sales agent for a ski equipment company, but later returned to Füssen and became, lacking any other possibility, a laborer in the same factory that had employed his father. He was disappointed and bitter—this was not the life he had hoped to live.

Upon returning from the war, defeated in battle but still believing in his future, Kögel joined the *Völkischer Block*, an extreme right, nationalist, militarist, and anti-Semitic organization, and later became a member of the *Bund Oberland*, formerly the *Freikorps Oberland*, the organization of discharged soldiers which, among other things, took part in the Beer Hall Putsch with Hitler. Kögel was probably among them on that occasion. He was among the first activists in the Nazi party.

Kögel married in May 1919 and two years later had a son. Some time thereafter his marriage began falling apart. Ten years after he married, his son, then 8 years old, died of the measles; immediately thereafter his wife submitted a request for divorce. The court ruled that the two "simply do not love each other anymore." A few months after his divorce Kögel joined the SS as a volunteer. At the same time he tried to make a new start, and asked to enlist in the Bavarian border police. For this he needed proofs of a clean past. He could not obtain this because of his former bankruptcy. In the meantime the Nazis gained power and soon thereafter Theodor Eicke wrote a letter to the Bavarian police on the stationery of the Dachau concentration camp:

At Dachau Kögel became one of my most trustworthy officers; I would unhesitatingly put thousands of marks into his hands. As far as I am concerned they can order him forever banished from Füssen. The village has not succeeded, apparently, in freeing itself from liberal ways of thinking. I demand that the authorities there be ordered to leave Kögel alone, once and for all. Likewise, I demand that he be promoted. I need Kögel at Dachau, for important work. The people of Füssen can go look for someone else for their nonsense.[74]

Only in the SS, and only under Eicke, could Kögel expect such backing; the SS could also support him in spirit after the death of his son and the crisis he suffered after his divorce. He also earned extremely high marks from his superiors. They described him as a man devoted to the movement, of strong character and perfect behavior, both on duty and off. They praised his thoroughness. After the war, a prisoner testified that Kögel, while serving as deputy camp commandant, had once come to Block 5 dressed in his black dress uniform. An order had previously been given to wash the floor. He entered the barracks, got down on the floor, and upon rising discovered a few grains of dust on his uniform. The punishment for all five prisoners responsible for the block was an hour on the "tree," hanging by their wrists, their arms tied behind their backs.[75]

When he joined the staff of the Dachau concentration camp he was 38 years old. The camp could not shock him—conditions there were still not as bad as they would later be, and Kögel had experienced greater horrors and brutalities, beginning with the death of his parents during his boyhood. Then there had been the war in which he had been wounded, and there had been the defeat and the economic disappointment, the failed marriage, and the dead son. As one of the first supporters of the movement he accepted the ideology which led to the establishment of the concentration camps, and later to the extermination of the Jews. Kögel remarried in 1934, and this time his marriage brought him to a higher social level than he had known previously.

His wife was the daughter of a successful engineer. Kögel therefore had good reason to make an effort to improve his status as an officer. As the years went by he also deepened his ideological identification with the organization. In 1935, for instance, he still listed himself as a Catholic. In 1936 he wrote that he had no religion. In 1940 he wrote the Nazi formula, "believer in God."

Kögel joined the General SS in July 1932 and began working full-time at Dachau in April 1933. He grew with the camps from the start. After three years in Dachau he already had a clear idea of what the camps were, even though he still had only indirect contact with the prisoners themselves. He was transferred to "Columbia House," the Gestapo prison in Berlin, and from there to Sachsenhausen for a few months. In January 1937 he was back in Dachau, this time as deputy camp commandant responsible for the prisoner compound. In September 1938 he served in the women's camp at Lichtenburg and when this was closed, he became the first commandant of the women's camp set up in its place, Ravensbrück. In 1942 he was in charge of the Majdanek camp in Lublin, the period when the extermination of the Jews began there. He supported this, and was already tough enough to direct the project. At the end of 1943 he was transferred to the Flossenbürg camp, where he remained until the end of the war, and where he was arrested by the American army. In June 1946 he was found dead in his cell.

"IN the concentration camps there were people who acted like pigs," Hans Hüttig said many years later. "All kinds of sadists and the like. They were everywhere in the camps. But a man could also follow the standing orders of the camp, and those who did were all right, if you read them the way we read them then." He acted only in accordance with orders, he claimed, as expected.[76]

Hüttig was born in Dresden, Saxony, on April 4, 1894, the eldest of three children, two boys and a girl.[77] His father worked first as a carpenter, but eventually succeeded in opening his own store, where, together with his wife, he sold chemical products and photographic equipment. The rest of the family was also involved in photography; one of them was among the founders of Zeiss-Ikon, a well-known lens factory. It was, in Hüttig's words, a good family of the middle class, very devout and strict in their Protestant faith. They said grace before each meal; the father punished the children frequently, as was normal then. "It made me into a man," Hüttig argued. His father dreamed that his son would be an officer in the standing army, but for that he needed a high school diploma. At that time Hüttig's father did not have the money to pay for high school, so he sent his son to a boys' boarding school in southern Germany which prepared its students for a year of service in the army without giving them a diploma. Studies there lasted only three years. Its graduates were not intended for service as officers, but if they met the requirements of the school and the army, they had a chance of becoming reserve officers. Hüttig's father saw a military career for his son as an opportunity to raise his status and improve his social prestige. Hüttig himself looked to the army for "danger, adventure, and manly heroism." They were both disappointed. In 1911 Hüttig failed his examinations and was not accepted into the army. "They told me that I wasn't good enough," he later said, still very upset. "If my father had only had enough money to send me to a better school, everything would have been different."[78] Hüttig was 17 years old. He reluctantly packed his bags, returned home, and became a salesman in his father's camera shop. That was not what he wanted to do with his life. A year or two later Hüttig left his parents' house and in March 1914 landed in one of the German colonies in East Africa, the agent of an import-export company. Five months later World War I broke out. Hüttig, still dreaming of becoming an officer, immediately volunteered for service in the East African corps of the German army. He participated in twenty-three battles all in all, reaching the rank of master sergeant, but was not made an officer.

Three years after enlisting, in December 1917, he was shot in the chest and sent to a military hospital that was captured three weeks later by the British army. He spent the next two years in a POW camp the British set up on the outskirts of Cairo, Egypt. Germany had been defeated in the meantime, the monarchy had collapsed, the army had been dismantled, and the colonies had been lost. So, in March 1920, Hans Hüttig returned to his parents' photography shop in Dresden disappointed, scarred, humiliated. He was now 25 years old. During the next six years he did "all kinds of things," in his words, working as clerk and bookkeeper in different firms. He changed jobs frequently. In the meantime the economic crisis worsened, but Hüttig was never unemployed. In December 1921 he married; two years later he had a daughter and five years after that a son. He was, nevertheless, restless. Even though he had never been interested in politics, he later said, he was bothered by what he read in the newspapers. In 1925 Hüttig joined the Stahlhelm. It was not concrete political consciousness that brought him there, he said, but a vague feeling that "something had to be done," if possible, in the company of other young men, veterans like him. They were all like him, uprooted men who had a hard time forgetting what the war had done to them. In 1926 he opened his own photography store, but the crisis of 1930 forced him to close it. He succeeded in finding work in a photography studio. In March 1932 Hüttig joined the SS. Something in him wanted to play soldier, he said, and would not leave him alone, as in his youth when he dreamed of being an officer. "I was already 38 years old. Tall, strong, just the type they were looking for. Only a little too old. But friends who joined before me told me, why not come? I was happy. They were younger than me. It was as if they returned my youth to me. Gave me another chance. I loved to be in the company of young warriors. I felt that I had something to offer them, and of course, the officer's rank they promised me tempted me. If not in the army, I thought, at least in the SS. And there was of course the same unique brother-hood-at-arms that prevailed there. It is still very dear to me today."

The organization still did not promise at this stage any material compensation. "I was not unemployed at that time and the organization did not pay. No, that wasn't the reason," Hüttig said. "At least not then. It was an elite unit. That was what attracted me. At least, that's how we saw it. I could not know that in less than a year we would win. I joined despite not knowing that we would win. Of course, I was a Nazi and I believed that the movement had a future. But I did not know that one day I would get a salary out of it. I found comradeship in the SS, and new faith in myself, and that was worth more than money." His personnel file shows that a few months before he joined the SS he was separated from his wife; a while later they divorced. A short time after he joined the SS, Hüttig became a member of the Nazi party.

His initial activity in the SS was restricted mostly to weekends. The members would meet for sports practice, and would some-times shoot, parade through town, protect party rallies, and from time to time get into fights with their opponents, the Communists and Social Democrats. Less than a year later, in January 1933, the Nazis gained power and Hans Hüttig found himself, for the first time in his life, among the winners. The SS now offered him a salary and a senior officer's rank and full-time employment. Hüttig accepted. He was placed in one of the Death's Head Formations. "A long time passed before I saw my first camp from inside. In November 1933 there was not yet much to see. In any case, I was involved in training soldiers. I was happy to make use of my experience in the world war. Think of it—at the age of 39 I still had something to contribute."[79] Hüttig had opportunities to visit the camps, including Dachau, where he was in a four-month advanced course in 1935. Six years, however, passed from the day he first joined the SS to the day he was stationed in one of the camps. In other words, he had enough time to adjust himself gradually to service in the camps, and could have avoided it entirely, had he wanted to, by leaving the SS. Such a possibility did not occur to him.

"I saw no reason to leave. First, I felt very good in the SS, and I've already told you why. Beginning in January 1933, when we came into power, I felt even better. As regards the moral aspect of the work, I would like to respond in this way: I saw no reason why enemies of the people, and that's what they were, should not be in concentration camps. Everything was done legally, and even more important—if we wanted Germany to move forward in the right direction—we had to put these people behind bars. It was very simple. And besides, I told myself more than once that, had they won instead of us, they would have done the same thing to us, and maybe worse. In other words, I had nothing against the camps in principle. I was in favor of them, you could say. The original idea was to put the prisoners through a process of re-education so that they, too, might become loyal Germans. We thought we could educate them through hard labor and strict discipline. That's how we had been educated, when we were children. I read the standing orders of the camp and I saw no reason to oppose them. True, people frequently acted in violation of those orders. You could see disgusting things. There were those who treated the prisoners with horrible cruelty. There were real sadists there, like Karl Koch, for instance. I was not like that," Hüttig claimed.[80]

Hüttig and Koch knew each other from Dresden. Hüttig was

appointed Koch's deputy. It was his first assignment in one of the camps. He was then 44 years old, a first lieutenant in the SS. According to Hüttig, he tried to restrain Koch, but did not succeed because his superior did not take criticism from his men. Koch, on his part, did not award Hüttig the usual praises in his evaluations of him, and sufficed with writing dryly: "Hüttig knows the standing orders well."[81]

Under Koch's command at Buchenwald Hüttig could learn everything he needed for his future work. It seems that he fit well into the atmosphere there. Camp prisoners testified after the war that he frequently mistreated and tortured them.[82] His superiors praised his personality and achievements. They described him as a man full of energy, sure of himself, a man who knew what he wanted and could establish friendly relationships with both his superiors and his subordinates. As evidence of his good character they noted the fact that he drank little—truly a rare quality.

His period of service at the Sachsenhausen and Flossenbürg concentration camps, both of them in Germany, gave Hüttig the reputation of a commander who could be counted on; for this reason he was often given special assignments. He oversaw the establishment of the Natzweiler camp in Alsace, the first concentration camp established in one of the western areas of occupation. It demanded a measure of tact and organizational ability. Afterwards, he was sent to set up a number of concentration camps and prison facilities in Norway, and then was moved, urgently, to the Hertogenbusch camp in Holland, where the commandant had been removed in the wake of an incident that caused the deaths of several prisoners. The incident created disquiet among the civilian population in the area and Hüttig had to calm things down. When the camp was closed, in September 1944, Hüttig was 50 years old. He had nothing left to do. He served in a police station until the end of the war.

Looking back, Hüttig commented: "During the war in Africa I saw great horrors, I was wounded, and I fell prisoner. Buchenwald still shocked me when I first went there. But, of course, after all the years in the guard units at the camps, I did not come there unprepared. I overcame it. Sachsenhausen, Flossenbürg, and all the others presented no problems after Buchenwald."[83]

5
"THEY ARE HERE TO DIE"

NOT long before he was executed in 1947, Rudolf Höss decided to write the story of his life. For more than a year they had been interrogating him almost nonstop on his part in the extermination of the Jews at Auschwitz. He knew he would be hanged. He nevertheless obediently cooperated with his interrogators and even appeared as a prosecution witness in one of the Nuremberg trials. His manuscript is neat and very pedantic and fills more than 200 pages. It is titled *My Psyche,* perhaps under the influence of conversations he had previously had with the American psychiatrist Martin Gilbert.[1] Exhibitionist and self-pitying, he was not always accurate, but he composed a valuable record of his involvement in the crimes of the Third Reich, from Dachau to Auschwitz. Höss remained faithful to his Nazi creed and did not repent. The extermination of the Jews, he wrote, was a "mistake," because it caused Germany more damage than good. The SS needed men like him. The organization knew it had to take others as well, but it was political soldiers like Rudolf Höss which allowed it to operate the concentration camps on such a scale and pattern.

Höss was born on November 25, 1900, the only child of a merchant from Baden-Baden, a city about 25 miles west of Stuttgart in south Germany.[2] Höss respected his parents but never loved them, he wrote. His father was often away from home on business trips. He was a lonely child, he added. His only friend was a black pony. For some reason, he was drawn to horses, as far back as he could recall. They spurred his imagination when he joined the cavalry in World War I, and afterward the SS mounted unit. He used to cross Auschwitz on horseback as well.

Höss described his father as a very religious man who intended that his son become a Catholic priest. One day, while still in elementary school, he discovered that his confessor, a priest whom he trusted unreservedly, had revealed one of his "sins," a fight with another student, to his father. The incident, Höss wrote, shocked him to the depths of his soul: his confessor had betrayed him. At 13 years old, he could no longer believe in God. Less than a year later his father died. Three months after that World War I began. Thus were three crises linked together in the life of an adolescent boy. There is no reason to doubt Höss's word that they were decisive in his development and were, perhaps, the beginnings of the hardening he underwent.

When the war broke out Höss was 14. He discovered the soldier in him. His father, grandfather, and great-grandfather had been officers. "Under no circumstances would I allow myself to miss this war," he later wrote. He immediately reported to the enlistment office. His mother, who had just been widowed, was naturally against her son's going off to war. From time to time Höss ran away from home for the army, but each time he was sent back. In the meantime he volunteered for work in a military hospital. "I saw the dying and the dead," he wrote. "It was a unique sensation that I cannot describe today." When he was 16 he succeeded in persuading one of the cavalry officers in the battalion his father had once served in to take him to the front against his mother's wishes and in violation of the law. He was a youth whose soul was storming, prisoner of the war hysteria that swept Germany.

By the time he returned home two years later Höss had been exposed to war in all its cruelty. Among the experiences he described he emphasized the brotherhood-at-arms, the intimacy among men in combat. This was, in his words, a set of relationships more powerful than anything he had previously known. "We were closer to each other than I had been to my father," he wrote. His closest friend, the officer who had taken him with him, fell in front of his eyes. And he learned to kill. "My first kill!" he cried out in his memoirs, still trembling. "A barrier went down. From then on I continued to kill and kill more just as they taught me." Among other things, he fought side by side with the Turks in Palestine, visited Jerusalem, and described with loathing the commercialism of the holy places. Wounded in his foot, he was hospitalized in a military hospital in Wilhelma, a German settlement near the Mediterranean coast of the Holy Land. While there he fell in love with one of the nurses, and first had sexual relations.

Höss returned to Germany at the head of a small cavalry unit that crossed the Balkans and the Alps in an audacious and dangerous journey lasting three months. At 18 he had become the youngest sergeant in the German army; he was among the heroes of the war.

Upon returning home Höss had nowhere to turn. His mother had died soon after he left for the front. Legally he was still a juvenile. His guardian demanded that he resume his studies towards the priesthood, as his father had wanted. Höss, of course, refused, but did not really know what to do with himself, like millions of other defeated, uprooted young soldiers. He was depressed. For the first time ever, he wrote, he missed his parents' house. "I was very lonely," he wrote. He did what thousands of other young men in his situation did, including many who later became concentration camp commandants. "I resumed being a soldier," he wrote, "and all my problems were solved." He joined First Lieutenant Gerhard Rossbach's Frei-korps. Rossbach and his men first set out for the Baltic region to fight in Posen, Lithuania, and Latvia. This was a sort of gang war among Germans, Lithuanians, Poles, and Russians. Höss described the horrors of battle there.[3] He once saw a farmhouse go up in flames with an entire family inside. It was worse than in Palestine. Afterwards the Rossbachers fought the French in the Ruhr district. The German army, forced to lay down its weapons, aided them with money and arms; the Republican government supported them halfheartedly. All this was of marginal legality. At one point, in November 1922, they tried to depose the government, and were outlawed. Rossbach joined the Nazi party that same day. His men, Rudolf Höss among them, followed him.

Some of them were later involved in the attempted putsch led by Adolf Hitler in a Bavarian beer hall.

In March 1924 Höss was sentenced to ten years in prison for his part in a murder. The victim was one Walter Kadow, another of Rossbach's men. Höss claimed it was an execution—Kadow was a Communist traitor and deserved death, he wrote. Rossbach's men were then living as laborers on a farm in the north. These were closed men's communes, part gang, part religious cult, with norms and values of their own. They suffered neither women nor foreigners. Höss was one of thirteen accused of the murder; among the others was Martin Bormann, later one of Hitler's aides. The court devoted much time to describing the political background of the murder, but ruled that Rossbach's men detested Kadow for personal reasons as well. They said he had spied on them and that he made a habit of borrowing money from them with no intention of returning it. The judgment recounted in great detail the intense relationships that formed among members of this closed group, with one of its members the focus of the hatred of all the others, young men under psychological pressures that they repressed but that threatened to break loose like steam from a pressure cooker. They did not mean to kill Kadow, only teach him a lesson, but they lost control of themselves. First they beat him, and their blows grew in force until he lost consciousness. Someone threw himself on him and cut his throat. Someone else—the court did not succeed in identifying whom—shot him to death. It was in a forest. All of them were drunk at the time. The court described what had happened as a sudden outbreak of evil impulses.[4] The murderers had difficulty explaining to themselves what they had done. For this reason they justified it ideologically, and said that Kadow had been "executed."

Höss wrote at length in his book about the mental and physical suffering he endured in prison, described in great detail the abuse of prisoners, both by guards and by other prisoners, and analyzed the options available to a prisoner who wants to preserve his sanity. In 1928, five years later, he was pardoned and released. He found himself, in essence, in the same place he had been ten years previously, upon his return from the war—like then, as a released prisoner without a profession, he did not know what to do with himself.

Within a short time he joined the *Artamanen*, and organization of young people training themselves for agricultural work. Höss heard of them while still in prison and was taken with their ideology. "All I wanted was to build myself a house in the country, live a healthy life with my family," he wrote. *Art* is an Old German word meaning "natural being" and suggesting a connection with the land. The Artamanen grew, as did other youth movements, out of nineteenth century German romanticism. They called for the renewal of the ecological balance between man and his land. Many of them came from the city to the county, rejecting industrialization and urbanization. They lived in agricultural communes and fostered what they saw as the true spirit of Germany, without nicotine, without alcohol, and with very little politics other than a vague, sentimental patriotism. In contrast to the Rossbachers, the Artamanen accepted women, and they were less violent. They did not see themselves as soldiers. A short time after joining them Höss met Helwig Hensel, 21, and married her. He was then 29 years old. At least one other concentration camp commandant, Walter Eisfeld, had been an Artaman; several others had decided in their youths to be farmers, and this, in those days, was a clear expression of conservatism and romantic nationalism. Himmler, with a degree in agriculture, was also involved with the Artamanen. He and Höss became friends. According to Höss, he could not decide immediately when Himmler suggested, in 1934, that he come over to the SS on a full-time basis. He had previously been a volunteer in the organization's mounted division, and according to his brother-in-law, "that revived his military instincts."[5] Höss was already a member of the Nazi party, and the party had in the meantime gained power. The Artamanen were not allowed to continue their separate existence, and were forced to become part of the Hitlerjugend. All this lent weight to Himmler's suggestion, but, according to Höss, he and his wife did not give up their dream of living in a small house in the country. Had they been able to, they would have done so after World War II, he claimed. But the new elite army of the movement fiercely attracted him. "I could not resist the temptation," he wrote.[6]

Hans Hüttig described this as "a passion for playing soldier."[7] Höss used the same expression.

After the Nazis gained power, the SS was given partial responsibility for internal security, including the operation of the concentration camps. For this it needed more personnel. For the first time since its establishment it could give its members paying jobs. Service in the SS was now prestigious, and it offered officer rank. Höss was stationed at Dachau; his new job also improved his finances. He was a 34-year-old father of three, a loyal Nazi, but lacked any professional experience. He had undergone experiences harsher than what he saw in Dachau when first stationed there, and in any case did not, at the start, have direct contact with the inmates. At first he was sent for six months of training. Then he was sent to guard a small group of prisoners, and then a larger group. Thus the years went by—Höss became part of the system and adjusted step by step to the mounting atrocities. Each stage prepared him for the next one as he rose in the ranks. In his book he describes his first lesson in how to whip a prisoner— tied to a specially designed post, in accordance with Theodor Eicke's disciplinary code. Höss was revolted. Even after all he had seen before he came to Dachau—as a youth, as a soldier, and as a prisoner—he had trouble taking what he saw, he wrote. The second time it was easier.

Höss's brother-in-law, Fritz Hensel, sometimes visited him. Once, in the Sachsenhausen canteen, he heard two officers dispute the most effective way of forcing a confession out of a prisoner: with a whip or by immersing his head in a bucket of water. Hensel, shocked, asked Höss why he allowed such things. Höss answered that it was forbidden to torture prisoners and that they were not tortured often, but there were unpreventable excesses, and there was nothing to be done about them.[8] In his book he frequently condemns the sadism he noticed among some of his comrades. In April 1940 Höss was sent to the east to set up a new concentration camp, Auschwitz. His brother-in-law asked him if it would be a second Sachsenhausen. Oh, no, Höss answered, it would be a model camp of an entirely new type. The inmates would receive re-education through agricultural training, in the spirit of the Artamanen.

In 1941[2] Höss was summoned by Himmler, who told him

that the Führer had decided to destroy European Jewry. Höss later claimed that he had not been the right man for the job, since he was too soft and opposed killing deep inside. "I did not have the courage to expose my softness to my men," he claimed. "And as an officer I had to act as if I supported what was being done." He may have believed in this after the fact, but there is no reason to think that, at the time, he did not favor the project. In any case, he did not break while it was being carried out. He was not all that soft.

Höss calculated that, if an average of 3000 bodies were burned each day for 27 months, the number of people killed was close to two and a half million. In his opinion, no more than one and a half million were killed, but he said he had no evidence to prove the accuracy of this number. Adolf Eichmann's judges decided not to determine the correct number.[9] The extermination of the Jews in any case developed gradually. First Soviet prisoners of war were liquidated—instead of shooting them, they were gassed. According to Höss it was Karl Fritsch who first tried this method. They died within minutes. "I thought it would be worse," Höss wrote. Auschwitz was not the first camp to gas Jews, and Höss knew what was going on elsewhere. Gassing was easier, from his point of view, than shooting, the method used in the ghettos and the forests. Höss heard that there had been horrible sights there, he wrote. There were wounded people who tried to escape, among them women and children, and it was necessary to chase after them and shoot them again, and there were screams and much blood. The victims were often forced to dig their own mass graves. "When we stood there by the pit," prosecution witness Rivka Joselevska related at the Eichmann trial, "I and my small daughter, she asked me, Mother, why are we standing and waiting, let's run. I turned my head. They asked me who to shoot first, me or the girl. I didn't answer. I felt how my daughter was torn from me, I heard the last screams, and then the shot. Then they came for me. I turned my head. He grabbed my hair and wanted to shoot me, too. I did not move. He shot and I fell into the body-filled pit. I did not feel a thing."[10]

Many SS men could not take it, Höss wrote: there were those who killed themselves and others who lost their minds. At Höss's Auschwitz everything was fast, efficient, quiet, and clean. Sometimes SS leaders came to observe the process. Himmler came, Eichmann came, and so did others. They told him that they did not envy him, but praised him for his accomplishments. It was not pleasant work, but it was not impossible. Sometimes it was very hard for him. He found comfort with his wife and children. He did it for them, for Germany, for the future he believed in, and because he had received an order, and those Jews, after all, were lesser creatures. That is the key.

The camp commandants believed that even before they served in the camps; the more the brutality increased and the inmates lost their human appearance, the more the theory of race and the subhuman *Untermensch* seemed to be proving itself. It made it easier for the men working at the concentration camps to perform their duties. "They were not human like us," said Ruth Kalder, Amon Göth's widow, in 1975. "They were so foul."[11] The court that heard Karl Chmielewski's case ruled that he was a sadist who murdered hundreds of prisoners, by dousing them with boiling water. This was not, however, a crime in his eyes. He did not see them as human beings like him, the court said.[12] "At some point," said Max Pauly's defense attorney, "they murdered people in the camps just as we do away with a bothersome fly or a bedbug."[13]

GITTA Sereny, a British writer and historian, spoke of this with Franz Stangl, once the commandant of the Treblinka extermination camp. She interviewed him in 1971 in the Düsseldorf Prison. "Could you not have changed that? In your position, could you not have stopped the nakedness, the whips, the horror of the cattle pens?" she asked.

Stangl: No, no no. This was the system. . . . When I was on a trip once, years later in Brazil, my train stopped next to a slaughterhouse. The cattle in the pens, hearing the noise of the train, trotted up to the fence and stared at the train. They were very close to my window, one crowding the other, looking at me through that fence. I thought then, "Look at this; this reminds me of Poland; that's just how the people

> looked, trustingly, just before they went into the tins—"

Sereny: You said "tins." What do you mean?

Stangl: —I couldn't eat tinned meat after that. Those big eyes—which looked at me—not knowing that in no time at all they'd all be dead.

Sereny: So you didn't feel they were human beings?

Stangl: Cargo. They were cargo.

Sereny: When do you think you began to think of them as cargo? The way you spoke earlier, of the day when you first came to Treblinka, the horror you felt seeing the dead bodies everywhere—they weren't "cargo" to you then, were they?

Stangl: I think it started the day I first saw the *Totenlager* in Treblinka. I remember [SS officer Christian] Wirth standing there, next to the pits full of blue-black corpses. It had nothing to do with humanity—it couldn't have; it was a mass—a mass of rotting flesh. Wirth said, "What shall we do with this garbage?" I think unconsciously that started me thinking of them as cargo.

Sereny: There were so many children, did they ever make you think of your children, of how you would feel in the position of those parents?

Stangl: No. I can't say I ever thought that way. You see, I rarely saw them as individuals. It was always a huge mass. I sometimes stood on the wall and saw them in the tube. But—how can I explain it—they were naked, packed together, running, being driven with whips like . . .[14]

Stangl officially joined the Nazi party soon after the German army invaded his homeland. Austria, in March 1938. He then served as a policeman in Linz. A few weeks after the *Anschluss* he turned 30. The persecution of the Jews now stood before a new stage. Within a few months, on the night of November 9, the pogroms of the *Kristallnacht* were to sweep the Reich. The dry statistics about the riots are that 191 synagogues were destroyed and 7500 Jewish-owned stores ransacked. Within a short time more than 30,000 Jews were arrested. Two and a half months later, in January 1939, Adolf Hitler would for the first time speak publicly of the physical destruction of European Jewry. Within two months World War II would break out; the soldiers would be followed by extermination units.

If they wanted to be faithful to their ideology and take it to its logical conclusion, the Nazis could not avoid an attempt to destroy all the Jews. The idea was part of the foundation of their creed from the beginning. The Final Solution was preceded, however, by several partial solutions. It developed step by step. Franz Stangl was involved in several stages which preceded Treblinka. A few months after the *Anschluss*, a concentration camp was opened in Mauthausen, a small village not from from Linz, where Stangl served in the political department of the secret police. He would later argue that he had no interest in politics and that he had joined the Nazi party out of fear.

He was born on March 26, 1908, in the town of Altmünster in Austria, where his father worked as a night watchman.[15] Stangl would later describe his father as a soldier in an elite unit of the Austro-Hungarian imperial army; his father never ceased to be proud of that, Stangl said. He ruled his family with an iron fist and in military style. "I was scared to death of him," Stangl related. "I knew since I was very small, I don't remember exactly when, that my father hadn't really wanted me. I heard them talk. He thought I wasn't really his."[16]

Stangl had a sister ten years older than he. Among his earliest childhood memories is one of his father beating him bloody over a minor misdeed. When he was 8 years old, and World War I had just entered its second year, his father died after a serious illness. When he was ten his mother remarried. Her second husband, himself a widower, was a metalworker. He had two sons from his previous marriage, one of them of Stangl's age. When he was 15, Stangl became a trainee at a textile factory. He did well. Three years later he passed his examinations and became a professional weaver, the youngest in Austria. He continued to work in the factory and, two years later, when he was 20, he was appointed foreman. He had fifteen workers under him. At night he gave sitar lessons, and on weekends he constructed a sailboat. "It was my happiest time," he later said, and his wife added that they were the first years of happiness he had ever known—his childhood, he once told her, had been miserable.[17]

In 1931, five years after becoming a professional weaver, he found himself at a crossroads. "Without higher education I couldn't get further promotion. But to go on doing all my life what I was doing then? Around me I saw men of 35 who had started at the same age as I and who were now old men."[18] He apparently had already met the young woman who would a few years later become his wife. She was the daughter of the owners of a cosmetics store, a high school graduate and, when she first met Stangl, a student at a social work school. The young textile worker thus had good reason to aim at improving his economic and social circumstances and bring them up to those of the woman he loved. He tried to get a job with the police. As a police officer he would wear a uniform and use a weapon, and he would gain something of the prestige of government work. His future as a public employee would be secure and he would have opportunities for advancement that an industrial worker did not have. It was a challenge—the entrance examinations were hard, and months passed before he received a response. He was accepted.

Studies in police school lasted for a year. "[The teachers] were a sadistic lot. They drilled the feeling into us that everyone was against us, that all men were rotten."[19] Stangl was successful and, upon finishing his studies, he was given various police assignments, from guiding traffic to breaking up demonstrations. He excelled at the latter. "During the Socialist uprisings in February 1934," he related, "there were terrific street battles in Linz. In one of them the Socialists entrenched themselves at the Central Cinema and we had to fight for hours to get them out. I was the one who flushed the last ones out that night at 11 p.m.—after well over 12 hours. I got the Silver Service medal for it."[20]

A few days after Chancellor Engelbert Dollfuss was assassinated in July 1934, Stangl discovered a Nazi weapons cache in a forest. His superiors saw that they had a diligent police officer. They gave him a second medal, and Austrian eagle decorated with a green and white striped ribbon, and sent him for an advanced course of the secret police. A year later he was assigned to the political department of the secret police in

Wels, a thirty-minute train ride from Linz and at that time, about three years before the German invasion, a focus of Nazi activity. Stangl now worked in civilian clothes, and his job was to keep tabs on the underground political activity of the Social Democrats, the Communists, and the Nazis. It was a large step forward in the career of a former textile worker of 27; at the end of that same year he married.

When asked years later what his attitude towards the activities of the Nazi party had been at that time, Stangl evaded answering. "I was just a police officer doing a job," he said.[21] But when the Germans invaded Austria he panicked. The eagle medal he had been awarded for flushing out Nazi weaponry could cost him his life, he feared, or so at least he argued a generation later. Three of the five police officers who had received the decoration with him were executed the day after the invasion, he claimed. Stangl rushed to a lawyer, a Nazi party activist, who for some reason owed him a favor, and the lawyer agreed to add his name to the list of members who had belonged to it illegally in 1936. In this way, Stangl said, he saved his life, by becoming a member of the party. It may be that this happened or it may be that Stangl lied. The Düsseldorf court did not believe the story. The judges ruled that Stangl had belonged to the party illegally beginning in 1936 and had supported it, as had many other Catholics in the area. His wife did not believe the story, either. In any case, Stangl, now a member of the party, continued to serve in the political department of the secret police, which was annexed after the *Anschluss* to the Linz office of the Gestapo. Some time thereafter Stangl signed a declaration in which he defined himself, according to the Nazi formula, as "a believer in God," instead of as a Catholic. This was an important step in the process of his gradual integration into the Nazi system of values. His wife, in those days a God-fearing woman, was deeply hurt when he told her he had signed the declaration, just as she was hurt later when it became clear to her that he had been a member of the Nazi party for two years without having told her. In her opinion, he was desecrating the principles of the church. When World War II broke out, Stangl was classified as an indispensable worker and was not drafted.

If he had then made an inventory of his life he would have

had good reason to be satisfied. He lived with his wife in a nice apartment, with a garden. A year after their marriage a daughter was born. Their family life was as happy as his life with his parents had not been. Stangl loved his work, he was promoted rapidly, and he reached a senior position much earlier then he could have expected when young. His achievements had not come easily; they were the product of his own hard work. As a party member, he had reason to believe that he would continue to advance.

In November 1940 Stangl was brought to Berlin to receive new orders; the summons was signed by Heinrich Himmler himself. He was invited to the national headquarters of the police force. "*Kriminalrath* [Chief Inspector] Werner told me that it had been decided to assign me to a very difficult and demanding job," Stangl related. "[Werner] said that both Russia and America had for some considerable time had a law which permitted them to carry out euthanasia—'mercy-killings'—on people who were hopelessly deformed. He said this law was going to be passed in Germany—as everywhere else in the civilized world—in the near future. But that, to protect the sensibilities of the population, they were going to do it very slowly, only after a great deal of psychological preparation. But that in the meantime the difficult task had begun, under the cloak of absolute secrecy. He explained that the only patients affected were those who, after the most careful examination—a series of four tests carried out by at least two physicians—were considered absolutely incurable so that, he assured me, a totally painless death represented a real release from what, more often than not, was an intolerable life."[22]

The truth is that the "mercy killings" were frequently carried out without such careful examinations having been made. They were done by authority of administrative orders signed by doctor-officials who had not even seen the candidate for death. They were at times influenced by economic or political considerations. Stangl did not yet know this, but in any case, he claimed, he tried to turn down the job.

"I . . . I was speechless. And then I finally said I didn't really feel I was suited for this assignment. He was, you know, very friendly, very sympathetic when I said that. He said he understood well that that would be my first reaction, but that I had to remember that my being asked to take this job was proof of their exceptional trust in me. It was a most difficult task—they fully recognized it—but that I myself would have nothing whatever to do with the actual operation; this was carried out entirely by doctors and nurses. I was merely to be responsible for security."[23] Stangl agreed to accept the assignment, for a few reasons, he said. He was influenced by their claim that mercy killings were already accepted in America and Russia. He was influenced by the fact that it would be carried out by doctors and nurses. He put his faith in the careful examination which was supposed to precede the decision about who would die and who would live. He was impressed by the intention of considering the sensibilities of the public, and he was afraid. A disciplinary action was in process against him at home—his superior, Georg Prohaska, had treated him badly, and he very much wanted to leave Linz.

The job carried a promotion with it—to security officer for the Hartheim castle, which would put him back in the green police uniform. Stangl was given a higher rank than that of the police chief in the nearby town. Upon arriving at Hartheim, Stangl met a friend who had served with him in the police, Franz Reichleitner, and later Christian Wirth as well. Both of them were later, like him, key figures in the daily operation of the Final Solution, and were police officers as he was.

Close to 400 men, among them doctors, psychiatrists, nurses, administrators, maintenance workers, and security personnel, were involved in the euthanasia program. Several tens of thousands of incurable invalids were killed during the course of the program, the great majority of them mentally ill or deformed. The program was headed by Professor Werner Heide, the psychiatrist who had once been assigned to care for Theodor Eicke. The euthanasia apparatus functioned from the beginning of the war until the autumn of 1941. From that time onward it served as a camouflage for the murder of thousands of concentration camp inmates. A mimeographed memorandum sent out in 1943 to all concentration camp commandants and containing details of changes in the euthanasia program is evidence that they all knew about the project. Close to 100 of the employees of the euthanasia program were later integrated, as was Franz Stangl, into the execution of the Final Solution. Their part in the euthanasia program also trained them psychologically for their roles in the extermination program.

The euthanasia program was presaged by the enactment of laws which required the sterilization of anyone with genetic disease, and allowed abortions when it was discovered that one parent suffered from such an affliction. The Nuremberg laws forbidding sexual contact between Jews and Germans were passed not long thereafter. By the time the Final Solution of the Jewish problem came up for consideration, there was already a clear definition of the right to life: it was conditioned not only on a person's racial identity, but also on certain mental and psychological attributes. In parallel, research on racial theory was being carried out in several places in Germany, involving medical experiments on concentration camp prisoners. Both reflected the unique conception of life and death adopted by the Third Reich.

For all Franz Stangl knew—and all he wanted to know—the patients brought to Hartheim were not fit to live. They were incurable; their death was approved by a medical team. His job did not require him to have pangs of conscience, since it did not contradict the moral values that had guided him up until now. Hartheim operated legally, in accordance with the Nazi ethic and government policy. He had personal reasons to prefer Hartheim to his previous assignment, under the command of a superior with whom he had trouble working, and his involvement with what was going on at Hartheim was indirect. He killed no one himself—he was responsible for security, for seeing that each patient brought the necessary forms with him, and for seeing that the death certificates were issued in good order. Later Stangl would tell of a working visit he made to a home for retarded children. The institution was run by nuns. One of them showed him a small boy of about five.

"'Do you know how old he is?' she asked me. I said no, how old was he? 'Sixteen,' she said. 'He looks five, doesn't he? He'll never change, ever.' Here was a Catholic nun, a Mother Superior, and a priest. And they thought it was right. Who was I, to doubt what was being done?"[24]

In August 1941 Hitler ordered the euthanasia program

halted, partly as a result of pressure from religious leaders and public opinion. It is estimated that, by that time, between 80,000 and 100,000 people had been killed in the framework of the project. Several thousand retarded children, political prisoners, criminals, homosexuals, and Jews were killed in the euthanasia institutions even after this date, as part of a project named after a form: "13F14." Stangl claimed later that he did not know about this project; he almost certainly lied.

With the end of the euthanasia campaign at Hartheim, Stangl was sent to assist with the dismantling of another of the euthanasia institutions, Bernburg, near Hannover. He remained there for a short time, dealt with administrative matters, returned equipment, dealt with insurance claims, and the like. The director of the Bernburg institution was Dr. Imfried Eberl, later the first commandant of Treblinka. Stangl's superiors allowed him, he said, to choose between returning to Linz and service in Lublin, under the command of Odilio Globocnik. Stangl, who remembered the tension between him and his superior in Linz, preferred working in Lublin. That was the spring of 1942.

Globocnik sent Stangl to take care of the establishment of the Sobibor camp. He told him that it was to be a military supply post. Soon after arriving at the site Stangl noticed gas facilities similar to those he had seen at Hartheim. Christian Wirth, who had been with him at Hartheim, explained what was going on. "I went there by car," Stangl recalled. "As one arrived, one first reached Belzec railway station, on the left side of the road. The camp was on the same side, but up a hill. The *Kommandantur* [headquarters] was 200 meters away, on the other side of the road. It was a one-story building. The smell—oh God, the smell. It was everywhere. Wirth wasn't in his office, I remember. They took me to him—he was standing on a hill, next to the pits—the pits—full—they were full. I can't tell you; not hundreds, thousands, thousands of corpses—oh God. That's where Wirth told me. He said that was what Sobibor was for. And that he was officially putting me in charge."[25]

According to Stangl, he told Wirth on the spot that he was not appropriate for the assignment given him; he had said the same when he was first sent to Hartheim. Wirth promised to pass Stangl's response on to his superiors. Nothing happened. The next day Wirth was in Sobibor to try out one of the new gas chambers. For this purpose twenty-five Jewish workers were put inside and killed. Stangl was there. From time to time, he would later claim, he asked for a transfer, which was not approved. Stangl was in charge of Sobibor between March and September 1942, and from that month until August of the next year he served as commandant of Treblinka, for a total of a year and a half. He had the possibility of opposing the continuation of his service; he did not do so, out of fear, he said. Thirty years later Stangl still remembered his first day in Treblinka.

"In Sobibor, unless one was actually working in the forest, one could live without actually seeing; most of us never saw anybody dying or dead. Treblinka that day was the most awful thing I saw during all of the Third Reich. . . . It was Dante's inferno. . . . When I entered the camp and got out of the car on the square . . . the hundreds, no the thousands of bodies everywhere, decomposing, putrefying,"[26]

Stangl was sent to Treblinka, among other reasons, to put the place in order. He had to rid the camp command of corruption. His predecessors took at least part of the money and valuables they found on the prisoners for themselves. According to Stangl, he saw himself the whole time as a police officer. He was not a sadist. The witnesses at his trial did not accuse him of personally abusing prisoners, in contrast to what they said about several of his colleagues at the camp. Neither was he accused of the corruption and orgies that were common among his fellows.

Franz Stangl may have once sat with his comrades and spoke with them about "what to do with the Jews." This was the phrase used in those days, in articles published in Nazi newspapers, in seminars organized by the party, and among friends sitting together in coffee houses or beer halls. If the ambitious secret police officer had been told in 1938 that within three years he would be put in charge of the extermination of hundreds of thousands of human beings, he would have dismissed it; he did not have much imagination. But if there had been among his friends someone who expressed the idea that the only way to get rid of the Jews was to exterminate them, it is likely that Stangl did not reject the idea out of hand. Stangl was a Nazi. Time after time he tested himself; time after time he found himself on a very narrow bridge, but never faced an obvious red light. So he continued on his way. At each stage of his advance he could have stopped—it was never too late. Had he wanted to, he could have gotten up and gone. Leaving, to be sure, involved discomfort, perhaps even risks. The career he had built with such great effort after rescuing himself from his status as a textile worker would have come, perhaps, to an end. They might have sent him to the front had he resigned. It is doubtful, however, whether he ever agonized over this. Everything he did was legal and was meant to advance the goals of the regime he served of his own free will. All the assignments he performed prepared him psychologically for what came next. He toughened and felt more and more apart from those led to death. At some point he ceased to see them as human beings like himself.

The mission he was given at Treblinka was not a pleasant one. Some months passed before he overcame his repulsion. According to Stangl, he suppressed what he saw and tried to make the place nicer. He planted flowers, built new barracks, new kitchens. He redid everything. There were hundreds of ways to suppress the reality of the horror and remove it from one's thoughts, and he used them all, he said. He sometimes got drunk. In the end he accustomed himself to it, just as he had accustomed himself to Sobibor and Hartheim. What he had done in both places, he thought, was the right thing. Treblinka was closed in the middle of 1943. Stangl and his superior, Christian Wirth, and Franz Reichleitner, his friend, were transferred to Trieste, where they worked against the Partisans. Wirth and Reichleitner were killed. Stangl escaped at the end of the war, with his family, to Damascus. He later emigrated to Brazil, where he worked at a German automobile factory, until he was arrested in 1967. He was extradited to Germany and brought to trial. The sentence was life in prison. In July 1971, while his case was being appealed, he died.

Fritz Hensel, Rudolf Höss's brother-in-law, asked Höss once what the term *Untermensch* meant. They sat in the commandant's house, in the evening, over glasses of wine. Höss sighed. "You always ask and ask," he said to his brother-in-law. "Look, you can see for yourself. They are not like you and me. They are different. They look different. They do not behave like human beings. They have numbers on their arms. They are here in order to die." Then they spoke about something else. Before they went to bed, Höss said suddenly, "Here you are on another planet. Don't forget that."[27]

In 1943 Höss was transferred from Auschwitz to SS headquarters in Berlin. He was with Himmler during the last days of the Reich. Himmler instructed his men to go underground. Höss succeeded in arranging a false identity for himself, as a sailor named Franz Lang. He passed several British checkpoints without being identified, but a few months later was captured and extradited to Poland. The Poles sentenced him to death. In his last letter to his wife he wrote, as he had in his book, that he believed in everything he had done.[28] According to his brother-in-law, this inner faith helped his widow bear his memory. She lived many years after him, managing a pastry shop in Fulda. The children left Germany to start new lives far away, one in America and one in Australia.

CONCLUSION

IT was not easy to interview these people; the fact that I came from Israel made it even more difficult. They agreed to talk with me because their past pursued them and they did not know how to escape it. The questions I raised had bothered them—and intrigued them—unceasingly for decades. This was the basis for our conversations. Each one hoped that he would succeed, if only a bit, in clearing his past. At the beginning, the three commandants I interviewed agreed, each one separately, only to talk about Theodor Eicke, their admired commander. Maybe they assumed that his image as a glorious military man would overshadow his crimes, and thus their own crimes as well. The conversations were very long, and were usually conducted as monologues—they spoke and I recorded.

Then they began, gradually, to speak of themselves as well, which was only natural. They were minor functionaries who had only done what they were supposed to do, they said, as expected—and this was true in general. They warned me not to believe everything written in books about the atrocities of the Holocaust. It is not pleasant to say this, they said, but there is a lot of Jewish propaganda in it. "What, don't you know?" Johannes Hassebroeck asked, his palm covering his mouth. "The Jews in America run everything." Each one of them also said, in admiration, that Israelis were very different from the Jews he had known. I heard all this, and the like, more than once from older Germans who had not been involved in the Reich's war crimes. It was tiring, nerve-wracking, and did not get me very far. Hours passed before we arrived at what I had come to ask them about: the motive.

During the first half of the 1960s people began talking about the "banality" of the Nazi evil and of human evil in general. That happened under the influence of a series of articles that the philosopher Hannah Arendt published in the wake of the Eichmann trial, first in the *New Yorker* magazine, and afterwards in a book titled *Eichmann in Jerusalem: a Report on the Banality of Evil*.[1] For a while these words were a sort of magic formula, an expression of a very pessimistic (and very fashionable) understanding of the nature of man—"we are all potential Eichmanns." I spoke with Arendt about this more than once while in New York. Sometimes she would snap at me: "Why do you have to ask why the concentration camp commandants did what they did or how they could have done it? They simply did and that's all there is to it. If they had not done it, someone else would have." In this, Arendt expressed a faith, a philosophy, maybe only a mood, not historical research. Injustice in the history of mankind, before the Nazi and after them, can constitute, of course, the foundation for such a view. The love, justice, and human righteousness in history provide a foundation for the opposite view. This is a philosophical debate over good and evil: which is the norm and which the exception. History supports everyone's views. Hannah Arendt did not like the widespread use made of the title of her book; were she writing now, she would not use those words, she told me. And, in fact, they do not adequately explain the commandants of the concentration camps.

They were mediocre people, without imagination, without courage, without initiative. From the personnel files, most of them seem to have had shallow personalities. Their grayness seems to have camouflaged them within the system in which they worked, allowing them to function somewhere around the middle management level; they did not frame ideology and did not establish policy. Most of the orders they sent to their subordinates came to them from their superiors. The system obviously did not require managers of any higher level. But their mediocrity is misleading: they were not Germans like all the Germans and not even Nazis like all the Nazis. It is not the banality of evil that characterizes them, but rather inner identification with evil. Most of the concentration camp commandants were among the early members of the Nazi movement or even its founders, and stood out from the beginning in their vehement support of its policies. Most Germans did not join the Nazi party. Most members of the Nazi party were not members of the SS. Membership in the organization reflected deeper involvement with the movement. The concentration camp commandants stood out even among the men of the SS. Service in the Death's Head Formations reflected particularly strong enthusiasm for the SS.

When I began studying Nazi war criminals, at the beginning of the 1970s, some historians were caught up with experiments in the use of psychology, and especially psychoanalysis, in their research. Psychohistory, as it was called, aroused great hopes. After 30 years of research based on tons of documents, it became clear to most scholars of Nazism that they could not properly understand Nazi war criminals and their crimes. Their colleagues in the psychology departments offered to help, and for a moment it seemed that they had found the theoretical key to the solution of the riddle. There is, for example, a well-known study which connects the attraction of the Nazi movement's military organizations with what the members of these organizations experienced when they were young, during World War I: fear, hunger, the absence of the father, his death at the front or his return, in defeat.[2] Even if it could be shown that most members of the SS actually had such experiences, and even if psychology were able to establish how these elements influenced their decision to join the organization, this would not be sufficient. After all, it was not so many years later that Germany began a new war. The young boys of World War II experienced the same fear and hunger, and their fathers were also absent, were killed, or returned defeated; but they, as if ridiculing the psychological theory, divided into two groups after the war: those who became loyal citizens of the Communist dictatorship in East Germany, and those who became part of the new democracy which arose in the West. This is not the only study of its kind. Some psychohistorical research broadens one's thinking, but in the end psychohistory promised more than it could deliver. In fact, it never went beyond theory, speculation, and guesswork.

There is evidence indicating that some of the concentration camp commandants were involved in overt acts of sadism; some lacked all feeling and may have acted like robots, as the psychiatrist who spoke with them, G. M. Gilbert, determined.[3] There were those who only obeyed orders, perhaps in response to the same instinct isolated in Stanley Milgram's laboratory.[4] Perhaps, but there is no way to be sure. None of them came to Nazism after having analyzed the situation methodically and examining the alternative ways of changing it. The major part of their decision was not rational, political or ideological awareness. Almost every one of them had personal and emotional motives which brought him to the movement. Sometimes, however, it was a matter of coincidence—had Frau Fritsch not asked for a house of her own before giving birth to her baby, her husband might not have gone to work in Dachau, and then probably, he would not have gone to Auschwitz. Some of them were simple opportunists. This is why it is necessary to examine the story of each one separately. Their personnel files do not suggest a psychological model— and perhaps such a model is unnecessary. The story of each commandant becomes clear within the circumstances of his life and times.

There are nevertheless common features, going beyond social origins, education, gray shallowness, and rabid identification with their movement. More than anything else, they were soldiers—by choice. Political soldiers, in the service of evil. The military was more then employment for them, more than a career. It was a way of life. Many of them chose to be army men even before World War I. Germany's defeat wounded and humiliated them more than it did others. The SS granted them a second chance. I asked them to recollect the day on which they joined the SS. "What brought you to the organization's enlistment office?" I asked again and again. Upon hearing the question, their faces—and even the faces of some of the relatives of those who were no longer alive— assumed an expression that combined mystery with nostalgia. "Only someone who was there can understand it," they said, still condescending and reticent, as if I had tried to enter a secret place uninitiated. Most of them joined the SS as volunteers. They spoke to me about honor and loyalty, about mission and challenge. I learned from them how powerful the emotional attraction of service in the SS army was. This did not tempt most Germans, who were not attracted to military service. The German army did not demand the tremendous identification that the SS did. But then the army did not require its men to operate concentration camps. The camp commandants were fully aware of the nature of the work they were doing; their identification with the work, its emotional force, and their personal motives set them apart from others and explain their readiness to work in the camps. Most of them served in concentration camps without feeling any revulsion. This requires additional explanation: even if a man could support the existence of the camps, how could he work in them?

Even when they earned a salary in exchange for their service in the SS, these men could have avoided being stationed in concentration camps, at least until the war began.[5] Most of them saw no reason to avoid it. The camps were meant to realize a creed they believed in, and were part of the Nazi system. They were meant to protect Germany from her enemies, and were considered legitimate institutions for the re-education of opponents of the movement, required by the first stages of the revolution, and afterwards by the country while at war. The camps were meant to operate within the general framework of the permitted and the forbidden (in the state and in the movement), according to routine orders and established regulations. This included the extermination of the Jews. A man could, therefore, serve in the concentration camps without suspecting that he was depraved; he could serve in the camps without others seeing him as depraved.

"How dare you ask me such questions," fumed Johannes Hassebroeck. Hans Hüttig said that he had been a good soldier and that whoever had been a good soldier had not been involved in the horrors. Afterwards, he said it had been terrible and broke into tears. Wilhelm Gideon suddenly said: "Excuse me. Are you referring to the Gideon who was commandment of the Gross Rosen concentration camp? Then you have made a mistake. I am not he. Excuse me for taking up your time," and he sent me away. Some of the commandants' widows and some of their children said that their husbands and fathers had not done the things they were accused of, so that the question of how they could have done such things was not relevant. Joseph Kramer said, "We came a long way from Dachau to Bergen-Belsen," and that, apparently, is the answer. They adjusted to their tasks at the camps from year to year, from camp to camp. Each stage prepared them for the next. They hardened. That their ruthlessness grew is clearly reflected by some of the personnel files. The brutality itself increased by stages, and the commandants accompanied that development. At the same time they rose in rank and acquired more responsibility. Kramer began as a simple guard at Dachau, in peacetime, and found himself a senior officer at Auschwitz in wartime. Others took a similar path, always in identification with the system.

"When it comes down to it, it is a very simple story," the elderly Hans Hüttig told me. "I was a Nazi." In saying that, he said almost everything.

NOTES

ABBREVIATIONS
BDCPF: Berlin Document Center Personnel File (SS Service Files), Berlin.
BAKO: *Bundesarchiv Koblenz* (German State Archives), Koblenz. Unless otherwise indicated,the quoted document is a mimeographed order sent to the camp commandments from Berlin.

INTRODUCTION
1. *The Attorney General of the State of Israel v. Adolf the son of Karl Adolf Eichmann*, District Court of Jerusalem, criminal case no. 40/61, June 7, 1961, Yad Vashem Archives, Jerusalem.
2. Fritz Hensel, interview with author, Hannover, March 3, 1975.
3. Polish estimate, in K. Dunin Warsowicz, *Oboz Koncentracyiny Stutthof*, Gdynia, 1960. Polish with English summary, available at the Yad Vashem Library.
4. Jörg Hoppe, interview with author, West Berlin, January 4, 1975.
5. Estimate of the *Encyclopedia Judaica*, Keter Publishing House, Jerusalem, 1971, vol. xii, p. 839

6. Hans Hüttig, interview with author, Wachenheim an der Rheinstrasse, March 8, 1975.

CHAPTER 1
JOSEPH KRAMER: FROM DACHAU TO BERGEN-BELSEN

1. Rosina Kramer, interview with author, Uetze, March 5, 1975.

2. "Nazis to Put Bavarian Foes in Concentration Camps," *The New York Times*, March 21, 1933, p. 1; *Völkischer Beobachter*, and other newspapers, all in the press clipping collection of the Wiener Library, Tel Aviv.

3. Joseph Kramer personnel file, BDCPF.

4. Raymond Phillips (ed.), *The Trial of Joseph Kramer and 44 Others*, His Majesty's Stationary Office, London, 1949, p. 125. (The trial record is included in a collection of Nazi war crimes trials known as "The Red Series.")

5. Rosina Kramer, interview.

6. Werner Schäfer, *Konzentrationslager Oranienburg*, Buch u. Tiefdruck Gesellschaft, Berlin, 1934.

7. Paul Berben, *Dachau—The Official History 1933–1945*, The Norfolk Press, London, 1975, p. 19.

8. The figures given here are minimums. For sources, see Tom Segev, "The Commanders of Nazi Concentration Camps," Ph.D. dissertation, Boston University, Boston, 1977, pp. 55 ff. and bibliography.

9. The best book on the history of the concentration camps is in French, Olga Wormser-Migot, *Le Système Concentrationnaire Nazi 1933–1945*, Presses Universitaires de France, Paris, 1968. See also Martin Broszat, "The Concentration Camps 1933–1945," in Helmut Krausnick and Others (ed.), *Anatomy of the SS State*, Walker and Co., New York, 1968, pp. 397 ff. A somewhat personal account of the concentration camps is given in Egon Kogon, *Der SS Staat*, Kindler, Munich, 1974. Surveys of a number of concentration camps can be found in: Martin Broszat (ed.), *Studien Zur Geschichte der Konzentrationslager*, DVA, Stuttgart, 1970. The International Red Cross published a list of concentration camps with a useful foreword, International Tracing

Service, *Vorleufiges Verzeichnis der Konzentration-slager*, ITS, Arolsen, 1969. Several of the postwar trials also heard a wide range of evidence about the concentration camps. See, for instance, *Justiz und NS Verbrechen*, University Press, Amsterdam, 1966. Important material is also included in the Nuremberg trials, especially in the trial of Oswald Pohl: see Trials of War Criminals Before the Nuremberg Military Tribunals Under Control Council Law No. 10, Nuremberg; October 1946–April 1949, vol. 5 (The Pohl Case), U.S. Government Printing Office, Washington, D.C., 1950. (The Trial is included in the collection of Nazi war crime trials known as "The Green Series." The best general survey of the extermination of the Jews is in Hebrew, by Leny Yahil, *Hashoah*, Schocken and Yad Vashem, Jerusalem, 1987). For others, see Raul Hilberg, *The Destruction of the European Jews*, Quadrangle, New York, 1961; Gerald Reitlinger, *The Final Solution*, Barnes and Co., New York, 1961; Nora Levin, *The Holocaust*, Shocken Books, New York, 1973. Lucy S. Dawidowicz, *The War against the Jews 1933–1945*, Holt, Rinehart and Winston, New York, 1975; Martin Gilbert, *The Holocaust*, Fontana, New York, 1987.

10. BAKO NS 3 439.

11. Trials of War Criminals Before the Nuremberg Military Tribunals ("The Green Series"), vol. 5, case 4 (The Pohl Case), U.S. Government Printing Office, Washington, 1950, p. 222.

12. Ibid.

13. Fritz Stern, *The Path to Dictatorship*, Anchor Books, New York, 1966, p. 206.

14. "Entlassung von Schutzhäftlingen," January 5, 1934, p. 10, BAKO R 58/264 fol. 1309 u. 198a.; Gerd Rüle (ed.), *Das Dritte Reich*, Verlag für Deutsche Literatur, Berlin, 1936, pp. 462 ff.

15. "Nazi Prison Camps to be Permanent," *The New York Times*, July 27, 1933, p. 7.

16. BAKO R 58/264 fol. 1309 u. 198a.

17. Ibid.

18. May 29, 1942, BAKO NS 19 320.

19. July 27, 1943, BAKO NS 3 426.

20. BAKO NS 3 vorl. 401.

21. Enno Georg, *Die Wirtschaftlichen Unternehmen der SS*, Deutsche Verlags Anstalt, Stuttgart, 1963.

22. Helmut Auerbach, 'Die Einheit Dirlewanger,' *Vierteljahreshefte für Zeitgeschichte*, vol. x, July 1962.

23. Johannes Hassebroeck, interview with the author, Braunschweig, March 1, 1975.

24. For example, *National Zeitung* (Essen), February 2 1941. Available at the press clipping collection of the Wiener Library, Tel Aviv.

25. Hans Helwig personnel file, BDCPF; November 10, 1942, BAKO NS 3 425.

26. Adam Grünewald personnel file, BDCPF.

27. November 9, 1941, BAKO R 58 264 fol. 1, 309 u. 198a.

28. September 2, 1942, BAKO NS 3 425.

29. September 2, 1942, BAKO NS 3 425 International Tracing Service Arolsen Hist. Abt. Buchenwald (149).

30. February 2, 1943, BAKO NS 3 425. January 19, 1942, BAKO NS 3 426.

31. Gitta Sereny, *Into That Darkness*, Andre Deutsch, London, 1974, p. 58.

32. *Völkischer Beobachter* (Berlin), June 13, 1939.

33. Max Domarius, *Hitler Reden*, vol. 3, R. Loweit, Wiesbaden, 1973, p. 1459.

34. *Münchner Illustruerte*, July 16, 1933; *Völkischer Beobachter* (Berlin), August 17, 1933; *Das Schwarze Korps*, January 16, 1936. Available at the press clipping collection of the Wiener Library, Tel Aviv.

35. Schäfer, *Konzentrationslager Oranienburg*, p. 247.

36. BAKO R 58 1027 fol. 1–291.

37. Ruth Göth, interview with author, Munich, March 12, 1975.

38. April 26, 1941, BAKO NS 3 425.

39. February 1, 1945, BAKO NS 3 388.

40. American Historical Association, Captured German Documents Microfilmed at the Berlin Document Center, T. 75 R. 216 2/752687 ff.

41. Herman Baranowski personnel file, BDCPF.

42. Otto Förschner personnel file, BDCPF.

43. Arthur Rödel personnel file, BDCPF.

44. July 12, 1943, BAKO NS 426.

45. Ibid., November 11, 1943.

46. Hans Loritz personnel file, BDCPF.

47. November 26, 1943, BAKO NS 3 405.

48. "Disziplinar u. Strafordnung für das Gefangenenlager Dachau," January 10, 1933, Nuremberg Document, 778 PS, Yad Vashem Archives, Jerusalem.

49. *Buchenwald Mahnung und Verpflichtung*, Kongressverlag, Berlin, 1961, p. 131.

50. BAKO NS 3 425.

51. January 8, 1935, BAKO R 58 264 fol. 309 u. 198a RSHA.

52. TV Befehlsblätter 1937, No. 5, p. 12, TV file, Berlin Document Center.

53. November 15, 1942, BAKO NS 3 425.

54. TV Befehlsblätter 1937, No. 5, p. 12, TV file, Berlin Document Center.

55. Buchenwald 47 (184), International Tracing Service, Historische Abteilung, Arolsen.

56. Hans Loritz personnel file, BDCPF.

57. November 7, 1944, BAKO NS 3 442.

58. BAKO NS 19/Neu 1542.

59. "Aufgaben und Pflichten der Wachposten," July 27, 1943, BAKO NS 3 426.

60. Ibid.

61. Buchenwald (14a), International Tracing Service, Historische Abteilung, Arolsen.

62. BAKO R 58/1027 fold. 1–291.

63. December 31, 1943, BAKO NS 3 425.

64. Ibid.

65. *Curiohaus Prozess: verhandelt vor dem britischen Militärgericht in der Zeit vom 18.3 bis zum 3.5. 1946 gegen die Hauptverantwortlichen des KZ Neuengamme*, vol. I, p. 19. Published in limited edition. Available at Yad Vashem Archives, Jerusalem.

66. BAKO R 58/1027 fol. 1–291.

67. August 19, 1942, BAKO NS 3 425.

68. "Natzweiler Routine Orders," February 25, 1943, American Historical Association, Captured German Docu-

ments Microfilmed at the Berlin Document Center, T. 75
R. 216 2/755081.

69. Ibid.
70. December 8, 1943, BAKO NS 3 426.
71. "Aufgaben und Pflichten der Wachtposten," July 27, 1943, BAKO NS 3 426.
72. Eicke to Himmler, May 7, 1938, BAKO NS 19/Neu 1542.
73. Ibid.
74. "Stutthof Kommandaturbefehle," July 17, 1944, Or. 492, International Tracing Service, Arolsen.
75. Ibid., July 16, 1943.
76. TV Befehlsblätter 1937, No. 3, p. 10, TV file, Berlin Document Center.
77. Häftlings Personalkarte, BAKO NS 3 379.
78. Josef Goebbels, "Der Papierkrieg," *Das Reich*, no. 12, April 12, 1942, BAKO NS 3 395.
79. January 11, 1943, BAKO NS 3 vorl. 426.
80. "Natzweiler Routine Orders," June 17, 1943, American Historical Association, Captured German Documents Microfilmed at the Berlin Document Center, T. 75 R. 216 2/755035.
81. Ibid.
82. TV Befehlsblätter 1937, No. 3, p. 10, TV file, Berlin Document Center.
83. February 11, 1943, BAKO NS 3 426.
84. "Natzweiler Routine Orders," American Historical Association, Captured German Documents Microfilmed at the Berlin Document Center, T. 75 R. 216 2/755060.
85. July 7, 1943, BAKO NS 3 386.
86. "Natzweiler Routine Orders," American Historical Association, Captured German Documents Microfilmed at the Berlin Document Center, November 24, 1943, T. 75 R. 216 2/755060.
87. October 29, 1942, BAKO NS 3 425.
88. Kommandaturbefehle Buchenwald, September 10, 1941, Buchenwald (149), International Tracing Service, Arolsen.
89. Ibid.
90. October 10, 1943, BAKO NS 3 395.
91. Buchenwald Library catalogue, BAKO NS 3 397.

92. December 3, 1945, BAKO NS 3 396.
93. January 1, 1943, BAKO NS 3 386.
94. "Natzweiler Routine Orders," American Historical Association, Captured German Documents Microfilmed at the Berlin Document Center, November 25, 1941, T. 75 R. 216 2/755129.
95. Stutthof Kommandaturbefehle, August 8, 1943, Or. 492, International Tracing Service Historical Abteilung, Arolsen.
96. December 15, 1943, BAKO NS 3 426.
97. August 8, 1943, BAKO NS 3 426.
98. February 2, 1943, BAKO NS 3 426.
99. *The Attorney General of the State of Israel v. Adolf the son of Karl Adolf Eichmann*, District Court of Jerusalem, criminal case no. 40/61, June 7, 1961, Yad Vashem Archives.
100. May 1943, 22, BAKO NS 3/ Vorl. 426.
101. May 15, 1943, BAKO NS 3 426.
102. Weiterversicherung von Häftlingen, BAKO NS 3 405.
103. BAKO NS 3 427.
104. April 21, 1936, BAKO R 58 264 fol. 1 309 u. 198a (RSHA).
105. BAKO R 58 1027 fol. 1 291.
106. January 22, 1943, BAKO NS 3 426.
107. November 11, 1938, BAKO R 58 264 fol. 1 309 u. 198a RSHA vol. 2.
108. May 21, 1942, BAKO NS 3 425.
109. August 24, 1943, BAKO NS 3 425.
110. August 5, 1942, BAKO NS 3 405.
111. *The Attorney General of the State of Israel v. Adolf the son of Karl Adolf Eichmann*, District Court of Jerusalem, criminal case no. 40/61 Judgment, paragraph 127 (unedited English version). Yad Vashem Archives, Jerusalem.
112. January 3, 1945, BAKO NS 3 380.
113. Hans Aumeier personnel file, BDCPF.
114. Wilhelm Goecke personnel file, BDCPF.
115. Rosina Kramer, interview.
116. Joseph Kramer personnel file, BDCPF.
117. Rosina Kramer, interview.

118. Ibid.

119. Ibid.

120. Ibid.

121. Ibid.

122. Phillips, *The Trial of Joseph Kramer and 44 Others*, p. 158.

123. Phillips, *The Trial of Joseph Kramer and 44 Others*, p. 161.

124. Phillips, *The Trial of Joseph Kramer and 44 Others*, p. 45.

125. Rosina Kramer, interview.

CHAPTER 2
THE UNDEFEATED ARMY

1. Günter d'Alquen, *Die SS: Geschichte, Aufbau und Organisation der Schutzstaffel der NSDAP*, Junker und Duhnof, Berlin, 1939; *Die Schutzstaffel*, vol. 1, no. I, November 1926; BAKO NSD 41/3.

2. *Statistisches Jahrbuch der NSDAP 1939*, BAKO NS 19/Neu 1669.

3. *Curiohaus Prozess: Verhandelt vor dem britischen Militärgericht in der Zeit vom 18.3. bis zum 3.5. 1946 gegen die Hauptverantwortlichen des KZ Neuengamme*, vol. I, p. 365, Limited edition available at Yad Vashem Archives, Jerusalem.

4. *Jahresbericht der SS Personalkanzlei 1938*, BAKO NS 19/Neu 1669.

5. BAKO NS 19/Neu 1652.

6. Hermann Foertsch, *Schuld und Behängnis die Fritschkrise im Frühjahr 1938*, Deutsche Verlags Anstalt, Stuttgart, 1951, p. 148.

7. William S. Shirer, *The Rise and Fall of the Third Reich*, Simon and Schuster, New York, 1960, p. 316.

8. Johannes Hassebroeck, interview with author, Braunschweig, March 1, 1975.

9. Hilmar Wäckerle personnel file, BDCPF.

10. Lorenz Kuchtner, *Das Köngl. Bayer Kadettenkorps* in *Deutsches Soldatenjahrbuch*, Schild, Munich, 1966, pp. 65–78.

11. Ibid.

12. Otto Staubwasser, *Das K.B. 2. Infanterie Regiment Kronprinz*, Bayerisches Kriegsarchiv, Munich, 1924, p. 50 ff.

13. Robert Waite, *Vanguard to Nazism*, Harvard University Press, Cambridge, Mass., 1952; also Ernst v. Salomon (ed.), *Das Buch vom Deutschen Freikorpskämpfer*, Wilhelm Limpert, Berlin, 1938.

14. Edgar V. Schmidt-Pauli, *Geschichte der Freikorps 1918–1924*, Robert Lutz Nachfolger Otto Schramm, Stuttgart, 1936 p. 396.

15. Translation of German military ranks to equivalent ranks in the U.S. Army is according to the table in Helmut Krausnick and Others, *Anatomy of the SS State*, Walker and Co., New York, 1968, p. 576.

16. Hans Helwig, Jakob Weiseborn, and Hermann Baranowski personnel files, BDCPF.

17. Wilhelm Goecke personnel file, BDCPF.

18. Wilhelm Gideon, interview with author, Oldenburg, March 4, 1975.

19. Friedrich Hartjenstein personnel file, BDCPF.

20. Karl Künstler personnel file, BDCPF.

21. Otto Förschner personnel file, BDCPF.

22. Hans Hüttig, interview with author, Wachenheim, March 8, 1975.

23. July 14, 1944, BAKO 19/Neu 1922.

24. Fritz Suhren personnel file, BDCPF.

25. Paul Werner Hoppe personnel file, BDCPF.

26. Johannes Hassebroeck personnel file, BDCPF.

27. Richard Baer personnel file, BDCPF.

28. Heinz Höne, *The Order of the Death's Head*, Ballantine, New York, 1971.

29. "Der Reichsführer SS/SS Hauptamt, Rassenpolitik" (Berlin 1934), in E.E. Knoebel, *Racial Illusion and Military Necessity: A Study of the SS Political and Manpower Objectives in Occupied Belgium* (Ph.D. dissertation, University of Colorado, 1965), pp. 22 ff.; American Historical Association, Captured German Documents microfilmed at the Berlin Document Center, T. 580 R. 88, file 436.

30. April 11, 1938, Verteiler V, BAKO NS 19/500.

31. Weltanschaulicher Unterricht 8, BAKO NS 41/268.

32. Joseph Altrogge personnel file, BDCPF. SS Handblätter

für den Weltanschaulichen Unterricht, BAKO 41/268; Josef Ackerman, *Heinrich Himmler als Ideologe*, Muster-schmidt, Göttingen, 1970.

33. Joseph Altrogge personnel file, BDCPF.
34. Johannes Hassebroeck, interview.
35. Joseph Altrogge personnel file, BDCPF.
36. "Verlobungs und Heiratsbefehl," December 1931, 31, BAKO NS 19 670.
37. Max Kögel personnel file, BDCPF.
38. Ibid.
39. Günther Tamaschke personnel file, BDCPF.
40. Heinrich Schwarz personnel file, BDCPF.
41. Franz Ziereis personnel file, BDCPF.
42. Arthur Liebehenschel personnel file, BDCPF.
43. Günther Tamaschke, Heinrich Schwartz, and Hilmar Wäckerle personnel files, BDCPF.
44. Marc Hillel and Clarissa Henry, *Of Pure Blood*, McGraw-Hill, New York, 1975.
45. "Der Untermensch," BAKO NSD 41/275.
46. "Lebensregel für den SS Mann," BAKO NS 19/Neu 1457.
47. Alfred Bauer personnel file, BDCPF.
48. Karl Lothar von Bonin personnel file; BDCPF; "Entwurf der 9 Lebensleitsätze für SS," June 25, 1935, p. 64, BAKO NS 19/Neu 1457.
49. Hans Helwig personnel file, BDCPF.
50. TV Befehlsblätter 1937, No. 4, p. 5, TV file, Berlin Document Center.
51. Ibid.
52. August 6, 1942, BAKO NS 3 Vorlg. 424.
53. Johannes Hassebroeck, interview.
54. Hans Buchheim, "Command and Compliance," in Krausnick, *Anatomy of the SS State*, p. 340.
55. BAKO NS 19/Neu 1711; Schumacher 469, November 16, 1943, BAKO.
56. Ibid.
57. Johannes Hassebroeck, interview.
58. Reimund Schnabel, *Macht Ohne Moral*, Röderbergverlag, Frankfurt, 1957, p. 32.

59. Kammeradschaft: Ihr Sinn und Ihre Pflege, November 1936, BAKO Schumacher 477.
60. Ibid.
61. Hans Loritz personnel file, BDCPF.
62. Günther Tamaschke personnel file, BDCPF.
63. Jakob Weiseborn personnel file, BDCPF.
64. Heinrich Deubel personnel file, BDCPF.
65. Albert Sauer personnel file, BDCPF.
66. Adam Grünewald personnel file, BDCPF.
67. Johannes Hassebroeck, interview.
68. July 7, 1942, BAKO NS 19/Neu 522.
69. SS Handblätter für den Weltanschaulichen Unterricht, No. 22, BAKO NSD 41/268; Rechtskräftige Urteil Strafverfügungen 1943, BAKO NS 19/1919.
70. BAKO NS 19/Neu 490.
71. BAKO NS 19/Neu 1863.
72. April 3, 1940; BAKO NS 19/Neu 453.
73. BAKO NS 19 500.
74. *Statistisches Jahrbuch der SS 1938*, BAKO NSD 41/1.
75. *Jahresbericht der SS Personal Kanzlei 1938*, BAKO 19/Neu 1669.
76. Günther Tamaschke personnel file, BDCPF.
77. *Statistisches Jahrbuch der SS 1938*, BAKO NSD 41/1.

CHAPTER 3
THEODOR EICKE AND THE DEATH'S HEAD FORMATIONS

1. Amalie Müller, interview with author, Bielefeld, March 6, 1975.
2. Ibid.; and Karl Leiner, interview with author, Bielefeld, March 6, 1975.
3. *Völkischer Beobachter* (Berlin), March 4, 1943.
4. *Völkischer Beobachter* (Berlin), April 16, 1943.
5. Eicke to Bürckel, March 12, 1933, and Bürckel to SS Gruppe Süd, February 20, 1933, Theodor Eicke personnel file, BDCPF.
6. TV Befehlsblätter 1937, No. 1, p. 9, TV file, Berlin Document Center.
7. Ibid., No. 2, p. 2.
8. *Statistisches Jahrbuch der SS 1938*, BAKO NSD 41/1.

9. BAKO NS 19/Neu 1652.

10. George H. Stein, *The Waffen-SS: Hitler's Elite Guard at War 1939—1945*, Cornell University Press, New York, 1966, p. xxxiii.

11. Charles W. Sydnor, *Totenkopf—A History of the Waffen-SS, Death's Head Division 1939–1945*, Ph.D. dissertation, Vanderbilt University, Nashville, 1971.

12. Johannes Hassebroeck, interview with author, Braunschweig, March 1, 1975.

13. Shlomo Aronson, *Reinhard Heydrich und die Frühgeschichte von Gestapo und SD*, Deutsche Verlags Anstalt, Stuttgart, 1971, p. 37.

14. *Merkblatt für die Einstellung bei den SS Verfügungstruppen und SS Totenkopfverbände*, December 1936, BAKO NS 19 500; July 1937, BAKO Schumacher 437.

15. *Der Weg eines SS Mannes*, BAKO NS 19 1457.

16. *Statistisches Jahrbuch der SS 1937*, Berlin Document Center Library.

17. TV Befehlsblätter 1937, No. 2, p. 1, TV file, Berlin Document Center.

18. *Jahresbericht der SS Personalkanzlei 1938*, BAKO NS 19/Neu 1669.

19. Rolf Holzapfel, "Monatlicher Financieller Überblick," Oranienburg, November 15, 1938, Rolf Holzapfel personnel file, BDCPF; BAKO NS 19/1669.

20. *Statistisches Jahrbuch der SS 1937*, Berlin Document Center Library.

21. *Der Weg eines SS Mannes*, BAKO NS 19 1457.

22. *Statistisches Jahrbuch der SS 1939*, BAKO NSD 41/1; *Statistisches Jahrbuch der SS 1937*, Berlin Document Center library.

23. *Statistisches Jahrbuch der SS 1939*, Berlin Document Center Library.

24. Ibid.

25. TV Befehlsblätter 1937, No. 1, p. 1 and No. 6, p. 6, TV file, Berlin Document Center.

26. Ibid.

27. Ibid.

28. TV Befehlsblätter 1937, No. 1, p. 9, TV file; Berlin Document Center.

29. Ibid., No. 1, p. 1; No. 3, p. 4.
30. Ibid.
31. Chef des SS Hauptamtes, May 10, 1939, FA 127, Institut für Zeitgeschichte, München.
32. Nuremberg Document 5792, Yad Vashem Archives, Jerusalem.
33. Merkblatt, BAKO NS 19 500.
34. Zeitungsnotiz, September 11, 1939, BAKO NS 19/Neu 1457.
35. "Lebensregel für den SS Mann," BAKO NS 19/Neu 1457.
36. Johannes Hassebroeck, interview.
37. TV Befehlsblätter 1937, No. 1, p. 4, TV file; Berlin Document Center.
38. Ibid., No. 5, p. 4.
39. Johannes Hassebroeck, interview.
40. TV Befehlsblätter 1937, No. 2, p. 3, TV file, Berlin Document Center.
41. Ibid., No. 6, p. 3.
42. Ibid., No. 4, p. 3.
43. Ibid., No. 5, p. 4.
44. Ibid., No. 3, p. 1.
45. Ibid., No. 1, p. 5.
46. Ibid., No. 1, p. 6.
47. Ibid., No, 1, p. 8.
48. TV Befehlsblätter 1937, No. 1, p. 8, TV file, Berlin Document Center.
49. Ibid., No. 4, p. 2, and No. 6, p. 3.
50. Ibid.
51. TV Befehlsblätter 1937, No. 1, p. 2, TV file, Berlin Document Center.
52. Ibid.
53. Ibid., No. 1, p. 6.
54. Amalie Müller, interview; and ibid.
55. Theodor Eicke personnel file, BDCPF.
56. Amalie Müller and Karl Leiner, interview.
57. Ibid.
58. Peter Hüttenberger, *Die Gauleiter*, Deutsche Verlags Anstalt, Stuttgart, 1969, p. 213.
59. Theodor Eicke personnel file, BDCPF.

60. Ibid.
61. Ibid.
62. Ibid.
63. Ibid.
64. Rudolf Höss, autobiographical notes written in jail, F 13/5, F 13/6, Institut für Zeitgeschichte, München.
65. *Buchenwald Mahnung und Verpflichtung*, Kongressverlag, Berlin, 1961, illustration 1.
66. Theodor Eicke personnel file, BDCPF.
67. Max Kögel personnel file, BDCPF.
68. Theodor Eicke personnel file, BDCPF.
69. Johannes Hassebroeck, interview.
70. Theodor Eicke personnel file, BDCPF.
71. Record owned by Amalie Müller, interview.
72. Rudolf Höss, autobiographical notes written in jail.
73. Theodor Eicke personnel file, BDCPF.
74. Ibid.
75. Ibid.
76. Aronson, *Reinhard Heydrich*, p. 213.
77. Amalie Müller, interview.
78. Ibid.
79. Theodor Eicke personnel file, BDCPF.
80. Amalie Müller and Karl Leiner, interview.
81. Theodor Eicke personnel file, BDCPF.
82. Karl Leiner, interview.
83. Rudolf Höss, autobiographical notes written in jail.

CHAPTER 4
WHERE CIRCUMSTANCES LED

1. Hans Helwig personnel file, BDCPF.
2. Dieter Frick (ed.), *Die Bürgerlichen Parteien in Deutschland*, vol. I, Bibliographisches Institut, Leipzig, 1968, pp. 774 ff.; Robert G. L. Waite, *Vanguard to Nazism: The Free Corps Movement in Postwar Germany 1918–1923*, Norton, New York, 1969, pp. 206ff.; Uwe Lohlam, *Völkischer Radikalismus*, Leibnitz, Hamburg, 1970.
3. Hans Helwig personnel file, BDCPF.
4. Heinrich Deubel personnel file, BDCPF.
5. Eduard Weiter personnel file, BDCPF.
6. Trials of War Criminals Before the Nuremberg Military

Tribunals Under Control Council Law No. 10, Nuremberg, November, October 1946–April 1949, vol. 5 (The Pohl Case), U.S. Government Printing Office, Washington; D.C., 1950, p. 222.

7. Wiener Library p. III H. Dachau, Buchenwald No. 234; Sachsenburg No. 689, No. 1058.

8. Arthur Rödel personnel file, BDCPF.

9. *Staatsanwaltschaft bei dem Landgericht Köln: Handakten gegen Arthur Rödel*, 24 Js 921/63 ha (Z) SH.

10. Johannes Hassebroeck, interview with the author, Braunschweig, March 1, 1975.

11. Nuremberg Document L 173; 1253; No. 2122; No. 5226. Wiener Library p. III h. 52 (Flossenbürg) p. 10. ff.

12. Wiener Library p. III h. 52 (Flossenbürg) p. 8, 12; Nuremberg Document No. 508; No. 5226; Hermann Langbein, *Der Auschwitz Prozess* Europäische Verlagsanstalt, Wien, 1965, pp. 117, 467.

13. *Schwurgericht des Lantages Ansbach Urteil*, ksl ab/61 (12/59), August 7, 1961, Yad Vashem Archives, Jerusalem.

14. See the discussion of the Koches later in this chapter.

15. Egon Zill personnel file, BDCPF.

16. Schwurgericht beim Landgericht München, II 12 ks 12/54, January 14, 1955; Yad Vashem Archives, Jerusalem.

17. May 12, 1944, American Historical Association, Captured German Documents Microfilmed at the Berlin Document Center, T. 75 R. 216 2/755144.

18. Karl Fritsch personnel file, BDCPF.

19. Fanny Fritsch, interview with author, Regensburg, March 8, 1975.

20. Arthur L. Smith, Jr., *Die "Hexe von Buchenwald,"* Bölau und Cie, Köln, 1983, p. 37.

21. *Justiz und NS Verbrechen: Sammlung Deutscher Strafurteile Wegen Nationalsozialistischer Tötungsverbrechen 1945–1966*, vol. VIII, University Press, Amsterdam, 1966, pp. 30–137.

22. Ibid.

23. Nuremberg Document 626, Yad Vashem Archives, Jerusalem; Franz Ziereis personnel file, BDCPF.

24. Smith, *Die "Hexe von Buchenwald,"* p. 69.
25. Ibid.
26. Karl Koch personnel file, BDCPF.
27. Smith, *Die "Hexe von Buchenwald,"* p. 67 ff.
28. Ibid.
29. Karl Koch personnel file, BDCPF.
30. "Ilse Koch's Posthumous Rehabilitation Sought by Son," *The New York Times*, May 7, 1971, p. 8.
31. Hermann Florstedt personnel file, BDCPF.
33. Adam Grünewald personnel file, BDCPF.
34. Schwurgericht des Landgerichts Ansbach, Urteil ksl ab/61 (12/59), August 7, 1961, Yad Vashem Archives, Jerusalem.
35. Ruth Göth, interview with author, Munich, March 12, 1975; Amon Göth personnel file, BDCPF.
36. Ruth Göth, interview.
37. *Law Reports of Trials of War Criminals Selected and Prepared by the United Nations War Crimes Commision, "The White Series"* vol. VII, case no. 37, His Majesty's Stationery Office, London, 1949. This is a condensation of the hearings. The full text, in Polish, may be found in the Yad Vashem Archives, Jerusalem.
38. Nuremberg Document d 626, Yad Vashem Archives, Jerusalem.
39. Franz Ziereis personnel file, BDCPF.
40. Friedrich Hartjenstein personnel file, BDCPF.
41. Hans Loritz personnel file, BDCPF.
42. Ibid.
43. Paul Berben, *Dachau: The Official History 1933–1945*, The Norfolk Press, London, 1975, p. 48.
44. Rudolf Höss, *Commandant of Auschwitz*, Weidenfeld and Nicolson, London, 1959, p. 202. This is the English version of Höss's autobiography.
45. Hermann Baranowski personnel file, BDCPF.
46. Ibid.
47. Ibid.
48. G. H. Täuber, interview with author, Bochum, March 7, 1975.
49. Paul Werner Hoppe personnel file, BDCPF.
50. Ibid.
51. G. H. Täuber, interview.

52. *Schwurgericht beim Landgericht in Bochum*, 17 ks 1/55 Urteil, June 4, 1957. Yad Vashem Archives, Jerusalem.
53. G. H. Täuber, interview.
54. *Curiohaus Prozess: Verhandelt vor dem britischen Militärgericht in der Zeit vom 18.3 bis zum 3.5 1946 gegen die Hauptverantwortlichen des KZ Neuengamme*, vol. II, pp. 434 ff. (Limited edition, in the Yad Vashem Archives, Jerusalem.)
55. Max Pauly personnel file, BDCPF.
56. *Curiohaus Prozess*, vol. I, p. 9.
57. Ibid.
58. p. iii, Denmark, No. 346, Weiner Library, Tel Aviv.
59. Max Pauly personnel file, BDCPF.
60. *Curiohaus Prozess*, vol. II, pp. 40, 469–495.
61. Johannes Hassebroeck personnel file, BDCPF.
62. Schwurgericht bei dem Landgericht Braunschweig 1 ks 1/67 Urteil gegen Johannes Hassebroeck, July 12, 1970; Budesgerichtshof 5 str 3171, November 11, 1971, Yad Vashem Archives, Jerusalem.
63. Johannes Hassebroeck, interview.
64. Ibid.
65. Ibid.
66. Schwurgericht, Urteil, Yad Vashem Archives, Jerusalem.
67. Johannes Hassebroeck, interview.
68. "SS-Führer Baer in Frankfurt," *Frankfurter Rundschau*, December 22, 1960.
69. Hermann Langbein, *Menschen in Auschwitz*, Europäische Verlagsanstalt, Vienna, 1966, p. 117.
70. Hermann Stoltig, interview with author, Düsseldorf, December 9, 1975.
71. Richard Baer personnel file, BDCPF.
72. Hermann Stoltig, interview.
73. Max Kögel personnel file, BDCPF.
74. Ibid.
75. Nuremberg Document L 173, Yad Vashem Archives, Jerusalem.
76. Hans Hüttig, interview with author, Wachenheim, March 8, 1975.
77. Hans Hüttig personnel file, BDCPF.
78. Hans Hüttig, interview.

79. Ibid.
80. Ibid.
81. Hans Hüttig personnel file, BDCPF.
82. Egon Kogon, *Der SS Staat: Das System der Deutschen Konzentrationslager*, Kindler, Munich, 1974, p. 233.
83. Hans Hüttig, interview.

CHAPTER 5
"THEY ARE HERE TO DIE"

1. G. M. Gilbert, *Nuremberg Diary*, New American Library, New York, 1947; G. M. Gilbert, *The Psychology of Dictatorship*, The Ronald Press, New York, 1950. Gilbert testified at the Eichmann trial on his conversations with Höss (*The Attorney General of the State of Israel v. Adolf the son of Karl Adolf Eichmann*, District Court of Jerusalem, criminal case no. 40/61, session 55, May 25, 1961, Yad Vashem Archives, Jerusalem).
2. Rudolf Höss personnel file, BDCPF. Höss's autobiography is quoted here according to the German original (*Kommandant in Auschwitz*, Deutsche Verlags Anstalt, Stuttgart, 1958). The English version is Rudolf Höss, *Commandant of Auschwitz*, Weidenfeld and Nicolson, London, 1959. An additional, unpublished, autobiographical manuscript by Höss can be found in the Yad Vashem Archives, Jerusalem, (023/5).
3. Robert G. L. Waite, *Vanguard to Nazism: The Free Corps Movement in Postwar Germany, 1918–1923* Norton, New York, 1969, pp. 94 ff.
4. *The Trial of Rudolf Höss and 12 Others*, fa/157, Institut für Zeitgeschichte, Munich.
5. Fritz Hensel, interview with author, Hannover, March 3, 1975.
6. Höss, Autobiography, p. 21.
7. Hans Hüttig, interview with author, Wachenheim, March 8, 1975.
8. Fritz Hensel, interview.
9. *The Eichmann Trial: Verdict and Sentence*, Government Information Center, Jerusalem, 1962, p. 148.
10. *The Attorney General of the State of Israel v. Adolf the son of Karl Adolf Eichmann*, District Court of Jerusalem,

criminal case no. 40/61, May 9, 1961, Yad Vashem Archives, Jerusalem.

11. Ruth Göth, interview with author, Munich, March 12, 1975.

12. Schwurgericht des Landgerichts Ansbach, Urteil ksl ab/61 (12/59), August 7, 1961, Yad Vashem Archives, Jerusalem.

13. *Curiohaus Prozess: Verhandelt vor dem britischen Militärgericht in der Zeit vom 18.3 bis zum 3.5. 1946 gegen die Hauptverantwortlichen des KZ Neuengamme*, vol. I, p. 366. Limited edition, Yad Vashem Archives, Jerusalem.

14. Gitta Sereny, *Into that Darkness*, Andre Deutsch, London, 1974, p. 201.

15. Franz Stangl personnel file, BDCPF. This file does not contain much material. Most of the material on these pages is based on Sereny's book.

16. Sereny, *Into that Darkness*, p. 25.

17. Ibid., p. 27.

18. Ibid., p. 27.

19. Ibid., p. 28.

20. Ibid., p. 28.

21. Ibid., p. 30.

22. Ibid., p. 51.

23. Ibid., p. 51.

24. Ibid., p. 58.

25. Ibid., p. 111.

26. Ibid., p. 157.

27. Fritz Hensel, interview.

28. Institut für Zeitgeschichte, Munich, F/13 1–8.

CONCLUSION

1. Hannah Arendt, *Eichmann in Jerusalem: A Report on the Banality of Evil*, The Viking Press, New York, 1963.

2. Peter Lowenberg, "The Psychological Origins of the Nazi Youth Cohort," *American Historical Review*, vol. 76, 1971, pp. 457–1502.

3. G. M. Gilbert, "The Mentality of SS Murderous Robots," *Yad Vashem Studies*, vol. 1963, pp. 35.

4. Stanley Milgram, *Obedience to Authority*, Harper, New York, 1974.
5. This is clear from testimony at a number of postwar trials. See *Gutachten des Institut für Zeitgeschichte*, Deutsche Verlags Anstalt, Stuttgart, 1958.

INDEX